Robert Wiedersheim

The Structure of Man an Index to His Past History

Robert Wiedersheim

The Structure of Man an Index to His Past History

ISBN/EAN: 9783337225285

Printed in Europe, USA, Canada, Australia, Japan

Cover: Foto ©ninafisch / pixelio.de

More available books at **www.hansebooks.com**

THE

STRUCTURE OF MAN

AN INDEX TO HIS PAST HISTORY

BY

Dr. R. WIEDERSHEIM

PROFESSOR IN THE UNIVERSITY OF FREIBURG I. BADEN

TRANSLATED BY

H. AND M. BERNARD

THE TRANSLATION EDITED AND ANNOTATED AND
A PREFACE WRITTEN BY

G. B. HOWES, F.L.S.

PROFESSOR OF ZOOLOGY, ROYAL COLLEGE OF SCIENCE, LONDON

WITH 105 FIGURES IN THE TEXT

London

MACMILLAN AND CO.

AND NEW YORK

1895

PREFACE

THE circumstances which led to the production of this work in the original German are sufficiently set forth in the annexed "Introduction," and no one would admit more readily than its author that it is largely supplementary to the classical treatises of Darwin and Huxley, quoted in its pages. Experience of the practical method of scientific education has shown that it is desirable to place in the hands of the student engaged upon a first investigation of individual types of animal structure, some sound treatise of a general character, which he may read while continuing his more systematic studies. Such works awaken the mind to the comparative method of inquiry, and to the higher educational and philosophic issues to which it leads. It was this consideration which prompted me to suggest this translation, in the hope that it might be of use, in the manner indicated, to the medical student while engaged in the study of anatomy. I am further hopeful that an educated public exists to whom a knowledge of the comparative morphology of Man and the Anthropoid Apes as set forth in these pages may be acceptable.

The truth of Evolution in organic nature is now generally admitted, but its application to man is not perhaps so widely acknowledged. This book, in no sense an exhaustive treatise, is an endeavour to set forth the more salient features in the anatomy of Man which link him with lower forms, and others in that of the lower forms which shed a special light on parts of the human organism. Such comparisons furnish a basis upon which to exercise judgment concerning Man's position in the series of organised beings.

In dealing with these comparisons, a word of caution is, however, needed. Our accepted views as to the inter-relationships between the greater groups of animals are largely based upon the assumption that similarity of gross structure implies community of origin. It is now becoming evident that an essentially similar definitive condition may be independently reached, under advancing modification along parallel lines, by members of independent groups of animals; and there is reason to suspect that some of our classificatory systems are unnatural and erroneous from want of appreciation of this principle of "convergence." We must, therefore, not lose sight of the possibility that some of the characters which modern Man and the higher Apes have in common may have been independently acquired. A notable instance is furnished by the ridges which connect the tubercles of the upper molar teeth, described by Huxley and Topinard. On comparing the little worn upper molars of, say, a female Chimpanzee and Man, one might at first sight be disposed to conclude that modern Man has descended from ancestors hardly differing from the modern Apes. On comparing the entire Man-Ape series, however, it is found that these ridges, and more especially that of Topinard, are extremely variable and not infrequently absent in individuals of both Men and Apes, and it becomes therefore evident that such a conclusion, if not unwarranted, is premature. If for no other reason than this, it will be obvious that considerable interest attaches to the more precise determination, in the future, of the limits of detailed structural variation in Man and the Anthropoid Apes. With regard to variation in Man some very useful results have been obtained, during the last five years, under the auspices of a "Collective Investigation Committee" of the Anatomical Society of Great Britain and Ireland, of which I have the honour to be a member. Subjects chosen for investigation year by year are taken in hand in the leading dissecting rooms throughout the kingdom. The work of the student, becoming thus a research work, is ennobled; and the reports embody a mine of accurate information which, edited and tabulated, is of great service to both the surgeon and scientific anatomist.

Our views on some of the topics dealt with in this volume may become very much modified as work of the above-mentioned order proceeds. There seems, however, no escape from the conclusion that Man and the Apes must have had a common ancestor in the remote past, and we await with especial interest further discoveries of fossil remains which may throw light upon their inter-relationships and upon the ancestors of Man.

Remains of Early Quaternary Man, few and far between, have been unearthed during the last fifty years in England, on the European Continent with Gibraltar, and in North America. The valley of the Meuse is now famous for having yielded the "Naulette" and "Spy" remains, which there is very strong evidence for believing to belong to the Palæolithic Age. The salient features of these ancient men are a low retreating and contracted forehead and an inwardly shelving occiput (indicative of a primitive type of brain and of powerful neck muscles), a high temporal ridge and an expanded palate (indicative of powerful jaws and jaw muscles); and further, the presence of ape-like brow ridges (for which the famous Neanderthal calvaria is so notorious) appears also to have been a racial character. Dr. Eugène Dubois has recently described some remains from the banks of the Bengawan River in Java, which he believes to be those of a creature structurally intermediate between the types represented by modern Man and the modern Anthropoids. In this he has been proved by Pettit, Cunningham, Turner, and others, to be mistaken. The Bengawan calvaria and the bones associated with it are strictly human. The calvaria shows a cephalic breadth index[1] of 70, as compared with 72 for the Neanderthal, and its smaller capacity and other characters render it perhaps representative of a race more primitive than any

[1] As mentioned in the body of this work (*infra*, pp. 51, 52), the cranial capacity of the Caucasian may average 1500 c.cm., and that of the Veddah may be but 950 c.cm. Thirty Australian skulls measured by Turner gave a maximum capacity of 1514 c.cm. and a minimum of but 930 c.cm., and 100 modern Parisian skulls, worked out by Topinard, varied between 1850 c.cm. and 1150 c.cm., while Testut describes a skull of Quaternary Man from the Dordogne with a capacity of 1730 c.cm. Individual variation being thus extensive, it is clear that for purposes of study of the inter-relationships between races of mankind, a method which deals with *relative* measurements, in such a way as to eliminate differences due to stature, is desirable. The above-named "cephalic breadth index" method has been found to be one of the most serviceable under existing circumstances. It is computed as follows: multiply the maximum transverse diameter by 100 and divide by the maximum long diameter, as determined by a line drawn between the superciliary ridges and through the most projecting mid-occipital point.

hitherto discovered. During the passage of these pages through the press, my friend and colleague, Mr. E. T. Newton, has described[1] from the Thames Terrace-Gravel, at Galley Hill, in Kent, some remains of a human skeleton which there is good reason for believing to belong to the Palæolithic Age, and to be perhaps slightly older than the Spy example. The Belgian remains were found in caves, those from Galley Hill were embedded in a Pleistocene river deposit; and it is a significant fact that the skull of the latter gives a cephalic breadth index of but 64.

The posterior molars or "wisdom teeth" of modern Man are exceedingly variable structures (cf. text, p. 159). Even when most fully developed, their crowns are as a rule less extensive than those of the teeth in front of them. In remains from reputed Palæolithic deposits hitherto described, in which jaws and teeth have been preserved, the crowns of the "wisdom teeth" are as large as, if not a trifle larger than those of the other molars in front of them. This greater development of the last molar is characteristic of the oldest known human jaws, but is only very rarely met with in those of recent Man. In its most expanded condition the crown of the wisdom tooth of both recent and fossil Man may be beset by numerous tubercles, its posterior and external cusps being subdivided and replaced by a series of smaller ones. The same variation has been observed among the Anthropoid Apes. This is an intensely interesting fact, as it approximates the molar of Man and the higher Apes with that of the multitubercular type, occurring among the oldest fossil and in the young of one of the two lowest living Mammals (*e.g. Ornithorhynchus*). Concerning the general question of mammalian tooth-genesis, choice to-day lies between the theory of "Trituberculism," originated by Rütimeyer and Cope, and staunchly upheld by the American Palæontologists, and that of "Polybuny" or "Multituberculism" founded and recently developed by Forsyth-Major. The advocates of the former would derive the various types of mammalian cheek-teeth from a

[1] Paper read before the Geological Society, London, 22nd May 1895. An admirable critical review of the subject of Fossil Man, by Dr. A. Keith, giving full references to original treatises up to the time of Newton's important work, will be found in *Science Progress* for July 1895.

tricuspid prototype, by extension, subdivision, and superaddition of parts, and those of the latter from a multicuspid, by reduction, confluence, and suppression.[1] Osborne has endeavoured to show [2] that the human molars may have been evolved out of a tritubercular type. I would point out, on the other hand, that during the tooth changes of the human subject of to-day, there is indicated, on the part of the cheek-teeth, a progressive reduction of that type of tooth represented by the first molar. The detailed facts concerning this process (cf. text, p. 160) appear to me to be more in accord with the theory of multituberculism; and on this basis the suggestion arises whether the first molar may not stand in a similar relationship to the wisdom tooth of the multitubercular order as the deciduous molars do to it, the entire series of modifications being those of advancing reduction of a multitubercular type of tooth.

No opportunity should be lost of excavating the Quaternary deposits of all parts of the world, especially where mixed with clays likely to be favourable to the preservation of human and other remains. Now that the African continent is being opened up, the scientific mind waits with longing for the careful investigation of its Tertiary Lacustrine deposits. Hugh Falconer long ago predicted that human remains would be forthcoming in the Tertiary deposits of India, and no one conversant with recent work in Mammalian Palæontology would doubt that the remains of ancestral Man must be sought thus far back in time. This prediction has been confirmed, by the discovery in 1894, by Noetling, in the Yenangyoung Oil-field, Burma, of flint flakes of early Pliocene date. I could desire no higher reward for the labour expended in placing this book before the English-speaking public than that it might help to awaken the interest necessary to ensure such investigation. It may be added, as an appropriate comment, that the interest in Dwarf Races, recently revived through African exploration and the fuller study of the natives of the Andaman

---

[1] For a fuller account of the history of these theories, and of the leading facts upon which they rest, cf. Osborne, *Americ. Naturalist*, vol. xxii. p. 1067; and Forsyth-Major, *Proc. Zool. Soc.*, Lond., 1893, p. 196.

[2] *Anat. Anzeiger*, Bd. vii. p. 740. Cf., however, the observations of Rose cited in this volume (*infra*, pp. 158 and 159).

Islands, has vastly increased, through the discovery that formerly dwarf races were widely distributed, evidence of their existence having been obtained in North Africa, Sicily, Switzerland, and the Pyrenees in the Old World, and in Central America in the New.

In editing this work, I have spared no pains to bring it up to the standard of English requirements. In the course of the revision a free rendering, rather than a translation, of the original German has been deemed in many places desirable; and paragraphs dealing with incidental and controversial topics have been for the most part put into small type. Important alterations and intercalations are enclosed in square brackets, and for these I hold myself responsible. My friend Professor Arthur Thomson of Oxford has done me the great service of looking through the proof-sheets, and to him and my friends Dr. Forsyth-Major and Mr. Oldfield Thomas, I tender my sincere thanks for advice upon special topics.

G. B. HOWES.

ROYAL COLLEGE OF SCIENCE, LONDON,
SOUTH KENSINGTON, S.W.,
May 1895.

PREFACE TO THE SECOND, REVISED AND ENLARGED, GERMAN EDITION

THE book "*Der Bau der Menschen*" made its first appearance in the year 1887 in the form of an academic treatise, intended only for a limited circle of readers. There were no illustrations, and the method of treatment of the material was very brief, indeed, in many parts a mere sketch of the subject was given. Notwithstanding this, I received letters and questions which showed me that my treatise had awakened interest in a circle of readers wider than that for which it was originally intended, and I therefore decided to reissue it in a more complete form.

The leading ideas are the same, although I think I may claim to have improved upon the manner and form in which they have been carried out. The large number of illustrations which accompany the text, as well as the wider foundation of comparative anatomy and ontogeny on which the subject rests, have, I hope, both made it more intelligible and greatly increased its usefulness.

An index has been added, giving a review of the material dealt with, and also, for the use of the lay reader, a glossary of the zoological terms employed.

I must express my hearty thanks to my publisher for the friendly assistance he has shown me.

It is my earnest hope that this work in its new form may once more win recognition, since it aims at assisting man to know himself.

THE AUTHOR.

FREIBURG, I. BADEN,
May 1893.

TABLE OF CONTENTS

	PAGE
PREFACE	v
PREFACE TO THE SECOND, REVISED AND ENLARGED, GERMAN EDITION	xi
TABLE OF CONTENTS	xiii
LIST OF ILLUSTRATIONS	xvii
INTRODUCTION	1
THE INTEGUMENT AND THE TEGUMENTAL ORGANS	3
Hair	3
Nails	11
Cutaneous Glands (Mammary Glands)	12
THE SKELETON—	
The Vertebral Column	26
The Ribs and Sternum	36
The Skull	48
Skeleton of the Limbs	67
The Pectoral (Shoulder) and Pelvic (Hip) Girdles	68
The Skeleton of the Free Limbs	76
The Skeleton of the Fore-Limb	77
The Skeleton of the Hind-Limb	81
Comparison of the Fore- and Hind-Limbs of Man	91
Changes of Position of the Limbs in relation to the Trunk	94
MUSCULAR SYSTEM	97
Retrogressive Muscles of the Trunk	98
The Muscles of the Cervical and Cephalic Regions	102
Muscles of the Limbs	109
Muscles which appear occasionally, and may be considered Atavistic	112
Progressive Muscles	114
Retrospect	120
THE NERVOUS SYSTEM	123
The Spinal Cord	123
Brain	127

	PAGE
Peripheral Nervous System	138
The Sympathetic System	139
THE SENSE ORGANS	140
Integumental Sense Organ	140
The Olfactory Organ	141
Jacobson's Organ	143
The Projectile Nose	147
The Eye	147
The Auditory Organ	150
THE ALIMENTARY CANAL AND ITS APPENDAGES	155
Palatal Ridges	155
Teeth	156
The Sublingua	161
Thyroid and Thymus	162
Bursa Pharyngea	164
Œsophagus and Stomach	164
The Vermiform Process	167
The Liver and Pancreas	171
THE RESPIRATORY SYSTEM	171
The Larynx	172
The Lungs	175
THE CIRCULATORY SYSTEM	180
The Heart	180
The Arterial System	181
The Venous System	184
The Spleen	186
THE URINOGENITAL SYSTEM	187
The Pronephros and the Primitive Kidney	187
Müllerian Duct	189
Hymen	194
The Cloaca	194
External Genital Organs of the Female	195
Male Genital Glands (Descensus Testiculorum)	196
Suprarenal Bodies	199
CONSPECTUS OF THE ORGANS MENTIONED IN THE TEXT, ARRANGED ON THE BASIS OF THEIR PHYSIOLOGICAL CONDITION	200
Organs showing Retrogressive Characters	200
Organs showing Progressive Characters	204

CONTENTS

LIST OF THE ORGANS AND TOPICS CONSIDERED IN THE TEXT, CLASSED
ACCORDING TO THE SYSTEMS TO WHICH THEY RELATE . . 206
- Integument and Integumental Organs 206
- Skeletal System 206
- Muscular System . . 207
- Nervous System . . . 208
- Sense Organs 208
- Alimentary System 208
- Respiratory System . . 208
- Circulatory System . . 209
- Urinogenital Apparatus 209

SOME ORGANS AND VESTIGES OF ORGANS WHICH SHOW REVERSION TO
THE CONDITION OF VERY PRIMITIVE VERTEBRATE TYPES . 210
CONCLUDING REMARKS 212
GLOSSARY OF TECHNICAL ZOOLOGICAL TERMS OCCURRING IN THE TEXT 219
INDEX 223

LIST OF ILLUSTRATIONS

FIG. | | PAGE
1. FACE OF AN EMBRYO FIVE MONTHS OLD, with the embryonic covering of hair. After A. Ecker 4
2. THE DISPOSITION OF THE HAIR-TRACTS ON THE HUMAN BODY. After Eschricht 6
3. THE VERTEX COCCYGEUS OF THE HUMAN EMBRYO. After A. Ecker 7
4. FOVEOLA COCCYGEA IN A HUMAN EMBRYO. After A. Ecker . 7
5. AND. JEFTICHJEFF, the "Russian Dog-man" 7
6. A, JULIA PASTRANA. B, HAIRY AINO, from the north-east coast of Yesso. After D. Macritchie . . . 8
7. YOUNG ORANG-UTAN, head from the side . 9
8. YOUNG ORANG-UTAN, head from the front 10
9. DIAGRAMMATIC REPRESENTATIONS OF THE EARLY DEVELOPMENT OF THE LEADING TYPES OF MAMMARY GLANDS. Modified from Gegenbaur 12
10. DISSECTIONS OF A BROODING FEMALE OF *Echidna hystrix*. A, Ventral aspect; B, dorsal inner view 13
11. THE "MAMMARY LINE" IN THE PIG'S EMBRYO, AT DIFFERENT STAGES. After O. Schultze . . . 15
12. THE ARRANGEMENT OF THE TEATS IN A DOG 16
13. EXAMPLE OF POLYMASTY. After D. Hansemann . . . 19
14. CASE OF POLYMASTY IN A YOUNG JAPANESE GIRL NINETEEN YEARS OLD 21
15. FRONT VIEW OF THE BODY OF A HOSPITAL ASSISTANT, TWENTY-TWO AND A HALF YEARS OLD, showing teats and hair vortices. After O. Ammon 23
16. SCHREINER VON SCHONACH, of the 16th Baden Infantry Regiment, showing supernumerary teats and teat areas. After O. Ammon 24
17. TWO YOUNG HUMAN EMBRYOS, showing freely projecting tail . 27
18. TAILED HUMAN EMBRYO. After L. Gerlach . . . 28

FIG.		PAGE
19.	"TAILED" CHILD, MOI, AGED TWELVE	29
20.	DIAGRAMMATIC RECONSTRUCTION OF THE TAIL END OF A HUMAN EMBRYO, length of trunk 8 mm. After F. Keibel .	30
20A.	DIAGRAMMATIC RECONSTRUCTION OF THE TAIL END OF A HUMAN EMBRYO, entire length 4 mm. After F. Keibel .	30
21.	THE PELVIS, showing variations in sacrum, promontory, and associated parts	35
22.	A, TRANSVERSE SECTION OF THE THORAX OF A LOWER MAMMAL (OR OF THE HUMAN EMBRYO); B, THE SAME OF A MAN .	36
23.	DIAGRAMS OF THE VERTEBRAL AND COSTAL SKELETON. A, IN THE QUADRUPED; B, IN MAN	37
24.	PART OF THE THORACIC, AND THE WHOLE LUMBAR, SACRAL, AND COCCYGEAL SECTIONS OF A YOUNG HUMAN VERTEBRAL COLUMN, dorsal aspect	40
25.	DIAGRAM OF A TRANSVERSE SECTION OF THE HIP GIRDLE AND SACRUM: A, OF A SALAMANDER; B, OF MAN, showing detailed constituents	41
26.	A, FIRST THORACIC SKELETAL SEGMENT, FOR COMPARISON WITH B, FIFTH CERVICAL VERTEBRA, OF MAN	41
27.	A, PORTION OF THE THORACIC SKELETON OF AN ADULT FEMALE POSSESSED OF A PAIR OF FREE CERVICAL RIBS. B, EXAMPLE OF THE REDUCTION OF THE FIRST PAIR OF THORACIC RIBS, IN AN ADULT MALE	42
28.	SHOULDER GIRDLE OF ORNITHORHYNCHUS . . .	46
29.	EPISTERNUM OF AN EMBRYO MOLE. After A. Götte .	47
30.	EPISTERNAL VESTIGES IN MAN	48
31.	A, SLIGHTLY DIAGRAMMATIC MEDIAN LONGITUDINAL SECTION THROUGH THE HEAD AND ANTERIOR PORTION OF THE TRUNK OF A HUMAN EMBRYO, SEVENTEEN TO EIGHTEEN WEEKS OLD. After W. His. B, EMBRYO TORPEDO, as seen by transmitted light. After H. E. and F. Ziegler	49
32.	SKULL OF IMMANUEL KANT. After C. von Kupffer .	50
33.	SKULL OF A CHILD SEVEN YEARS OLD . . .	51
34.	SKULL OF AN AUSTRALIAN FROM THE MURRAY RIVER . .	51
35.	SKULL OF A YOUNG ORANG-UTAN . . .	52
36.	SKULL OF AN ADULT ORANG-UTAN	52
37.	MEDIAN SECTIONS THROUGH THE HEAD OF A DEER, A BABOON, AND A MAN	54
38.	A to C, VARIOUS FORMS OF THE OS INCAE. D, E, DIAGRAMS OF THE BONES OF THE OCCIPITAL REGION IN THE EMBRYO. Partly after Ficalbi	56

LIST OF ILLUSTRATIONS

FIG.   PAGE

39. SKULL OF A GIRL TWO YEARS OLD, showing broad ala magna of sphenoid 59
40. SKULL OF AN ABORIGINAL AUSTRALIAN, showing contracted ala magna of the sphenoid 59
41. SKULL OF A NEGRO EUNUCH, showing epipteric bone . . 61
42. SKULL OF A TURCO, with the temporal bone nearly reaching the frontal 62
43. SKULL OF A TWO-YEAR-OLD CHIMPANZEE, from the side . . 62
44. HARD PALATE OF A CAUCASIAN, A NEGRO, AND AN ADULT ORANG-UTAN 63
45. HEAD OF A HUMAN EMBRYO OF THE FOURTH MONTH, to show the auditory ossicles, tympanic ring, with Meckel's cartilage, and the hyoid and thyroid apparatus 65
46. SKULL OF A TAILED AMPHIBIAN (*Menopoma*) 66
47. TRANSVERSE SECTION THROUGH THE EMBRYO OF A SHARK (*Pristiurus melanostomus*), showing limb buds . . . 67
48. DIAGRAM ILLUSTRATING THE DEVELOPMENT OF THE FINS OF A FISH 68
49. DIAGRAMMATIC REPRESENTATION OF THREE SUCCESSIVE STAGES IN THE DEVELOPMENT OF THE PELVIC FINS OF A SHARK . 69
50. AN ATTEMPT TO DEPICT DIAGRAMMATICALLY THE PROCESS BY WHICH THE LIMBS OF TERRESTRIAL VERTEBRATES WOULD APPEAR TO HAVE BEEN PROBABLY DERIVED FROM THE FINS OF FISHES 70
51. PECTORAL GIRDLE OF A TAILED AMPHIBIAN, ventral aspect . 71
52. RIGHT BLADE-BONE OF A NEW-BORN CHILD, showing ossification of the coracoid 72
53. PELVIS OF A FEMALE CHIMPANZEE, TWO YEARS OLD . . 75
54. RIGHT HUMERUS OF A NEGRO, showing perforation of the olecranon fossa 77
55. DISTAL EXTREMITY OF THE HUMERUS, to show epicondylar foramina, in *Hatteria*, *Lacerta*, the Cat, and in Man . . 78
56. SKELETON OF THE HIND-LIMB OF A TAILED AMPHIBIAN (*Spelerpes fuscus*) 79
57. DIAGRAMS OF THE HUMAN CARPUS. A, EMBRYO; B, ADULT . 80
58. PROXIMAL HALF OF A LEFT HUMAN FEMUR POSSESSED OF THREE TROCHANTERS 82
59. THE ANKLE-JOINT, in a Chimpanzee, an Australian native, and a Caucasian 84
60. SKELETON OF THE LEFT PES OF A CHIMPANZEE, dorsal aspect 85
61. SKELETON OF THE LEFT HAND, dorsal aspect . . . 86
62. SKELETON OF THE LEFT FOOT, dorsal aspect . . . 87

FIG.		PAGE
63.	FORE- AND HIND-LIMBS OF A TWO MONTHS' HUMAN EMBRYO, to show the position of the thumb and great toe . . .	89
64.	POSTERIOR END OF THE BODY OF TWO HUMAN EMBRYOS, with left hind-limb and umbilical cord	90
65.	LARVAL SALAMANDER. After Hatschek. A, with limbs turned down; B, with limbs turned up	92
66.	SKELETON OF A YOUNG BEAR, illustrating the positions of the limbs. After Hatschek	93
67.	DIAGRAM OF THE DISTRIBUTION OF THE PLATYSMA OVER THE HEAD. After Gegenbaur	104
68.	SUPERFICIAL MUSCULATURE OF THE FACE IN *Lepilemur mustelinus*. After Ruge	105
69.	FACIAL MUSCLES AND NERVES OF THE LEMUROID *Propithecus*. After Ruge	106
70.	MUSCLES OF THE EPICRANIAL REGION IN MAN, WITH CERTAIN OF THE FACIAL MUSCLES. After Gegenbaur	107
71.	THE PINNA, in Man, a Baboon, an Ox, *Macacus* and *Cercopithecus*. After Schwalbe and Henle	108
72.	SUPERFICIAL MUSCLES AND TENDONS OF THE DORSUM OF THE FOOT. After Rauber	111
73.	DEEP MUSCLES OF THE FLEXOR SIDE OF THE FOREARM. After Rauber	116
74.	MEDIAN PLANTAR MUSCLES IN THEIR CONNECTION WITH THE FLEXOR TENDONS. After Rauber.	117
75.	DEEP DORSAL MUSCLES OF THE FOREARM. After Rauber .	118
76.	LOWER PORTION OF THE SPINAL CORD, WITH THE CAUDA EQUINA AND THE DURA MATER, dorsal aspect. After Schwalbe .	124
77.	BRAIN OF A DOG-FISH (*Scyllum canicula*), three views . .	126
78.	CEREBRUM OF A FEMALE CHIMPANZEE TWO YEARS OLD, showing asymmetrical development	128
79.	BRAIN OF A FEMALE CHIMPANZEE TWO YEARS OLD, lateral aspect	128
80.	CEREBRUM OF THE GIBBON (*Hylobates*), lateral aspect . .	129
81.	CEREBRUM OF A SEVEN TO EIGHT MONTHS' HUMAN EMBRYO, dorsal aspect	129
82.	CEREBRUM OF A SEVEN TO EIGHT MONTHS' HUMAN EMBRYO, lateral aspect	130
83.	HYPOTHETICAL MEDIAN-LONGITUDINAL SECTION THROUGH THE SKULL AND BRAIN OF A VERTEBRATE EMBRYO. Partly after Huxley	131
84.	BRAIN OF A RABBIT, three views	132
85.	LONGITUDINAL SECTION THROUGH THE PINEAL ORGAN OF A REPTILE (*Hatteria punctata*). After Baldwin Spencer . .	133

LIST OF ILLUSTRATIONS xxi

FIG. PAGE
86. MEDIAN LONGITUDINAL SECTION THROUGH THE HEAD OF A
   NEWLY-HATCHED LARVA OF THE LAMPREY (*Petromyzon planeri*) 136
87. LATERAL VIEW OF THE NASAL CHAMBER OF A HUMAN EMBRYO . 141
88. SAGITTAL SECTION THROUGH THE NASAL AND BUCCAL CAVITIES
   OF THE HUMAN HEAD. 142
89. A-D, STAGES IN THE DEVELOPMENT OF THE SO-CALLED JACOBSON'S
   ORGAN OF THE URODELA. E, THE SAME ORGAN IN A GYMNO-
   PHIONE. F-H, THE NOSE AND JACOBSON'S ORGAN IN
   Lacerta, A PLACENTAL MAMMAL, AND *Ornithorhynchus*. H,
   after Symington 144-145
90. HEADS OF TWO HUMAN EMBRYOS AT SECOND AND THIRD MONTHS 147
91. HUMAN EYE 148
92. DIAGRAM TO ILLUSTRATE THE SHIFTING OF THE LACHRYMAL
   GLAND, WHICH HAS TAKEN PLACE IN THE COURSE OF
   PHYLOGENY 149
93. EYE OF A MONGOLIAN, WITH THE EPICANTHUS 150
94. DIAGRAM TO ILLUSTRATE THE METAMORPHOSIS DURING DEVELOP-
   MENT OF THE VISCERAL SKELETAL ARCHES 151
95. PALATE OF A HUMAN EMBRYO AT THE EIGHTH MONTH . . 155
96. PALATAL FOLDS OF THE RACOON (*Procyon lotor*). . . . 156
97. HUMAN MOUTH, IN WHICH THE DEVELOPMENT OF THE UPPER
   OUTER INCISORS HAS BEEN SUPPRESSED 158
98. HUMAN STOMACH 166
99. THE CÆCUM AND PROCESSUS VERMIFORMIS IN A HUMAN
   EMBRYO 167
100. THE CÆCUM AND VERMIFORM PROCESS OF A HUMAN EMBRYO . 168
101. THE CÆCUM AND VERMIFORM PROCESS IN A KANGAROO 169
102. HUMAN LARYNX IN FRONTAL SECTION 174
103. A SERIES OF WHOLLY DIAGRAMMATIC FIGURES TO ILLUSTRATE
   THE COMPARATIVE MORPHOLOGY OF THE URINOGENITAL
   ORGANS OF THE VERTEBRATA 191
104. DIAGRAMMATIC REPRESENTATIONS OF THE CHIEF TYPES OF
   UTERUS OCCURRING IN THE PLACENTAL MAMMALS . . . 193
105. A, PARTLY DIAGRAMMATIC REPRESENTATION OF THE EMBRYONIC
   URINOGENITAL APPARATUS OF A MALE MAMMAL, showing its
   relations to the Ventral abdominal wall. B, THE PENIS AND
   SCROTUM OF A HUMAN EMBRYO, 15 cm. long. Both figures
   founded on the work of Klaatsch 197

THE STRUCTURE OF MAN

INTRODUCTION

SOME thirty-four years have elapsed since the publication of Charles Darwin's work *On the Origin of Species by Means of Natural Selection*. A short period of time, and yet important enough to throw into the shade all previous centuries, so profound is the significance of the results obtained in it, in the field of Natural Science.

Darwin's book brought about a reformation not only of Zoology, but of our whole knowledge of surrounding Nature. It marked, in fact, the commencement of a new epoch, and of a new cosmology. This has been said so often and demonstrated so thoroughly, that the topic need not be further enlarged upon here. I cannot, however, refrain from briefly sketching the condition of the natural sciences during the last two centuries, since it is only on such a background that a correct picture of the enormous transformation which has since been effected in the intellectual life of all cultured nations can be obtained.

In spite of the great discoveries made, in the sixteenth and seventeenth centuries, by such men as Kepler, Newton, Harvey, Schwammerdam, Malpighi, and Leeuwenhoeck, the Aristotelian philosophy, which had been stirred to new life at the period of the Reformation, was universally accepted. Its exegetical principle rested on the assumption of the existence of an intelligent design, to which the phenomena of nature were subordinated. The teleological speculations which arose out of it, and the resulting anthropocentric and anthropomorphic cosmology, outlived the centuries named. Indeed, in spite of all progress in science, they continued to count many of their most brilliant advocates among distinguished scientific men, even into the fifties of the present century. This philosophy was deeply rooted in human vanity, receiving immense support from the Mosaic cosmogony, which assigned to Man a sovereign position over nature, and especially over the animal kingdom. Every attempt to shake this sovereignty was regarded as heresy. Even the laity persistently refused to submit Man to the same strict scientific analysis which, with increasing clearness, was being applied to the surrounding forms of life by the existing schools of natural philosophy.

In spite of this opposition, however, the theory of descent steadily gained ground, and its advance was especially favoured by new and surprising results attained in the three closely allied branches of science—Palæontology, Comparative Anatomy, and Embryology. The proofs of the great changes which must have taken place in both the animal and vegetable kingdoms, during the immeasurable periods consumed in the development of our planet, became more and more convincing.

The earlier assumption of repeated separate acts of creation gave way to a more satisfactory and strictly scientific conception of the fundamental unity of all organic nature. "Blood relationship, and not some unknown plan of creation, forms the invisible band which unites organisms in various degrees of similarity," and in this great family Man must find his place. He forms but a link in the chain, and has no right to consider himself an exception. To claim for himself a special act of creation, in order to account for his appearance in the series of living creatures, would be nothing less than a denial of the unity of physiological science.

It may be that we have not as yet succeeded in tracing back the primitive history of Man beyond diluvial times by the light of palæontological discoveries, for no certain proof of the actual existence of tertiary Man has been obtained. But this "break in the record" cannot in the least impair the evidence of morphology as to the real ancestry of Man. Comparative morphology points not only to the essentially similar plan of organisation of the bodies of all Vertebrates, and to the agreement in their entrance into life, individual existence, and final dissolution, but also to the occurrence in them of certain organs, or parts of organs, now known as "vestigial."

By such organs are meant those which were formerly of greater physiological significance than at present. In the course of generations, in consequence of the adaptation of the body to special conditions of life, they have been, so to speak, put out of the running, subjected to reduction or degeneration, and now persist as mere vestiges. Such organs, which remain inexplicable by the doctrine of special creation or upon any teleological hypothesis, can be satisfactorily explained by the theory of selection. They are found alike in the lower animals and in Man; and it is evident that these relics of a long vanished epoch are of peculiar interest in this latter case, where Palæontology offers us no help. Their closer study, therefore, has a fascination for us which we cannot resist.

In the attempt to track the primitive Man, *i.e.* to follow up the traces of Man's ancestry, we shall find indications—here of progression—there of retrogression. These will help to throw light on Man's position among the Vertebrata.

Thirty-one years have passed since Huxley published his *Evidence as to Man's Place in Nature*. When we remember how much work has been done since, and what results have been attained in physical Anthropology, Anatomy, and Embryology, it will, I think, be evident that the time has come once more to look back, to gather together into a whole the new material which now lies scattered far and wide, and from it to attempt once more to estimate what Man is, what he was, and what he may become.

THE INTEGUMENT AND THE TEGUMENTAL ORGANS

In Man, as in all Vertebrata, two of the three germinal layers take part in the formation of the integument, the outer (ectoderm) and the middle (mesoderm). The ectoderm gives rise to the epidermis (cuticle or scarf-skin) and the mesoderm to the corium or dermis.

The epidermis, again, consists of a superficial and a deep layer, of which the latter is of the greater physiological importance, all the so-called cutaneous or tegumental organs owing their origin to it. To these belong (1) the various corneous structures, such as hair and nails; (2) many different kinds of glands; and (3) the terminal apparatus of nearly all the sensory organs.

Hair

Man is the least hairy of all the Primates; indeed, his skin may be called almost smooth. Apart from the head, the only parts of the body abundantly supplied with hair are, as a rule, the pubic, perineal, and axillary regions, although a careful examination of the skin shows that hair follicles are to be found over its whole surface. In males, in addition to the parts already mentioned, hair is frequently strongly developed on the ventral and dorsal regions of the trunk, *i.e.* on the breast and abdomen, and on the buttocks and neck, and on the limbs.

These facts alone would suffice to render it probable that man was in primitive times far more hairy than at present, but still stronger evidence can be brought forward.

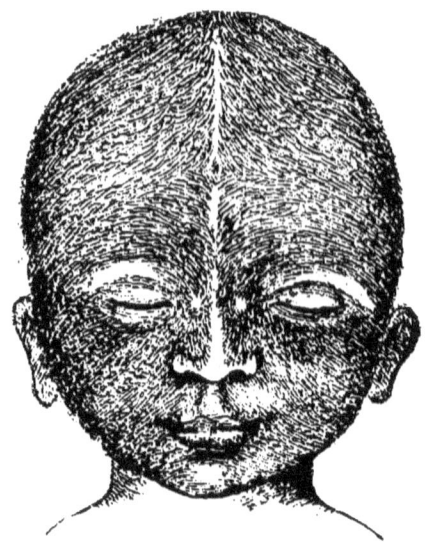

FIG. 1.—FACE OF AN EMBRYO FIVE MONTHS OLD, with the embryonic covering of hair. (After Ecker.)

The first traces of hair appear, in the human embryo, as early as the twelfth or thirteenth week, the earliest being found about the forehead, the mouth, and the eyebrows, *i.e.* in those parts of the body where, in the lower Mammals, the so-called " whiskers " (vibrissæ) or tactile hairs usually appear. It is evident that, morphologically, the hairs about the mouth and eyebrows in Men belong to this same category. The hairs begin to break through the integument at the end of the fifth month, and they continue to do so till the seventh month, those of the head being the earliest and those of the limbs the latest to appear.[1] In the

---

[1] The fact of the appearance of hair in different parts of the body in regular order, the lower limbs being the last to become thus clothed, has apparently attained popular recognition in the very old proverb "he has hair on his toes," which may doubtless be referred to a time when boots and shoes did not play the part they now do. From what I have gathered in conversation with inhabitants of Berne (Ober-

sixth month, the whole body of the embryo, except the surface of the hands and feet, the red edges of the lips, the glans penis and clitoridis, and the inner surface of the foreskin, is covered with abundant soft woolly hair (lanugo).[1]

In certain parts of the body the hairs are arranged closely and quite regularly in tracts, just as birds' feathers are arranged in the so-called "*pterylæ.*" These hair-tracts (Fig. 2) are vortex-like in arrangement, diverging over some areas, converging over others.

In the former (cf. the hair of the head) the hairs point with their free ends outwards, from the vertex as a centre ; in the latter, on the other hand, the direction of the hairs is the reverse of this, their free ends being directed inwards, *i.e.* towards the centre of the vortex. This latter, converging, disposition is only found, both in the lower Mammals and in Man, at parts where an organ either projects during life, as in the case of horns and antlers, or has projected at some period in ontogenetic or phylogenetic development.

An excellent example of this is afforded by the radial arrangement of hairs often found in the male sex in the region of the navel, or still better by the "*vertex coccygeus*" (Fig. 3) described by Ecker. The position of this latter exactly corresponds in the embryo with the point at which, before the bending of the os sacrum took place, the extremity of the coccyx pushed against the skin ; *i.e.* with the point where the coccyx formerly projected as a free tail, the cauda humana (cf. pp. 27, 28).

Just before birth the position of the vertex coccygeus shifts, a hairless area being developed (Glabella coccygea) which may sink in to form a pit (Foveola coccygea, *fv*, Fig. 4) (Ecker). On the other hand it frequently attains such a degree of development,

deutschen) and of Holland (Niederdeutschen), I am convinced that "on his toes" (Zehen) is the right version of the proverb, and not "on his teeth" (Zähnen).

Many similar perversions of old popular sayings, or of words of which the original meaning has gradually been lost in later generations, are to be found ; for instance, the expression "to have his sheep (Schäffchen) in the dry" originated on the coast, where "to have his ship (Schiffchen) in the dry" is still heard. Again, the Schönberg near Freiburg was originally called Schynberg, from Schyn, which means a witch, a word which has been retained in the "Witch's Valley" at the foot of this hill, and in the Swabian term of contempt "Schyn-Aas" (literally witch carcase).

[1] In the fourth or fifth month the human embryo has a distinct stratum corneum with an epidermal layer outside it, which corresponds with the epitrichium of Reptiles and of many Mammalian embryos (Edentata, *Dicotyles*, *Sus*, and others). After the sixth month of embryonic life the latter disappears from most parts of the body. The epitrichial layer covers the hairs and the glands, being able to some extent to keep back the secretions of the latter. In this way it provides for the accumulation of a rich secretory deposit, the so-called "vernix caseosa."

even in the sixth or seventh month, that the hair may be twirled between the fingers like a moustache.

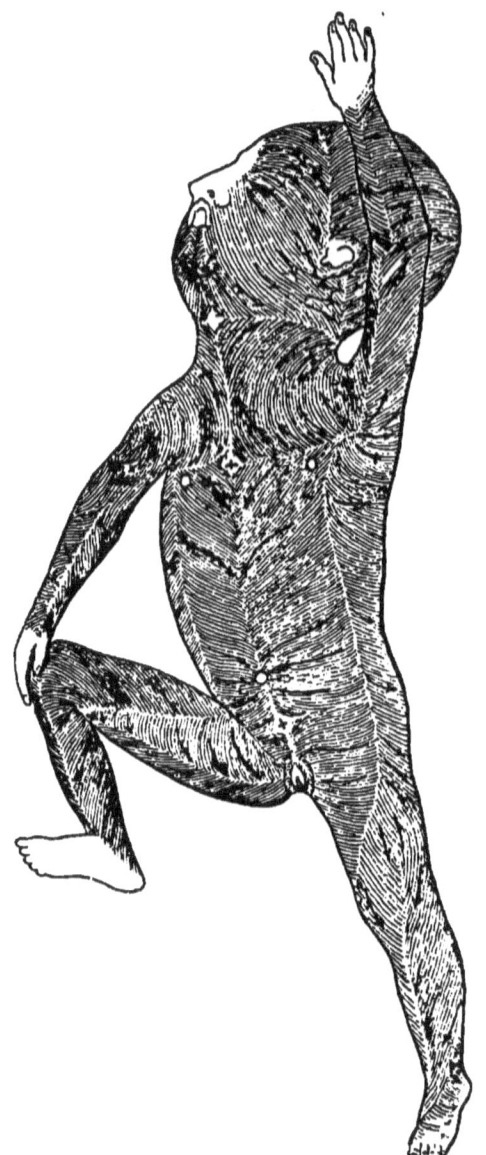

Fig. 2.—The Disposition of the Hair-Tracts on the Human Body.
(After Eschricht.)

TEGUMENTAL ORGANS 7

Hypertrichosis, or excessive hairiness, which also not in-

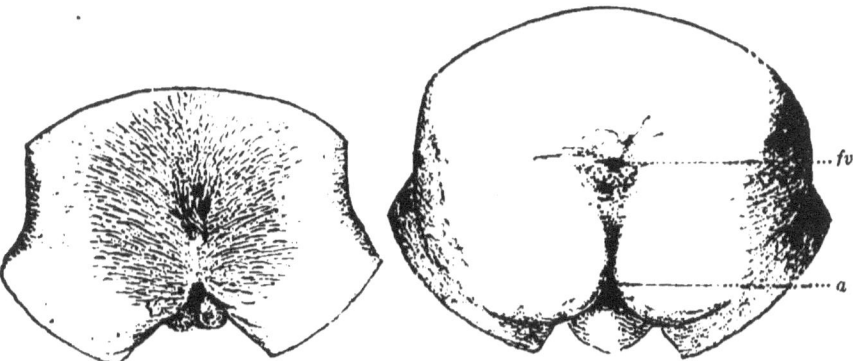

FIG. 3.—THE VERTEX COCCYGEUS OF THE HUMAN EMBRYO. (After Ecker.)

FIG. 4.—FOVEOLA COCCYGEA IN A HUMAN EMBRYO. (After Ecker.) a, anus ; fc, foveola coccygea.

FIG. 5.—AND. JEFTICHJEFF, the "Russian Dog-man."

frequently occurs in adults of both sexes, is a very interesting phenomenon. By far the greater number of such cases, as

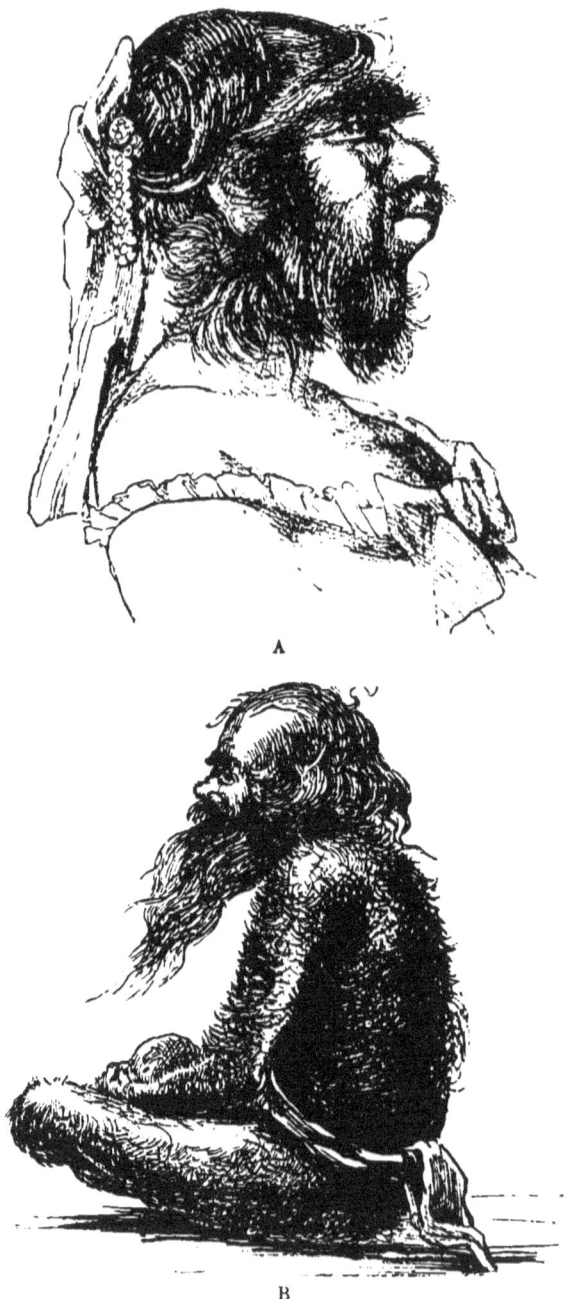

FIG. 6.—A, JULIA PASTRANA. B, HAIRY AINO, from the north-east coast of Yesso. (After Macritchie.)

Ecker has specially pointed out, appear to be due to a temporary arrest in the development of the hairy covering, and the persistence and subsequent growth in post-embryonic life of the fœtal woolly covering or lanugo. We can describe this as Pseudohypertrichosis lanuginosa (Bonnet), since normally the greater part of the lanugo is said to be shed, and to be replaced by stronger medullated hairs.

FIG. 7.—YOUNG ORANG-UTAN. *Zeitschrift für Ethnologie (Anthropolog. Gesellschaft)*, Bd. viii.

To this category belong all the well-known cases of "Dog-men," or hairy men,[1] *e.g.* the Ambraser hairy family, Barbara Uslerin, and Mrs. Lent (commonly known as Zennora Pastrana II.); also the Russian Dog-man Jeftichjeff (Fig. 5), his son Fedor, and the Burmese Shwé-Maong and his family. In the cases of Jeftichjeff senior, and Shwé-Maong, the whole face, except the red edges of the lips, was thickly covered with delicate, soft, and partly curly hair, such as also projected from the orifices of the ears and nose. The body of the Russian was somewhat

[1] In these cases defects in the dentition and other traces of arrested development (*e.g.* retarded puberty) not infrequently occur.

less hairy than that of the Burmese, the whole of whose trunk and limbs was covered with hair from 4-8 inches long.

The extreme hairiness of the Ainos (Fig. 6, B) may probably also be referred to Pseudohypertrichosis; but this point requires closer investigation.

In all the cases mentioned above, the persistence of the vestigial lanugo must undoubtedly be regarded as a return to a

FIG. 8.—YOUNG ORANG-UTAN. *Zeitschrift für Ethnologie (Anthropolog. Gesellschaft)*, Bd. viii.

primitive hairy condition in Man; whereas true hairiness, or "hypertrichosis vera," is quite a different thing. This, which was well exemplified in the once famous dancer Julia Pastrana I., is due to an excessive development of the secondary covering of hair. In her case (Fig. 6, A) the greater part of the primary hairy covering (the lanugo) must be considered to have been shed during embryonic development.

Bonnet rightly points out that "in Man and the domestic animals, the accessory structures of the epidermis accurately register the balance of nutrition," and that various circumstances, such as climate, domestication, natural and artificial selection, influence the hairy covering. Further, the development of this may be in inverse ratio to the thickness of the integument, and particularly of the epidermis (Leydig), the hair and the epidermis supplementing one another in the work of protecting the body. This is illustrated, on the one hand, by animals which have a delicate epidermis and thin skin and a thick covering of wool or fur; and on the other by animals like the Rhinoceroses, Hippopotami, some Armadillos, and Scaly Ant-Eaters, in which, while the epidermis is so thickened as to form a hard carapace, the hair is very scanty.

I cannot leave this subject without touching upon the question of the origin of the Mammalia, especially as this chapter in morphology has recently been ably dealt with by Max Weber, who deduces reasons for taking up the following position. The first Mammals, as descendants from primitive scaly Reptiles, were covered with scales, differing from those of the Reptiles only in minor points. Behind the scales of the primitive Mammals there first appeared a few small hairs, the origin of which it is difficult to explain with certainty. By degrees, as a constant temperature was maintained by the body, the covering of hair attained a greater development and the scales degenerated. Scales, somewhat specialised, are still retained as a covering for the mammalian body in a few cases, *e.g.* Armadillos and Scaly Ant-Eaters. Among other Mammals they are found, as a rule, only on the tail and limbs. The recurrent arrangement of the hairs, however, due to their original development behind scales, has very generally persisted, and on this basis hairs may be considered to imply the earlier presence of scales.

NAILS

The nails of the fourth and fifth fingers (and especially the latter) most nearly suggest the claws of the lower animals, in being decidedly arched from side to side. As the thumb is approached the nails become more and more flat, and the like is true of the great toe as compared with the four lesser toes. This condition commences with the Lemuroidea [although among the lower Mammalia the Squirrels, for example, bear a flattened nail upon the pollex].

On the under edge of the nail, between it and the ball of the finger, is found the last vestige of a structure which in the Apes is covered with a thickened layer of epidermis.[1] This structure undergoes considerable degeneration, even during intra-uterine life, through the advancing development of the ball of the finger (Gegenbaur).

[1] This structure is most conspicuous in the Ungulata, and it is there known as the "frog."

CUTANEOUS GLANDS (MAMMARY GLANDS)

The cutaneous glands of Man fall into two classes: sweat-glands and sebaceous glands, with their modifications. Certain of these glands play an important part in Mammals on account of their odoriferous secretions. In Man the secretion of the axillary and anal glands is well known to have a penetrating odour, but the significance of this we have so far failed to discover.

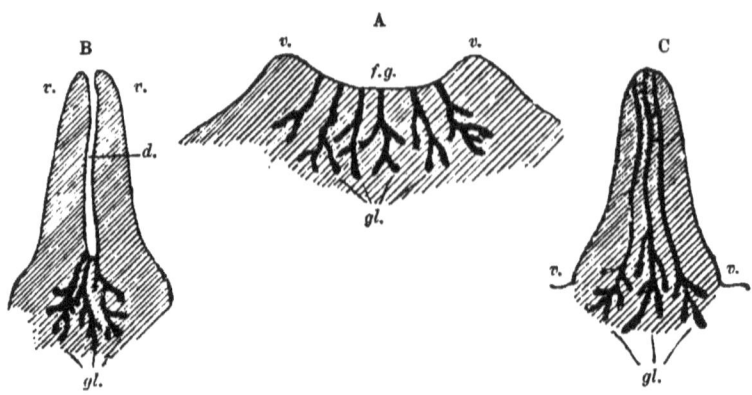

FIG. 9.—DIAGRAMMATIC REPRESENTATIONS OF THE EARLY DEVELOPMENT OF THE LEADING TYPES OF MAMMARY GLANDS. (Modified from Gegenbaur.)
A, First or undifferentiated (mammary pit) stage ; B, stage of the false teat ; C, stage of the true teat ; *v. v.*, rim (or rampart) of the glandular area ; *f.g.*, glandular area ; *gl.*, mammary glands; *d.*, mammary canal.

The mammary glands, in all Mammals higher than the Monotremata,[1] must be regarded as aggregates of much modified sebaceous glands. This is attested not only by their whole structure, and by the nature of their secretion, but also by the fact that the sebaceous glands lying immediately around the teat in the female, the so-called Montgomery's glands, grow larger when lactation begins, many of them yielding milk. This functional transition from sebaceous to mammary glands furnishes the best evidence for their homology (Gegenbaur). In rare cases sebaceous glands still farther from the teat may also take part in lactation, instances being known in which such glands extended as far as the axillary region.

These facts lead us to believe, *à priori*, that all parts of the skin may be capable of producing mammary glands.

[1] The mammary organ of the Monotremata is derived from sweat-glands, so that we have a diphyletic origin for the mammary glands collectively considered (Gegenbaur).

The development of mammary glands and teats is always initiated by a shallow depression of the integument (*f.g.*, Fig. 9, A), the mammary pit; the base of this pit is the glandular area, and the surrounding border (*r*) the rampart of the gland. The Malpighian stratum of the epidermis at the base of the glandular area, by inward proliferation, gives rise to the glandular tissue.

The mode of development of the teats is not the same for all

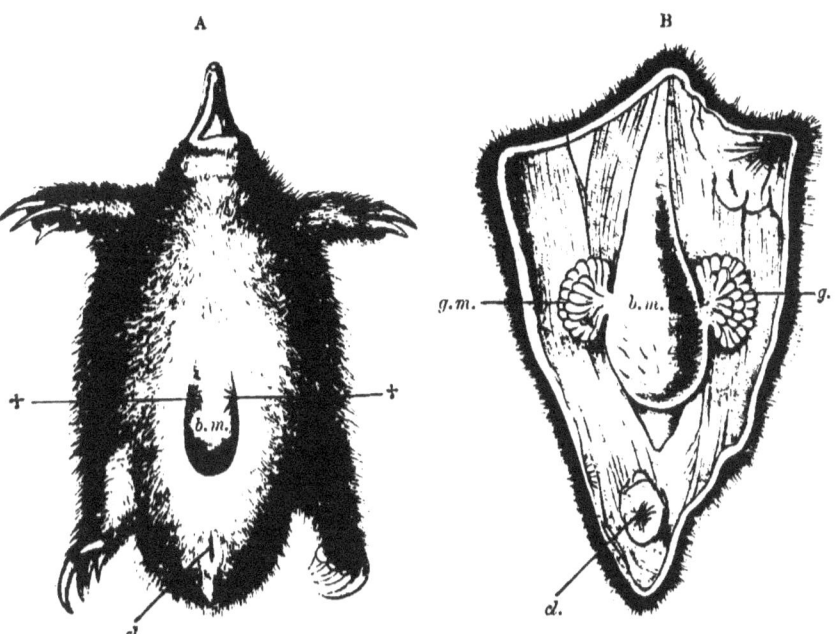

FIG. 10.—DISSECTIONS OF A BROODING FEMALE OF *Echidna hystrix*. A, Ventral aspect; B, dorsal inner view. † †, The two tufts of hair, in the lateral folds of the mammary pouch from which the secretion flows. On each side of the pouch (*b.m.*), which is surrounded by strong muscles, a group of mammary glands (*g.m.*) opens; *cl.* denotes the cloaca in each figure. (After W. Haacke.)

Mammals. Either (Fig. 9, B) the rampart which borders the depression rises and forms a tube (the lumen of which is known as the mammary canal), into the base of which the true ducts open, or (Fig. 9, C) the glandular area rises in the shape of a papilla, while the rampart degenerates. The latter, in which the nipple must be considered as a secondary formation, is exemplified in the Marsupials, the Lemuroidea, Apes, and Man; in the former, which obtains in the Carnivora, Pigs, Horses, and Ruminants, it is a primary formation. The first indications of the primary formation are found in certain Marsupials (*Phalangista vulpina*) and among placental Mammals as high as Carnivora (Gegenbaur).

The question now arises, whether the developmental stages of the mammary glands point to primitive conditions which in any degree persist in the lower Mammals? An examination of the Monotremata shows that this may be the case; and to make this clear we must enter somewhat further into detail.

In the Monotremata, in which as yet there are no teats, the ducts of the mammary organ open in a group on the ventral integument. As the reproductive period approaches, if fertilisation has taken place, a temporary depression of the ventral integument occurs, which gives rise to a pouch (*b.m.*, Fig. 10). The egg is deposited in this pouch, and the mammary fluid is probably carried to the young animal to which the egg gives rise, by means of the pointed tufts of hair which project around the apertures of the glands. Closer examination shows that the ducts open into two cutaneous depressions, which lie near the tufts just mentioned, in the lateral folds of the mammary pouch. These may be called mammary pits, and are of considerable importance, because they are repeated in the development of the various forms of nipples and mammary organs occurring in the higher orders of Mammals. We have here a glandular area which, like that already described (Fig 9, A), is nothing more than a depressed portion of the external integument, with all its characteristic derivatives, such as hairs, glands, and pigment.

Before passing to the question of the disposition of the mammary glands on the body, an important discovery, for which we have to thank Oskar Schultze, must be mentioned.

In young embryos of Mammals, *e.g.* the Pig, a ridge-like prominence (*l.m.*, Fig. 11) is found on each side, running from the base of the anterior limb, which is at this period a mere stump, towards that of the posterior limb and into the inguinal furrow. This is due to a linear thickening of the developing epidermis, and especially of the stratum Malpighi. This lateral epidermal ridge represents the common epithelial rudiment of the mammary glands, and may be called the "Mammary Line." Along this line a row of fusiform thickenings develop (Fig. 11, B and C), the whole presenting the appearance of a regularly varicose fibre. These protruding "primitive teats" flatten out again at a later stage, and in no way represent the teats which form later, although they generally correspond in number with the centres of origin of the future glands.

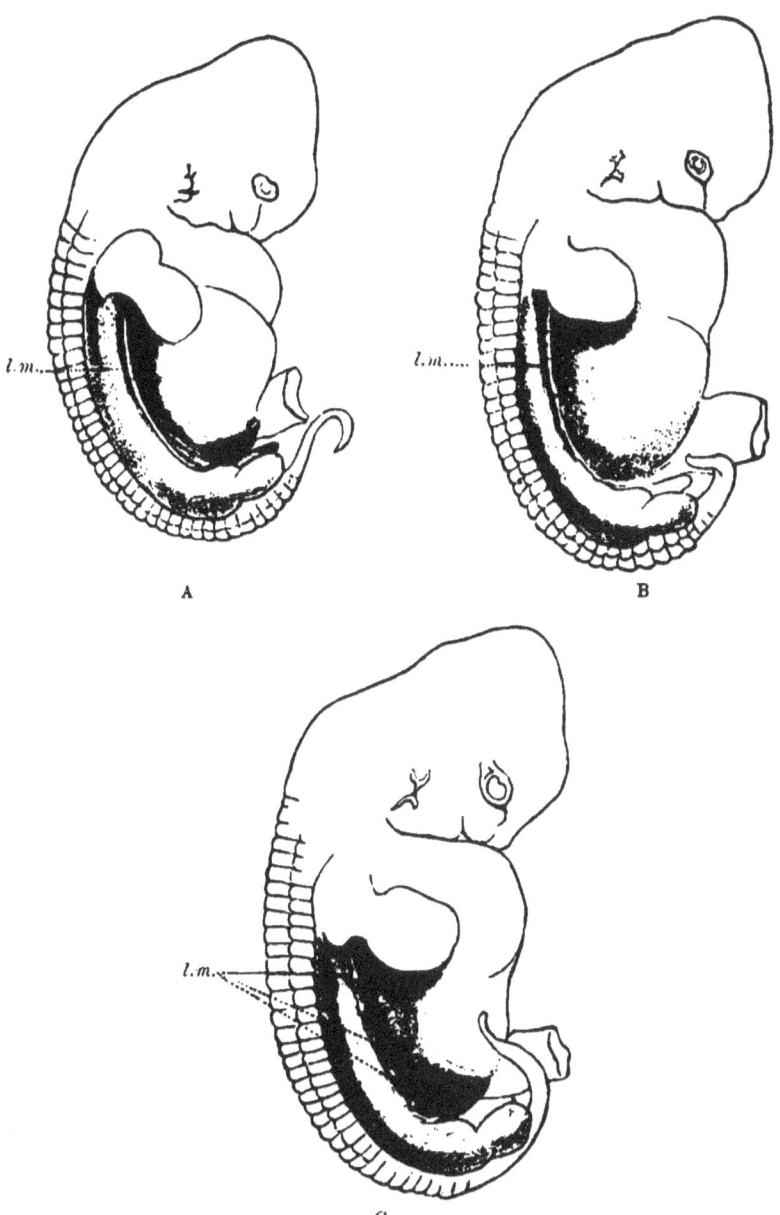

Fig. 11.—The "Mammary Line" (*l.m.*) in the Pig's Embryo at Different Stages. (After O. Schultze.)
A, embryo I, 5 cm. (from head to coccyx); B, embryo I, 7 cm. long; C, embryo I, 9 cm. long.

Resorption of those portions of the mammary line which lie between the primitive teats soon begins to take place, and in such a manner that the originally elongated and fusiform eminences become rounded. At a later stage, as above stated, these flatten out, and extend at the same time into the subjacent tissues. In this way they form the well-known button-like epidermal proliferations, which have generally been considered to mark the first stage in the development of the mammary glands, a stage which is immediately followed by the formation of the so-called mammary pits.

Later on we shall have to refer to the conclusions, with respect to Man, to be drawn from Schultze's observation, but we may now turn to the question of the disposition of the mammary glands on the body.

Although the position of these organs may vary greatly, the ventral side of the body has the preference on account of the greater facility with which the young can reach the teats. The position in the postero-ventral region, i.e. in the region of the groin, may be considered the most primitive. The udder of some Ungulates, as is well known, is found in this position, and the same is also the case in the Cetacea. In the great group of the Carnivora, and in the Pigs, the teats are found on the thoracic and abdominal regions (Fig. 12), arranged in two rows converging towards the pelvic region. In other groups, again, they are confined to the pectoral region (e.g. Elephants, Sirenia, many Lemuroidea, Chiroptera, Apes, and Man).

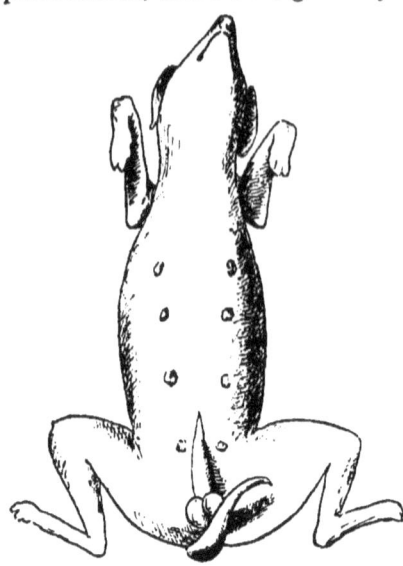

FIG. 12.—SHOWING THE ARRANGEMENT OF THE TEATS IN A DOG, in two longitudinal rows converging towards the pelvic region.

The great range of variation in the position of the teats and mammary glands deserves careful attention, since it enables us to satisfactorily explain the existence of so-called supernumerary mammary glands and teats, which often occur in human beings of both sexes. The term polymasty is used to denote the former condition, and polythely[1] the latter.

During the last three decades an immense number of cases of this kind have been recorded; and as it is quite impossible to consider them all here, we must limit ourselves to a few of the more characteristic. We may remark at the outset that the increase in number of the mammary glands or teats, in both men and women, may be regarded as a return to a primitive condition in which many glands were developed and many young were produced at a birth. The change from polymasty to bimasty can be observed at the present day in the Lemuroidea. In these animals the teats of the groin and abdomen are functionless and clearly degenerating, whereas the pair which occur in the pectoral region are well developed. In accordance with this most Lemuroids give birth to only two young, which they carry about at the breast. This habit permits of the greatest freedom of movement (for example in climbing), and renders explicable the gradual degeneration of the other teats.

But how are we to explain the presence of such pronounced vestigial organs as the teats of the male human being?

It is usually considered that they are inherited from the female, and it is possible that this explanation is correct. But when we find that in the Monotremata the mammary glands are almost equally well developed in both the male and the female, it seems not improbable that originally both sexes may have taken an equal share in the bringing up of the young.

It is certain that a functional condition of the mammary glands (gynækomasty) may occur in men.[2] [Humboldt records a case, to which he bore ocular testimony, of a man who, at the age of thirty-two, was left in charge of a sucking child by the death of his wife. Not knowing how to rear it, he in despair pressed it to his own bosom; and it is alleged that hypertrophy of his breast, with milk secretion sufficient for the rearing of the infant, was thereby induced.][3] It is also known that boys, both

[1] Either well-developed or rudimentary supernumerary teats are not infrequently found in various Mammalian orders, for instance two rudimentary teats often occur behind the four normal teats of the cow.

[2] [I can testify to this in person, for, while bathing with friends on the Welsh coast at the age of thirty-six years, milk, sufficient to cover a threepennypiece, issued from my left breast on contact with the towel. This state of affairs continued for three days, the right breast remaining inactive.—G. B. H.]

[3] [During the passage of these pages through the press this subject has been comprehensively dealt with by Schaumann (*Verhandlg. d. physik.-medic. Gesellsch.*, Würzburg, Bd. xxviii. p. 1)].

soon after birth and at the time of puberty, may produce milk (so-called "witch's milk") from more or less swollen breasts.[1] Milk has also certainly been obtained from male goats and from castrated rams, and this has been found on chemical analysis to be even richer in caseine than ordinary milk.

[In this connection it is interesting to note that Dobson has called attention (British Museum Catalogue of the Chiroptera, Lond., 1878, pp. 79 and 83) to the great development of the teats in the males of certain frugivorous Bats. He points out that while many Bats are known to bring forth two young at a birth, he has never found a mother with more than one clinging to her body; and he inclines to the belief that in such cases the male may relieve the female of the charge of one of the young ones (as the weight of two might render flight difficult or impossible). He suggests that "instances of the male performing the office of nurse are probably not uncommon among Bats."]

The following results on the subject of supernumerary breasts and teats were obtained by Leichtenstern, from the study of extensive data:—

Cases of polythely, with or without polymasty, were observed with almost equal frequency in the two sexes. On an average, one case may be expected in every 500 individuals.

In 91 per cent the accessory glands and teats were developed on the anterior side of the thorax, and in by far the greater number (94 per cent of these) they were found below (caudad of) the normal teats, in a convergent disposition.

The following is a table showing the position occupied by the accessory mammillæ in the 105 cases recorded by Leichtenstern:—

On the anterior side of the thorax	96 cases
In the axilla	5 ,,
On the back	2 ,,
Above the acromion	1 case
On the outer side of the hip	1 ,,

Rudimentary breasts occurring above (cephalad of) the normal ones are of rare occurrence (3 per cent), and these (Fig. 13, m'') always lie outside the normal mammary line in the direction of the axilla. Want of symmetry, especially on the left side, is common in all cases of rudimentary teats or mammary areas, in whatever part of the body they occur. The rarest condition

---

[1] Decided swelling of the breasts is sometimes found in youths of from twenty to twenty-one years of age, in cases of retarded puberty (Ammon).

(only one case being known) is that in which a supernumerary teat occurs in the same horizontal plane with the normal teats, either at or near the median line.

Hyrtl put forward the view that the greater development of the left breast is due to the habit of feeding the child from that, in order to leave the right arm free. Leichtenstern opposes this, but does not furnish any satisfactory explanation of the fact.[1]

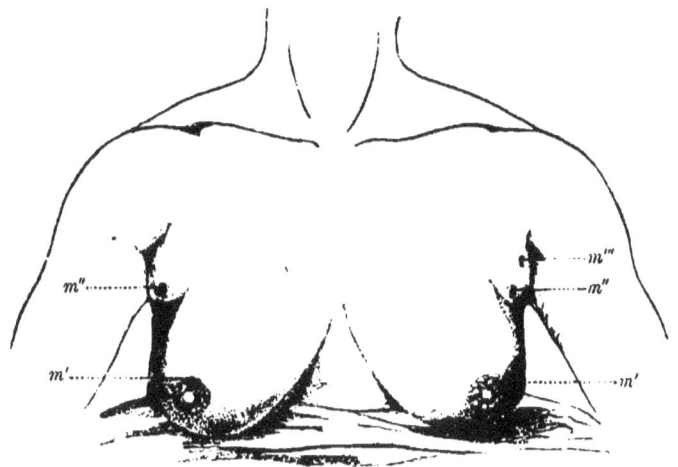

FIG. 13.—EXAMPLE OF POLYMASTY. (After Hansemann.)
The position of the supernumerary breast (m'') is superior and lateral to that of the normal (m'). The left accessory gland has a second teat (m''').

Rudimentary mammary organs were never found by Leichtenstern below the costal ridge or in the inguinal region.

In the Dog the normal number of teats varies from seven to ten, and Cuvier's dictum that the numerical variation in breasts is greatest where they are most numerous is thus confirmed.

Towards the end of the last century, Professor Socin of Basel, and subsequently the Medical Faculty of the University of Tübingen, were consulted by a lady with four breasts, as to whether she could marry without incurring the danger of having twins at every birth. The authorities decided that polymasty did not imply predisposition to bear twins, and the result proved the correctness of this opinion. Among seventy women with polymasty, twins are known to have been born in only three cases.

[1] [It may be remarked here that the young "vervet" (*Cercopithecus lalandii*) has been recently observed to suck both teats at once (*Proc. Zool. Soc.*, Lond. 1893, p. 615).]

If the supernumerary teat is sufficiently large, it can be used for suckling; but it is generally too small for this purpose, and is merely an encumbrance, since when the child is being fed from the normal breast, milk may dribble from the accessory one.

Hansemann has recorded the case of a married sempstress, forty-five years old (Fig. 13), who had, above and laterally to the normal breasts, two accessory ones, which possessed teats, but hardly any areolæ. Above the supernumerary teat of the left side there was another one showing distinct orifices. Glandular tissue could be discerned below all five teats, and many accessory apertures were found in the areolæ of the normal breasts. In the twenty-one years of her married life this woman had given birth to twelve children, twins being born twice, and had had seven advanced miscarriages; she had thus passed through seventeen pregnancies. All the breasts yielded milk, but a child could only be fed from the normal ones, since these alone were furnished with teats which could be seized by it.

Hansemann records in his treatise 262 cases in all: 81 males, 104 females, and 77 in whom the sex is not stated. The author refers to the goddesses Isis and Diana, who were represented with many breasts as a symbol of fruitfulness; but he rightly adds that, judging from data of the present day, the myth can have had no foundation in fact.

I have to thank my pupil Kenkitzi Horiuchi for the record of a case of polymasty, published in the *Weekly Medical Journal* of Tokio, of 4th July 1891 (No. 692), which may be added to Hansemann's series. It is that of a Japanese girl, aged nineteen, who was examined in the hospital of Fukui. Above the normal well-developed teats, at a distance of 4 cm., there was on each side (Fig. 14 m'') an accessory teat of the size of a pea, dark in colour, and in all respects like a true nipple. Above, and at some distance laterally from the normal breast on each side, a second smaller breast (m''') was found, with a teat. Fig. 14 is taken from a photograph of this case. The girl was in all other respects normal, and menstruation began at the age of fifteen.

In conclusion, I append some observations for which I am indebted to Otto Ammon, of Karlsruhe, distinguished for his researches into the anthropology of Baden. The data were obtained in connection with the recruiting for military service in the year 1890; and the manuscript bears the title, "Some Observations on the Occurrence of Supernumerary Teats, and on the Direction of the Hair on the Breasts." Out of 2189 men (of the Donaueschingen military district) supernumerary teats were found in sixty-six cases, one extra teat in sixty-two, and two in four, giving a proportion of one case in every thirty-three. Besides these sixty-six cases, forty-eight others showed traces of supernumerary teats, in the form of circumscribed patches of pigment (small areolæ). The nature of these patches was indicated by the fact that while on one side of the body there was the pigment patch and the teat, on the other, symmetrically

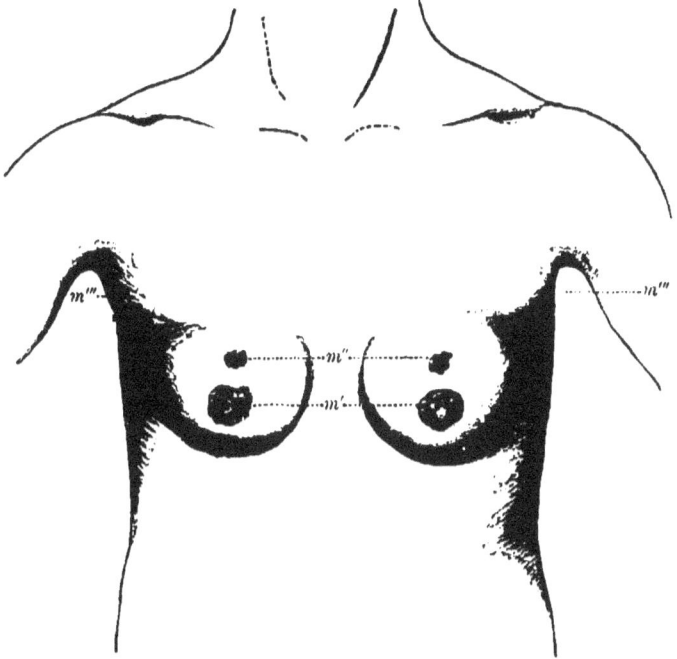

Fig. 14.—Case of Polymasty in a young Japanese Girl nineteen years old. m', normal teats; m'', supernumerary teats on the normal breasts; m''', supernumerary teats on accessory breasts.

placed, there was merely the patch. This condition was so often repeated, that there could be no doubt that these patches, situated as they were along converging lines, were the homologues of teats in an advanced stage of degeneration.

The above-named sixty-six cases, together with the forty-eight others in which only traces were found, testify to the occurrence of rudimentary mammary organs in various degrees of development in 114 of the 2189 men examined, *i.e.* in the proportion of 1 in 19. In every nineteenth man, then, we find the atavistic reappearance of supernumerary mammæ.

The following is an analysis of these cases:—

	On the right.	On the left.
One teat	24 cases.	36 cases.
Two teats	3 ,,	3 ,,
Other combinations	2 ,,	2 ,,
One trace	8 ,,	35 ,,
Two traces	3 ,,	7 ,,
Other combinations	2 ,,	2 ,,

The preponderance of teats on the left side is as 1·4 to 1, and in the case of traces of these organs it is still more striking, viz. as 3·38 to 1. This is no doubt to be associated with the well-known fact that the normal left breast in women is often (always ?) more developed than the right (cf. *ante*, p. 19), and it may be that the right, therefore, degenerates more rapidly than the left.

In those cases recorded in the literature of the subject in which one of the normal teats is entirely absent (amasty), the right nipple is more frequently wanting than the left.

In the cases recorded by Ammon (if we reckon together the number of teats and teat traces occurring singly) the proportion of those on the left to those on the right is 71 to 32. These results agree pretty closely with those of Leichtenstern.

In one of the cases with a pair of supernumerary teats, Ammon found these considerably to the side, quite near the anterior axillary fold formed by the edge of the pectoral muscle; and in a case described by Leichtenstern they had even entered the axillary area.

This shifting apart is explained by Ammon as connected with the upright gait of Man, *i.e.* with the position of the upper extremities, which is secondarily acquired as a result of it.

The following case, observed by Ammon, is particularly interesting, as a striking example of the extraordinary persistence of certain organs which, after becoming as a rule extinct, occasionally reappear.

On the upper part of the breast of a very hairy soldier, two diverging hair vortices occurred a few centimetres above the teats, but farther apart than these, and nearer the axillary folds (* Fig. 15). At the focal point of each of these vortices there was a light spot from which the hair grew upwards and outwards as from the crown of the head. These were evidently the sites of former teats—that is, of former orifices; for, as Ammon rightly remarks, the hair vortices agree with the diverging vortex found at the point where the canalis sacralis finally becomes closed—the glabella coccygea, or "sacral dimple," which lies above the coccygeal vortex. This latter, however, is a *converging* vortex,

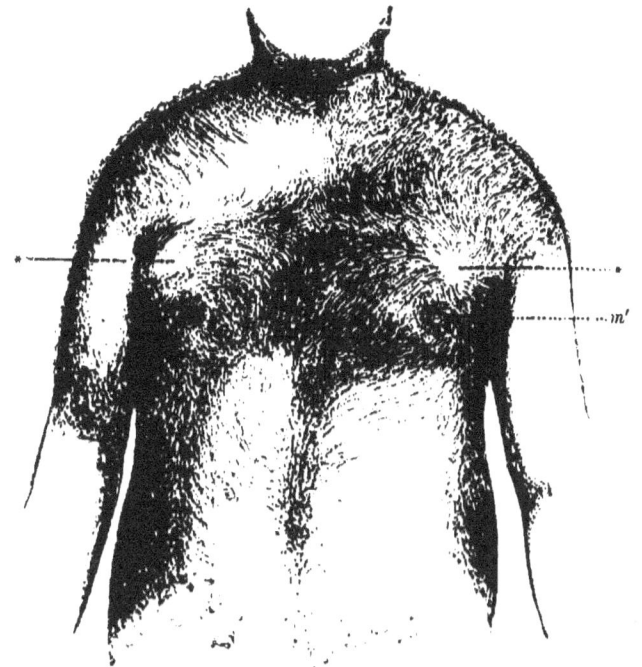

FIG. 15.—FRONT VIEW OF THE BODY OF A HOSPITAL ASSISTANT, TWENTY-TWO AND A HALF YEARS OLD. (After O. Ammon.)
m', normal teats; *, hair vortices above these, pointing to the former presence of supernumerary teats.

such as always occurs where a protuberance formerly existed (cf. *ante*, p. 5); but the glandular area of the breast, as Ammon further rightly argues, originally developed not as an elevation, but as a depression, out of which the teat rose up secondarily. According to Ammon there are, on the normal teats also, smaller diverging vortices, in which "the hairs course round and round the areolæ . . . but these are soon lost in the general course of the hair tracts."[1]

[1] I here reprint by permission a letter received from Herr Otto Ammon, on the 10th February 1892. I have refrained from commenting upon it, as I have not yet been able to confirm the observation recorded:—

"Allow me to draw your attention to another case which I have not yet recorded.

24 THE STRUCTURE OF MAN

The most interesting case yet recorded by any author, a case which is in fact unique, is that of a Triberg recruit

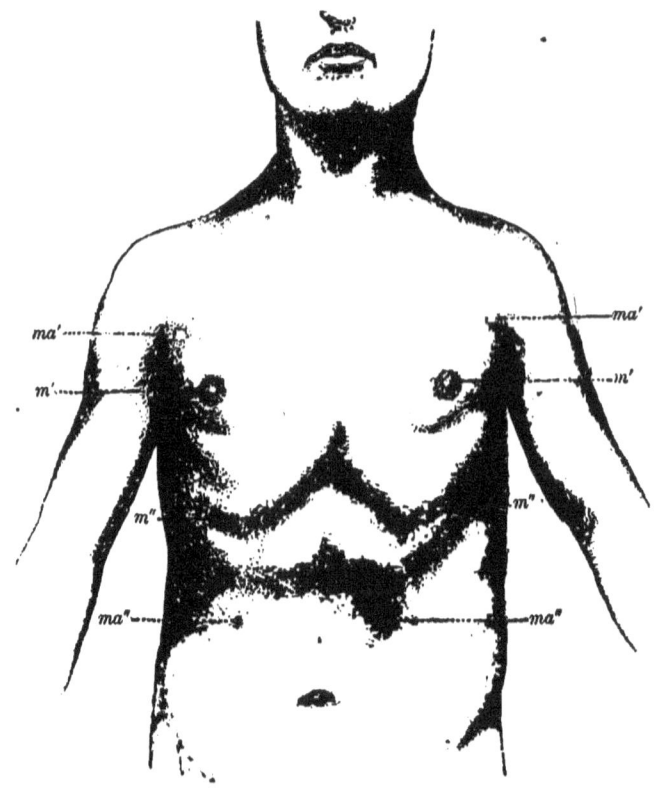

FIG. 16.—SCHREINER VON SCHONACH, aged twenty-two and a half, serving in 16th Baden Infantry Regiment, K. F. III. No. 114. (After Ammon.)
m', normal teats ; m'', supernumerary teats ; ma', supernumerary teat areas above the normal breasts ; ma'', the same below the normal breasts.

examined by Ammon. In this man (Fig. 16) there were four pairs of teats and teat traces. Above the normal teats (m') there were two teat areas (bilaterally symmetrical pigment spots,

As I am not sure of its significance, I simply give the facts, leaving you to decide whether it is anything more than a chance occurrence. In very hairy men there are often found all over the ventral surface small hairs (0·5–1·0 cm. long), disposed in the middle line lengthwise and at the sides horizontally, which gradually bend round and converge towards the navel. Above the navel they point downwards, below it upwards. The ordinary course of these hairs is broken at points where longer and stronger hairs grow, and these points occur where in other individuals

ma') lying in shallow depressions of the axillary folds, and thus still more lateral in position than in the case above described (Fig. 15). In descending order, below the normal teats, came a pair of tolerably distinct though small teats with areolæ (m''); and lowest of all two small rudiments (bilaterally symmetrical pigment spots, ma''') lying below the ribs.

This case suggests that the demonstration in the human embryo of a mammary line or ridge like that above described in the quadruped may be only a matter of time.[1]

supernumerary teats appear; they lie, however, below the normal teats, while in the man in your large photograph (Fig. 15) they lie *above* these.

"The greater development of hair at those parts of the body which correspond with the position of supernumerary teats below the normal ones, *i.e.* on the converging lines, has twice been observed by me, and in each case on both sides of the body. The stronger hairs do not form tufts, but lie parallel and close together, and follow the general course of hair, *i.e.* have the same direction as the rest; they are merely *longer, thicker,* and perhaps also darker. The fact that they do not form vortices deterred me from connecting them with rudimentary teats. The facts, however, are worth recording."

[1] Further information on the subject of supernumerary teats and mammary gland, can be obtained from the works of Mitchell Bruce (*Jour. Anat. and Phys.*, vol. xiii. p. 425) and Karl von Bardeleben (*Verhandl. d. Anatom. Gesellsch.*, München, 1891; and Wien, 1892). I would, however, warn inquirers against the danger of seeing a teat in every wart-like prominence!

THE SKELETON

THE VERTEBRAL COLUMN

THE vertebral column of an adult human being consists normally of thirty-three to thirty-four vertebræ, numerical variation being due to the inconstancy of those of the coccygeal or caudal series. As might be expected from the study of other related organs (*e.g.* the vertex coccygeus, the filium terminale, the arteria sacralis media, certain muscles and nerves, and the coccygeal gland), we here meet with evidence of degeneration and variation. This is specially the case during development. It is, above all, the caudal region which, in this respect, has claimed the greatest attention of morphologists; and incidentally to the study of this there arises the old controversy as to whether Man or his ancestors possessed a tail.

At an early stage of development the human embryo possesses at the posterior end of the body, clearly in direct continuity with its developing axial skeleton, a free projecting pointed appendage, bearing an undeniable resemblance to the tail of a lower animal. This is delineated in Fig. 17, *cd.*, and will be further discussed as we proceed. At later stages of development this organ is less conspicuous; it gradually becomes shorter and blunter, and is slowly, as it were, taken into the trunk. For some time, however, a caudal prominence remains; but this at last either disappears altogether, or leaves, at the point where its tip abutted against the integument, more or less distinct traces known as the "vertex coccygeus" (cf. *ante*, pp. 5 and 7). This is the normal course of development, but occasionally a tail-like appendage is found in extra-uterine life. An extensive literature exists on this subject,[1] and to it I

[1] Some of the alleged observations on this subject are not such as to awaken confidence, and others refer to pathological cases or abortions, in which, among other malformations, more or less developed caudal appendages occurred. Other

must refer the reader, as I can here only call attention to a few cases.

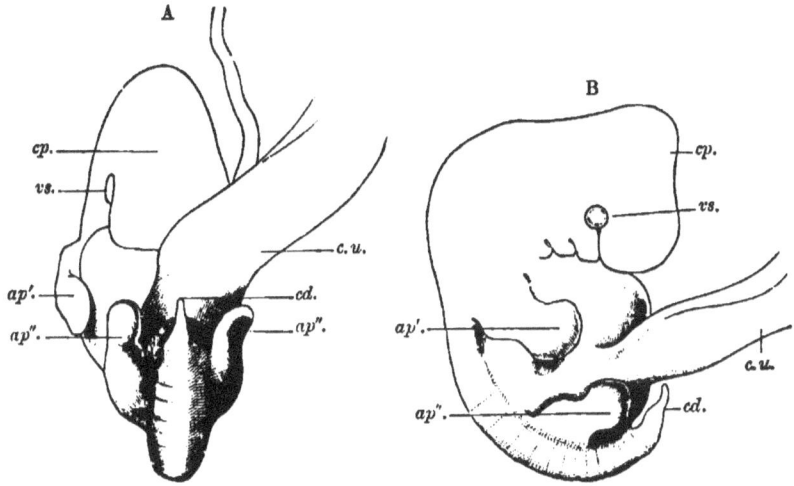

Fig. 17.—Two Young Human Embryos.
A, ventral; B, lateral view. (After Ecker.) Both figures are intended to show the freely projecting tail (*cd.*). *cp.*, head; *vs.*, eye; *ap'.*, fore-limb; *ap".*, hind-limb; *c.u.*, umbilical cord.

Gerlach records a very remarkable case of tail formation in an otherwise normal human embryo, in the fourth month of intra-uterine life, an age at which, as a rule, the tail-like appendage has disappeared. The length of the trunk was 7·6 cm., the total length 10·8 cm.; and as the tail (Fig. 18), which projected freely from the buttocks, measured from root to tip 17 mm., it was almost a sixth of the total length of the whole embryo. At its thickest part, where it left the body, it was 2 mm. broad, and it thence gradually narrowed towards its middle. Closer examination revealed the following facts:—The caudal appendage was not only connected with the last (fourth, and still cartilaginous) coccygeal vertebra, but the chorda dorsalis could be distinctly traced within it. Muscle bundles were also found, which from their whole position could be compared with nothing else than the M. curvator caudæ of the lower animals, *i.e.* with a true tail muscle. The existence of muscles further justifies

more recent observations, again, have been made on living subjects, where naturally no precise anatomical data could be obtained. One point can be maintained with certainty, viz. that in some of the observed cases, *e.g.* in those of de Maillet, a hereditary tendency was evident.

the assumption of the former presence of "proto-vertebræ" [or mesoblastic somites] in this region, and these, in turn, might indicate the prolongation of the spinal cord into the caudal region in earlier embryonic stages (cf. Fig. 20).

Fig. 18.—Tailed Human Embryo. (After Gerlach.)

We must not, however, assume, as Gerlach justly observes, that a true tail, supported by skeletal tissues, would have developed in this embryo had it lived longer; because the tissues lying in the region of the caudal filament showed no traces of conversion into permanent cartilaginous or osseous vertebræ. It was further observed, that at the point of junction between the posterior coccygeal vertebra and the proximal end of the caudal filament, the chorda dorsalis had already disappeared. These facts indicate an attempt to return to the normal. The tail showed every sign of degeneration; but this does not detract from the great morphological interest of the case, which has led me to describe it at some length.

Three other certified cases of tail formation in human beings may be cited.

The first is that of an Esthonian recruit, described by Max Braun in vol. iv. of the *Zoologischer Anzeiger*. The coccyx, in this case, did not recede into the groove of the buttocks under cover of the nates, but ended in an eminence, which, though not long, could be laid hold of and felt by the fingers. Thus examined, it was found to lie in a direct line with the vertebral column and to contain distinct vertebræ, the last of which was about the size of a pea. It could not be certainly ascertained in the living subject whether this tail was due to numerical increase in the number of vertebræ, or simply to a retention of the embryonic straight condition of the coccyx itself. It is a noteworthy fact, however, that Ecker's glabella and foveola coccygea, or sacral dimple, had persisted.

The second case is that of a newly-born female child, recorded by Lissner in 1872. Here also hard, irregular bodies, somewhat like the phalanges of a finger, could be distinctly felt in direct axial continuation of the vertebral column. Twelve years later, when the caudal appendage had reached the length of 12·5 cm., these could still be detected.[1]

I have to thank my friend and colleague, Professor G. B. Howes, for the knowledge of the third case.[2] It is described in the *Scientific American* of May 11th, 1889, p. 296, where an engraving taken from a photograph is also given. Fig. 19 is a copy of this, and represents a young Moi, twelve years old, who possessed a tail-like appendage 1 foot in length, and soft and smooth to the touch. As no skeletal elements could be felt, a prolongation of the vertebral column was certainly not present. It cannot therefore be considered a true tail, and this conclusion applies to a large number of similar formations which have erroneously been regarded as tails [some of which are purely pathological and due to spina bifida].

With regard to the number of caudal vertebræ definitively formed in Man, Steinbach has arrived at the following conclusions, after working upon a great accumulation of material.

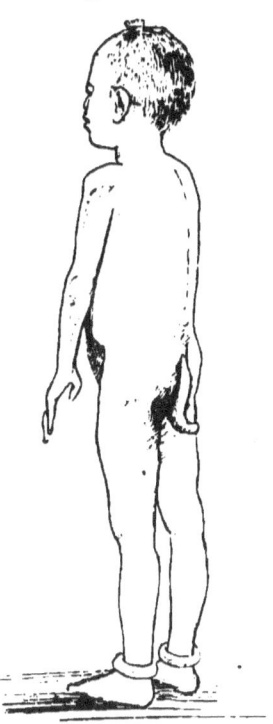

FIG. 19.—"TAILED" CHILD, MOI, AGED TWELVE.

The male embryo, from the end of the second month of intra-uterine life, has five post-sacral vertebræ; and indications of com-

---

[1] It is important also to note that similar reversionary formations have occasionally been observed in the Anthropoid Apes (Gorilla and the Orang), and this is the more remarkable, as in the latter the degeneration of the os coccygis, which consists as a rule of only three vertebræ, has gone still further than in Man. [It is worthy of remark here that this same maximum reduction of the caudal vertebræ to three occurs also in some Bats, and that the opposite extreme for the mammalian series is reached by a small insectivore from Madagascar (*Microgale longicaudata*) and the long-tailed Pangolin (*Manis macrura*) of the old world, in which the caudal vertebræ may be close upon fifty in number.]

[2] [And I, in turn, have to thank my friend Professor Johnson Symington, of Queen's College, Belfast, in conversation with whom my attention was first drawn to this case.—G. B. H.]

mencing fusion between the last two of these sometimes occur. Six vertebræ were once observed in a boy four weeks old; and

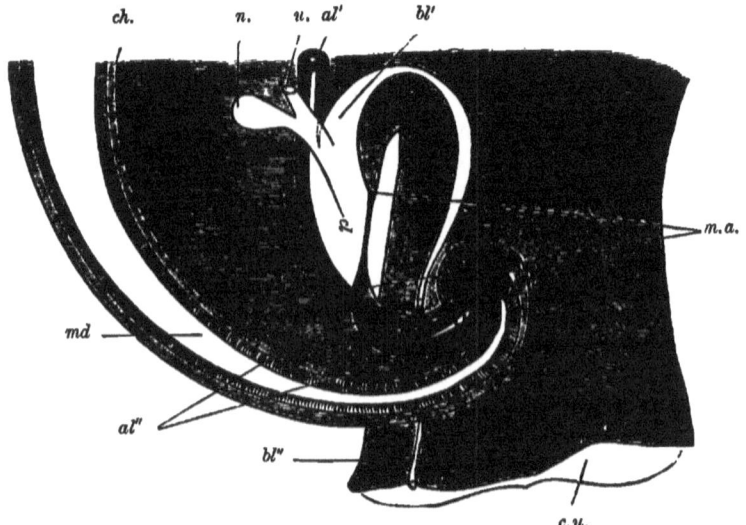

Fig. 20A.—Diagrammatic Reconstruction of the Tail End of a Human Embryo (length of trunk, 8 mm.)
ch., notochord; *n.*, Wolffian tubule; *u.*, duct of primitive kidney; *al'*, intestine; *bl'*, urinary bladder; *m.a.*, anal membrane; *md*, medullary tube; *al"*, post-anal gut; *bl"*, neck of allantois; *c.u.*, umbilical cord. (After Keibel.)

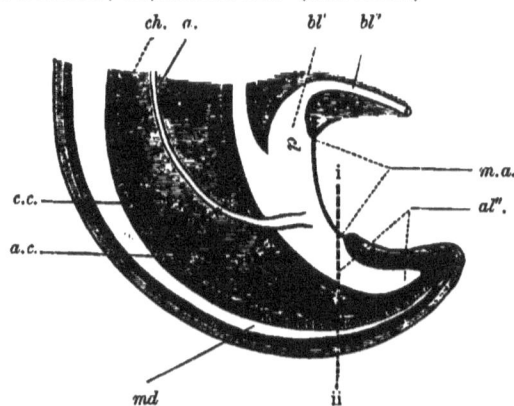

Fig. 20B.—Diagrammatic Reconstruction of the Tail End of a Human Embryo younger than Fig. 20A (entire length, 4 mm.). (After Keibel.)
Lettering as above; in addition *c.c.*, caudal limit of the cœlom; *a.c.*, caudal limit of the hind-limb; i-ii, line drawn through the anterior limit of the tail.

Leboucq has recorded the same number in an embryo 25 mm. long. The opposite extreme is reached where only three vertebræ occur. In the adult man the regular number of caudal vertebræ is five, whereas the number may be either four or five in the adult woman.[1]

In the female embryo four such vertebræ are found as early as the end of the third month, and the end of the caudal portion of the vertebral column is in the female at all times more liable to variation than in the male. On the other hand, the whole vertebral column of the female is much more constant, with regard to the limits and detailed characters of its separate sections, than that of the male.

The complete development of the caudal vertebræ is not concluded at birth, for their ossification has not then commenced; they are in this condition subject to the most varied influences, which may cause further fusion, reduction, or deviation from the sagittal plane (lateral curvature of the terminal vertebræ) (cf. Fig. 24).

But what defines the human tail? In answering this question we cannot do better than follow Keibel, who rightly points out that the definition of the tail in human anatomy must be in strict harmony with that of Comparative Anatomy, and that therefore so much of the vertebral column as is posterior to that (sacrum) which attaches the pelvic girdle is caudal. Since, however, the relation of the limbs to the axial skeleton is of a secondary nature, Comparative Anatomy cannot help us in the important early stages. We can only deal with this difficulty by dividing up the body of the embryo into regions, each containing a certain number of segments, and in so doing we cannot avoid ascribing to the regions the number of segments which are found in the adult. In Man, therefore, whom we are now considering, we refer the first seven vertebræ to the cervical region, and the twelve which follow to the thoracic; the lumbar and "sacral" regions each have five, and the remainder belong to the caudal.

In all Vertebrates, however, a shifting of the pelvic girdle which occurs during embryonic development has to be taken into account; and in this case the definitions borrowed from the adult are not altogether applicable. His, Fol, and Keibel,

[1] The most reduced vertebral columns are always those of females. Sexual requirements probably account for this, and for the fact that synostotic union of the first coccygeal with the last sacral vertebra is less frequent in females than in males. In the latter, the connection between the cornua sacralia and coccygea may even give rise to a fifth pair of sacral foramina, and in such cases the sacrum appears to consist of six vertebræ.

agree in attributing to human embryos of 4 to 6 mm. an externally visible and segmented tail, with a nervous axis and a post-anal gut (cf. Fig. 20B), in comparison with which the peculiar permanent internal tail of the adult is a very degenerate organ. In this early embryonic stage the tail consists of only two or three segments, but at a later period there are six caudal segments, the terminal mesodermal mass being reckoned merely as one. At this stage the tail consists of a number of segments, which are but very rarely retained permanently or even for a long time.

The post-anal gut seems to be constricted off from the cloaca at this stage, but it is continued for the greater part of its course along the whole length of the embryonic tail. It apparently reaches its maximum length at this period (cf. Fig. 20, al'').

At a later stage of development also, when thirty-six somites or body segments are formed, the post-anal gut can still be traced, but is no longer tubular. The caudal region at this stage possesses four spinal ganglia with three related nerves. At a later stage the post-anal gut degenerates altogether.

To sum up, we have the following purely anatomical facts which indicate that Man's ancestors possessed a tail :—

(1) The coccyx of the adult consisting of three to six caudal vertebræ.

(2) The two caudal spinal nerves.

(3) The caudal musculature, the existence of which, further, is a direct proof that the tail was external and functional (cf. p. 27).

(4) The vortex coccygeus and the foveola and glabella coccygea (cf. p. 5).

(5) The variability of the caudal region in general.

The other divisions of the human vertebral column also furnish many interesting points. One of the most characteristic peculiarities of the human backbone is its typical mode of curvature. The lumbar portion (cf. Fig. 23, B), which extends to the promontory of the sacrum and is convex anteriorly, deserves special attention. This lumbar curvature might appear to owe its origin to statical and mechanical causes connected with the upright gait, but while it is less markedly developed in the anthropoid Apes, [it has been shown by Cunningham and Charpy to be at least anticipated in certain quadrupedal Mammals].[1]

[1] [Huxley was the first to appreciate the existence of the lumbar curvature in the anthropoid apes, and Cunningham, Turner, and Symington have more recently drawn

Of special interest, however, are the variations of the separate divisions of the vertebral column, in relation to other parts of the skeleton which have become secondarily attached to it, such as the ribs and the pelvic girdle. These variations, though effected ontogenetically, have a phylogenetic significance, and may therefore be described in further detail.

Although the pre-sacral portion of the column consists normally of twenty-four vertebræ, Embryology and Comparative Anatomy show that this cannot be regarded as a primitive condition, and that the pelvis formerly lay much farther back than at present, that is, that the trunk was originally longer than now. (We shall see later that a more extensive body-cavity or cœlom was connected with this greater length of the vertebral column.)

Rosenberg has demonstrated that in the course of human development the first sacral vertebra becomes incorporated in the sacrum later than the second, and that later than the third, and so on. And further, since a primary relationship between the vertebræ which become the two anterior coccygeal of the adult and the developing sacrum is discoverable, it is evident that while new sacral articulations are formed anteriorly, detachment of vertebræ which were formerly sacral takes place posteriorly, the latter being transformed into coccygeal vertebræ.[1] *A forward shifting of the sacrum and pelvic girdle is thus ontogenetically proved.*

attention to the detailed differences in the condition of the lumbar vertebræ of the European and certain dark-skinned races, and the anthropoid Apes.]

[Cunningham has shown (*Mem. R. Irish Acad.*, No. II. 1886) that Acby's denial of the existence of a lumbar curvature in the Gorilla is untenable. His own test for a lumbar curvature is a line drawn from the centre of the anterior border of the upper surface of the first lumbar vertebra to the centre of the anterior border of the lower surface of the last lumbar vertebra. The distance of the most prominent point on the ventral surface of the lumbar section of the column from this line, multiplied by one hundred and divided by the length of the line, gives the index of curvature.] Little is known concerning the lumbar curvature of the savage races of mankind; but the cousins Sarasin, on the examination of dried skeletons of the Veddahs of Ceylon, report the lumbar vertebræ to be distinctly concave anteriorly. [From what has been said above, it would appear more than probable that the application of the Cunningham method to the study of the Veddah backbone, in the fresh or specially prepared state, would reveal a lumbar curvature according to the above, its most recent and rigid, definition. And, from what is known of the backbones of other races (ex. the Australian), it would appear probable that the observation of the Sarasins is rather indicative of a greater suppleness of the column during life, induced by habitual resort to certain postures, such as squatting, which lead to a greater compression of the vertebræ, and a corresponding greater tendency towards obliteration of the curvature after death.]

[1] Distinct indications of a shifting of the pelvic girdle are traceable in the lower animals also, such shifting being in some cases in a proximal and in others in a distal

These changes come to an end when the twenty-fifth vertebra, by virtue of its apposition with the hip-girdle, becomes the first sacral, and the promontory attains its full differentiation between it and the last lumbar vertebra, *i.e.* between the twenty-fourth and twenty-fifth vertebræ of the whole column. This later assimilation anteriorly of sacral vertebræ is further evident in the fact that synostosis between the separate parts of the sacrum always takes place from behind forwards.

The tendency of the human pelvic girdle to extend even farther forwards is revealed, in cases in which the last or fifth lumbar vertebra enters into the constitution of the sacrum. The number of pre-sacral vertebræ is in such a backbone reduced to twenty-three, and this is the normal condition in the Orang and Chimpanzee, and the general, though not the invariable, condition in the Gorilla.[1] This change is accompanied in Man by the depression of the promontory, which becomes duplicated (Fig. 21, C' C''). The sacrum appears deeply sunk into the pelvis; although such sinking may also occur, as is shown in Fig. 21, A' A'' without any incorporation of the fifth lumbar vertebra in the sacrum. In both cases the iliac crests rise almost to a level with the upper edge of the penultimate lumbar vertebra (*l.iv.* of Figs.).

In contrast to this reduction of the lumbar vertebræ to four, the shifting of the pelvic girdle during development may be arrested one vertebra behind the normal; in such cases, which are rare, we have twenty-five pre-sacral vertebræ. This has become the normal condition in the Gibbon (*Hylobates*).

Similar variations are found in individual Orangs, Gorillas, and Chimpanzees. In the Orang and Gorilla, for instance, the

direction. Credner, by comparing young with old specimens, has proved that in a fossil Amphibian (*Branchiosaurus*) a distal shifting of the pelvic arch along six to seven vertebræ took place ontogenetically.

[1] [In this animal, the last lumbar vertebra, although it may take on the relationships and detailed structure of a sacral vertebra, always retains its independence (*i.e.* it does not become co-ossified with the other vertebræ of the sacral series as in the Orang and Chimpanzee). The presence of a highly differentiated articulation between the last lumbar vertebra and the anterior border of the ilium is an invariable characteristic of certain Armadillos. The joint thus formed is a transverse one, which comes into especial use when the animal rolls itself up, and is therefore of a purely adaptive nature. It is well to guard against confusion between this condition and that of incorporation of lumbar with sacral vertebræ under extension or forward translocation of the hip-girdle, in which the extra articulation is a longitudinal one lying on the inner border of the iliac head. (Cf. Symington, *Jour. Anat. and Phys.* vol. xxiv. p. 42.; and Paterson. *Trans. R. Dublin Soc.*, vol. v., Ser. 2, p. 123.]

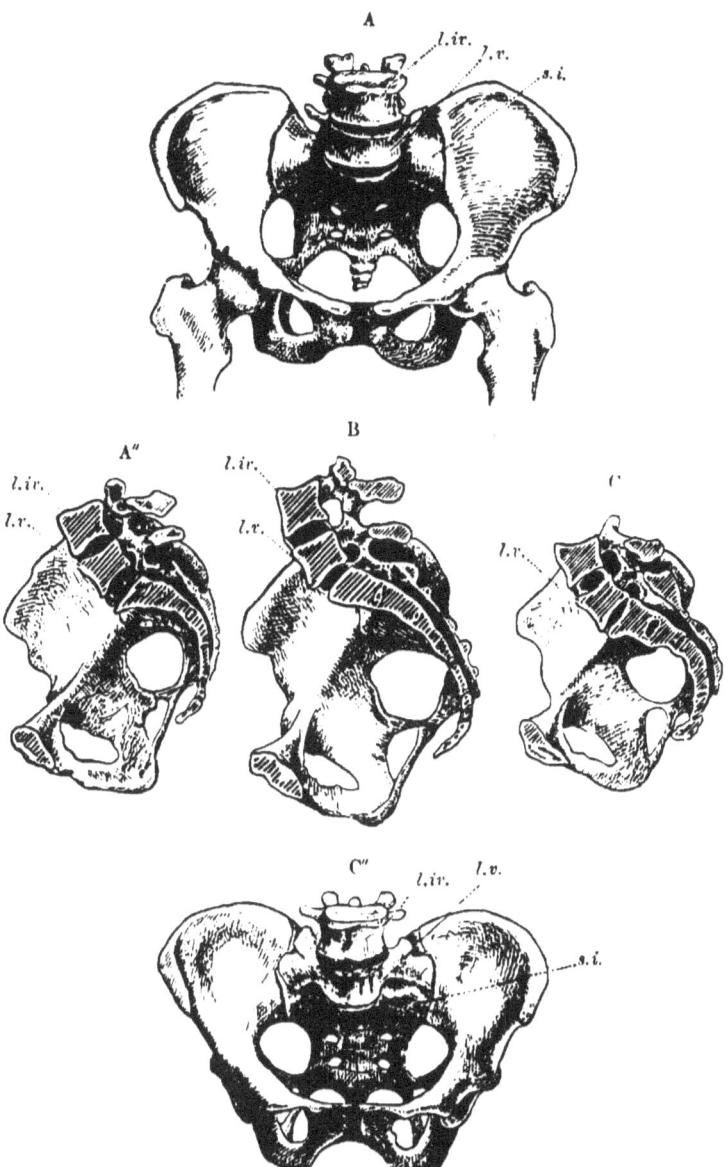

FIG. 21.—THE PELVIS.

A′ A″, with depressed ; B, with high standing promontory (A′ ventral view ; A″ and B, median longitudinal sections). In A″ the highest point of the iliac crest almost reaches the level of the upper edge of the penultimate lumbar vertebra ($l.iv.$). In B, on the contrary (which is the original condition, and that still found in children), the upper edge of the last lumbar vertebra ($l.r.$) is hardly reached. C′ C″, pelvis with double promontory, caused by assimilation of the last lumbar vertebra with the sacrum (C′, median longitudinal section ; C″, ventral view). In the latter the appearances are as if the pelvis had shifted forward along the vertebral column. (After Froriep.)

lumbo-sacral boundary may be shifted back a vertebra, and in the Chimpanzee even two vertebræ. In the former case the position normal to Man is attained.

It is evident that shifting of the pelvic girdle (and, as will be seen later, of the pectoral girdle also) cannot take place without concomitant variations in other organs. To this question we shall return.

THE RIBS AND STERNUM

Two types of variation of the thorax are to be distinguished in Mammals, a primary and a secondary type. The former is

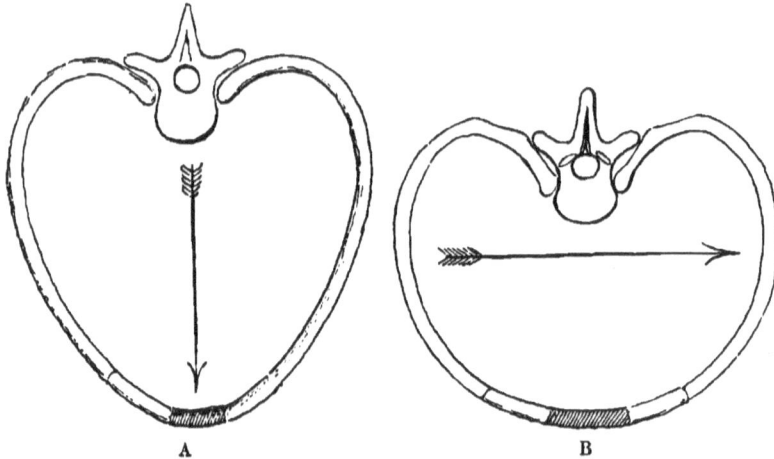

FIG. 22.—A, TRANSVERSE SECTION OF THE THORAX OF A LOWER MAMMAL (OR OF THE HUMAN EMBRYO); B, THE SAME OF A MAN.
In the former it is the vertical diameter which is the greater, in the latter it is the transverse, as indicated by arrows.

far more common than the latter, and is found in most Mammals, including the lower Apes. The thorax of this primary type (Fig. 22, A) is elongated, its dorso-ventral greatly exceeding its transverse diameter (carinate or keeled type).

The secondary type (Fig. 22, B) is found in Anthropoid Apes and in Man. The dorso-ventral diameter is here greatly diminished and the transverse is increased in proportion; the broad thorax is somewhat barrel-shaped, and often compressed antero-posteriorly. This secondary type is preceded, both ontogenetically and phylogenetically, by the primary.

It is evident that the associated modifications, viz. the

shortening of the thoracic wall, the shifting of the thoraco-abdominal boundary, the changes in the axial skeleton, and the numerical reduction of the thoracic metameres, must have a far-reaching influence on the whole anatomy of the trunk, *e.g.* on the position of the thoracic viscera (lungs, heart), and on the relationships of the pleural cavities. Thus Ruge has shown, in a series of excellent papers, that as the secondary type of thorax begins to develop, the pleural boundary gradually recedes along the anterior and inner wall of the thorax, so that the heart, which in the primitive thorax almost always lies remote from the sternum, approaches nearer the anterior thoracic wall. As a consequence of this, the anterior edges of the pleural sacs, which are primarily apposed behind the sternum, are forced apart, so that in Man, for example, they are often separate as high as the fourth rib.

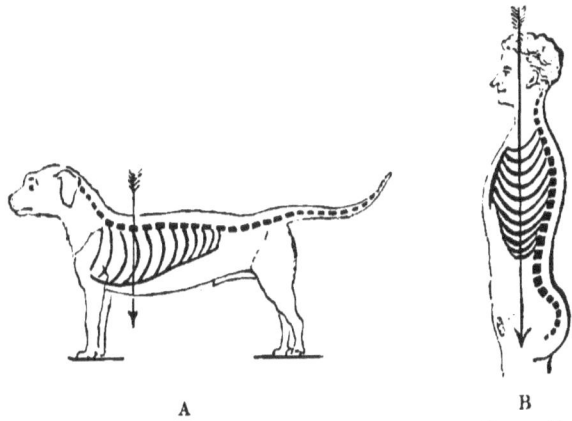

A   B

FIG. 23, A AND B.—DIAGRAMS OF THE VERTEBRAL AND COSTAL SKELETON.
A, IN THE QUADRUPED ; B, IN MAN ; the arrows indicate the line of direct pressure of the thoracic viscera upon the wall of the thorax.

Among the various factors recognisable as having played a continuous *rôle* in the evolution of the Primates, not the least weighty is the assumption of the upright position. The alteration in the shape of the thorax above described, by shifting back the centre of gravity of the body, favours the upright position; and the inter-dependence of these two modifications is evident.

To the same category, it appears to me, belongs the gradual diminution in number and size of the sternal ribs. It is easy to see how, with the shifting of the centre of gravity towards the dorsal side of the body, and a consequent diminution of pressure on the ventral, the ribs which in the quadrupeds are the more necessary for enclosing and supporting the viscera, might degenerate in the abdominal or lumbar region. The pressure of the viscera is no longer in the ventral, but in the caudal direction (cf. Fig. 23). We find, in consequence, a compensating expansion of the iliac fossæ of the bones of the pelvic girdle. The fact that this change is specially pronounced in women is easily explained by functional (sexual) adaptation, and it thus tends to confirm the above theory.

The shifting of the centre of gravity towards the dorsal side explains why the vertebral ends of the lowest ribs are so firmly attached, and also why the dorsal portion of the thoracic bony skeleton is much longer than the ventral. In this connection we have naturally to take into account the great muscles which are statically and mechanically required by the axial skeleton, and for which these ribs furnish points of origin and insertion. But even supposing that the ribs were not required for this purpose, there are other related structures which, to a certain extent, favour their persistence. The chief of these is the serratus posticus inferior muscle, which is inserted into the four lower ribs, and the latissimus dorsi which partly arises from the last three.

It may be remarked, however, that the mere presence of these two muscles, as will be seen later on, is insufficient to account for the persistence of the lower ribs. Indeed, the latter might well be degenerating so far as the former are concerned, for not only is the serratus posticus inferior distinctly rudimentary, but the parts of the latissimus dorsi attached to these ribs are quite insignificant in comparison with the rest of the muscle. But, notwithstanding this, the action of the serratus to a certain degree favours the retention of these ribs (cf. p. 45).

Returning now to the more important factors which determine the transformation of the thorax, we must, as Ruge rightly points out, take into account the influence of the fore-limbs. As the latter developed into seizing organs, their muscles became more powerful and more specialised, and reacted, in turn, on the form of the ribs and the arch of the thorax. Further consequences of this are seen in the greater compactness of the internal organs, in the gradual fusion of certain lobes of the liver and lungs, and in the approximation and final union of the pericardium and diaphragm, which may also imply the gradual depression of the heart. It is, moreover, evident that the change undergone by the heart and diaphragm, due to the forcing of the former out of the median plane and the shifting of its longitudinal axis towards the ventral and left side of the body, must again react upon the form and limitations of the pleural cavities.

Slight changes in the limitation of the pleural cavities occur also in the lower Mammals; but how far these may be related to each other, or in any way to those occurring in the Primates, is not very clear. The original causes of the changes are very various, but their close dependence upon the skeleton is evident.

The tendency towards a gradual diminution in the number of ribs, previously referred to, requires further consideration.

The presence of free ribs, as is well known, distinguishes the thoracic vertebræ of the adult from those of the cervical and lumbar regions. The limits of the thoracic region, however, are liable to variation, akin to that already described as occurring in the lumbar and sacral regions. Twelve pairs of free ribs are present normally in Man, as in the Orang, but a comparison with other (and chiefly lower) Vertebrates points to the earlier existence of a larger number. This view is supported by Ontogeny, as well as by the occasional occurrence of so-called supernumerary ribs. These are less frequently found at the upper than at the lower end of the thorax; and in either case, the thirteenth rib is subject to great variation both in form and size. For example, a thirteenth rib at the lower end of the human thorax may vary in length from 2 to 14 cm.; but thirteen is the normal number of ribs in the Gorilla and the Chimpanzee, and Hylobates has thirteen or fourteen. Where a free rib is borne by the seventh cervical vertebra, the number of these vertebræ naturally appears to be reduced to six. Where a thirteenth rib occurs in the thorax, the lumbar vertebræ similarly appear to be reduced to four—unless the embryonic forward shifting of the pelvis has been arrested at the twenty-sixth pre-sacral vertebra, as is not unfrequent under these circumstances, for it has been observed that the thirteenth rib, which always appears in the embryo, begins to degenerate as soon as the twenty-fifth pre-sacral vertebra is incorporated in the sacrum.

We have further evidence that Man has inherited more than twelve pairs of free ribs, in the fact that reduced ribs are found in the embryo, not only in connection with the first but with all the lumbar vertebræ (Fig. 24, *r.l.*), and in the sacral region also (Fig. 25, B *r.s.*).[1] From this it is clear that the pelvis in Man,

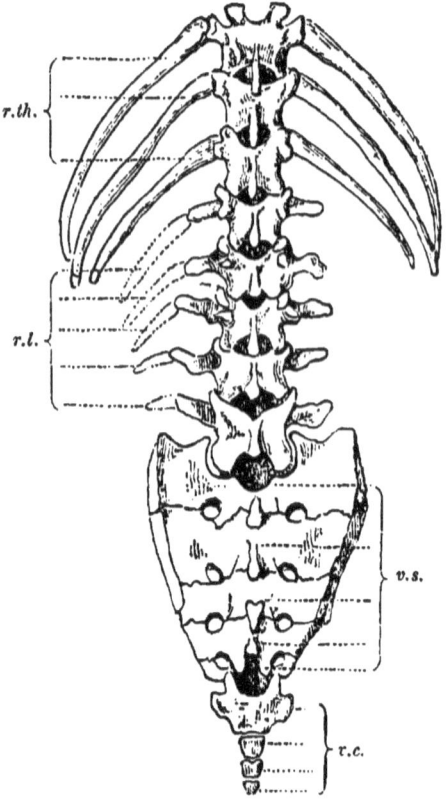

FIG. 24.—PART OF THE THORACIC, AND THE WHOLE LUMBAR, SACRAL, AND COCCYGEAL SECTIONS OF A YOUNG HUMAN VERTEBRAL COLUMN. (Dorsal aspect.) The lateral processes of the first to the fifth lumbar vertebræ are on one side prolonged (by dotted lines) for diagrammatic delineation of the formerly existing lumbar ribs (*r.l.*), which are present in the embryo. The sacrum is still subdivided into its five component parts, *i.e.* consists of five distinct vertebræ (*v.s.*). *v.c.*, caudal (coccygeal) vertebræ; *r.th.*, the three lower thoracic ribs.

like that of all terrestrial Vertebrates, is carried by ribs, which, however, become early united with the sacral transverse processes.

[1] In the twenty-first and twenty-second pre-sacral vertebræ of the embryo, the ribs are still separated from the vertebral arches by membranous tissue, but in the succeeding vertebræ they are more and more completely united with them. It would thus appear that the reduced ribs are early incorporated in the so-called transverse processes of the lumbar vertebræ.

As already stated, the presence of a free rib in connection with the last cervical vertebra (Fig. 27, A) is somewhat rare in

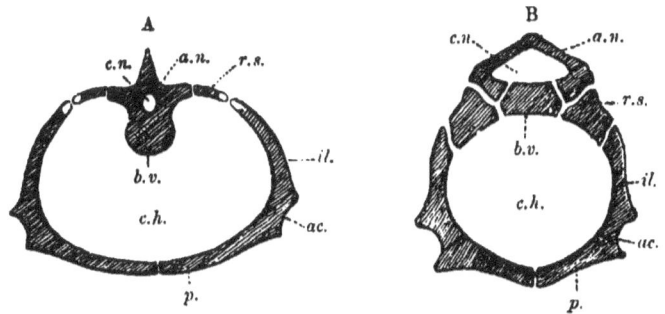

FIG. 25.—DIAGRAM OF A TRANSVERSE SECTION OF THE HIP GIRDLE AND SACRUM: A., OF A SALAMANDER; B., OF MAN (young stage in which the separate parts of the sacral vertebræ are still distinct).

b.v., body of sacral vertebræ; *a.n.*, arch of same; *r.s.*, sacral rib; *il.*, ilium; *p.*, pubis; *c.h.*, cœlom; *ac.*, acetabulum.

adults, but the vestige of such a rib, and even of a second (somewhat less attached) near the sixth cervical vertebra, is almost always

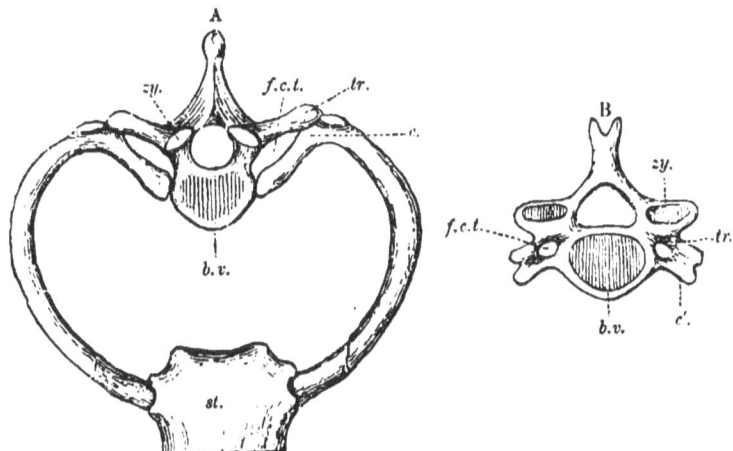

FIG. 26.—A, FIRST THORACIC SKELETAL SEGMENT FOR COMPARISON WITH B, FIFTH CERVICAL VERTEBRA (MAN).

c., first sternal rib; *c'*, cervical (rib which has become united with the transverse process (*tr.*)) the two enclosing the costo-transverse foramen (*f.c.t.*); *zy.*, articular process of the arch (zygapophysis); *b.v.*, body of vertebra; *st.*, sternum.

found in the embryo. The five anterior cervical vertebræ show no such distinct vestiges, although their former presence is clearly indicated by the detailed characters of the transverse processes (Fig. 26, b). [In the Platypus (*Ornithorhynchus*) reduced cervical ribs remain for life distinct on six of the seven neck vertebræ, being absent from the atlas only, and one or more cervical ribs may occasionally retain their independence among the quadrupedal Mammals generally.[1]]

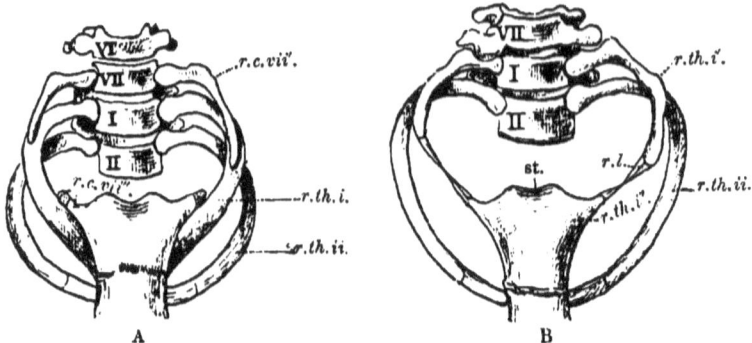

FIG. 27.—A, PORTION OF THE THORACIC SKELETON OF AN ADULT FEMALE POSSESSED OF A PAIR OF FREE CERVICAL RIBS.
The twelve normal pairs of thoracic ribs were present. Length of the right cervical rib 3·5 cm., of the left 6-7 cm. *r.c.vii.'*, vertebral end of the cervical rib ; *r.c.vii."*, sternal end of the same, fused with the manubrium sterni (the vertebral and sternal ends being in life connected by a ligamentous band, not indicated in the figure), *r.th.*, first and second sternal ribs.

B, EXAMPLE OF THE REDUCTION OF THE FIRST PAIR OF THORACIC RIBS (AN ADULT MALE).
There were twelve pairs of free ribs present, the first pair being reduced both in length and calibre. The left of these was 9, the right 8, cm. long. *r.th.i.'*, vertebral end of the first rib ; *r.th.i."*, its sternal end, synostotically united with the manubrium sterni (*st.*) ; *r.l.*, fibrous band, formed by retrogression of the missing portion of the rib.
In both figures, I, II denote the first and second thoracic vertebræ, VI, VII the two last cervical vertebræ. (Adapted from Leboucq.)

The greatest development of the seventh cervical rib would naturally be that of uninterrupted extension round the neck. Such an extraordinary condition has only apparently been once observed (by P. Albrecht). Cases in which the rib in question unites with the first thoracic rib by its cartilaginous extremity, before reaching the manubrium, are far more frequent. Sometimes only the sternal and vertebral ends are found (in either a bony or cartilaginous state), the intermediate part being represented by a fibrous band. In spite of the reduced con-

---

[1] [Mivart has figured and described (for example) what appear to be practically stages in the redevelopment of the last cervical rib on opposite sides of the same vertebra of a Binturong (*Arctictis*), *Proc. Zool. Soc.*, Lond., 1882, p. 461.]

dition, however, the internal and external intercostal muscles between this cervical and the first thoracic rib are well developed in cases like that above figured; indeed this is so even when (as occasionally happens) the fibrous connecting band is wanting (Leboucq). The sternal portion of the rib is as a rule very weakly developed, sometimes free, sometimes partly fused with the first thoracic rib. The vertebral end varies much in form, size, and articulation upon the vertebral column; and further, its relations to the first thoracic rib may, as Leboucq has shown, vary greatly. It may either be altogether fused with the latter, merely loosely attached to it by connective tissue, or actually articulated with it. In the first case, the first thoracic rib appears forked at its vertebral end, and this (according to P. J. van Beneden) is the rule in many Cetaceans.

Apart, however, from such cases as these, a further proof of the former existence of cervical ribs in Mammals is derived from the study of the adult Edentata. Among these, *Cholœpus* has normally only six cervical vertebræ [defined as those destitute of free ribs].[1] *Bradypus infuscatus* and *B. tridactylus* illustrate the other extreme, possessing normally nine such vertebræ; while *B. cuculliger* has either eight or nine. In the latter cases the upper end of the thorax has undergone greater reduction than in any other Mammal.

The fact that in Man the first thoracic rib is probably beginning to degenerate,[2] and is at the present time in process of atrophy, is established by the not infrequent recurrence of undoubted cases of its abortive development. Such have been recorded by Struthers, Grosse, Hunauld, Gruber, Turner, Leboucq, and others (cf. Fig. 27, B). The description given above of the seventh cervical rib might, in these cases, be applied to the first thoracic. Nevertheless, I believe, for reasons to be given later, that should reduction at the upper end of the thorax advance, it will do so far more slowly than at the lower, or indeed that it may even be arrested for an indefinite period (cf. p. 45).[3]

[1] A similar numerical reduction of the cervical vertebræ occurs also in the Manatee [but there is reason for believing that it is in that animal due to the excalation of at least the body of one of these, and not to the assumption of thoracic characters by the last of the series.]
[2] I should like here to raise the question whether this tendency to reduction at the upper end of the thorax may not be a determining factor in the degeneration so frequently found to be commencing at the top of the lungs? (cf. *infra*).
[3] It is interesting here to note that ventrally to the transverse process of the sixth cervical vertebra, there often arises, on either side, a projection, which might be claimed as a vestigial structure, since in most Mammals it stands out prominently

From the above facts it is sufficiently evident that the vertebral column was ancestrally furnished with a far greater number of ribs than at present, and that the pleuro-peritoneal cavity or cœlom was once more capacious both at its cephalic and caudal ends. Even at the present time, as already shown, its modifications are not permanent. This is manifest, not only from the reappearance of (so-called "supernumerary") ribs, but also from the decidedly rudimentary character of the eleventh and twelfth ribs, which is rendered evident in several ways, more especially in connection with variation in their size. The twelfth rib, as might be expected, has a much wider range of variation (2 to 27 cm.) than the eleventh (15 to 28 cm.); neither pair of these reaches the sternum, and both show degeneration in their detailed relationship to the vertebral column. These ribs have no tubercle, and, consequently, no costo-transverse articulation; and the articulation of the head (capitulum) of each of them is vertebral, instead of inter-vertebral, as in the case of those in front of them. Occasionally a tendency to similar conditions appears in the ninth and tenth pairs. Ontogeny shows that the reduction of the eleventh and twelfth ribs is comparatively recent, since the rudiment of the costo-transverse articulation (tubercle) of the eleventh rib is still developed in the embryo.

Turning now to the ensiform (or xiphoid) process of the sternum, the variations in its shape, and more especially the presence of occasional median fissures or foramina in it, show that it arose from paired cartilages. It is, in fact, constricted off from the eighth, and possibly also from the ninth pair of ribs. The cartilages named, undoubtedly, at one time took part in the formation of the "sternal bands" to be described later, and thus the number of ribs reaching the sternum may once have been greater

as a strong process (Gegenbaur). These *lower lateral* spinous processes [anapophyses] which are found only in *Hylobates*, among Anthropoids, arising from the bases of the arches of the last two thoracic and sometimes from the first lumbar vertebræ, according to Broca, occasionally occur in Negroes. It has been observed, further, that the spinous processes of the cervical vertebræ, which are, as a rule, forked in Man, are simply pointed in the Hottentots; and we here encounter a persistence of the original simple condition which is normal among Anthropoids (R. Blanchard).

Finally, it should be mentioned, that the groove on the dorsal side of the arch of the human atlas for the reception of the vertebral artery is sometimes overarched with bone, and converted into a foramen, such as is always found in most Primates, Carnivora, and various other Mammals (Sappey). [And it is here worthy of remark that the costo-transverse foramen, and its homologue the vertebarterial canal, may in a similar way become completely surrounded by the transverse process (*Hippopotamus, Man?*). Cf. *Jour. Anat. and Phys.*, vol. xxvii. p. 545.]

than at present. This conclusion is strengthened by the fact that the eighth rib not infrequently reaches the sternum even in adults.[1]

Eight sternal ribs are found in the lower Apes (which may have as many as ten), and may occur in the higher Apes, with the exception of the Orang. It is certain that in all Mammals those ribs which have their ventral ends in any way attached to one another were once connected with the sternum.

On the other hand, the union of only six ribs with the sternum is not rare in Man; and the existence of this condition is a clear indication of the gradual degeneration (shortening) of the thoracic skeleton and sternum. In such cases the distal end of the xiphisternum may bear two lateral prongs, which correspond with the sternal ends of the seventh pair of ribs.

There are certain considerations which confirm the statement above made that the process of degeneration at the upper end of the thorax is slower than that at the lower end, to which latter, indeed, no limits of variation can be foreseen. We have first the rhythmic respiratory mechanism, which is so closely connected anatomically and topographically with the complete ribs; and, second, the attachment to this part of the thorax of the musculature of the shoulder girdle (I refer especially to the serratus magnus and the pectoralis major). [These muscles under certain conditions play an important part in effecting the movements of respiration], and in order to secure a sufficient range of activity they must necessarily be inserted into a certain number of fixed points. Such points are supplied by the bony framework formed by the seven upper pairs of ribs, the sternum, and the clavicles; and as long as these muscles remain indispensable, the bones named cannot well degenerate further. We have here a striking example of the important reciprocal relation and close interdependence existing between the various organs and systems which, so to speak, hold each other in check.

We learn both from Ontogeny and Comparative Anatomy that the sternum (which is first formed by the fusion of a couple of sternal bands) consisted, in the ancestors of Man, of a row of

[1] [Cunningham and Robinson have recorded the existence of an eighth sternal rib on one or both sides in 20 per cent of (seventy) subjects examined (*Nature*, vol. xxxix. p. 248, and *Jour. Anat. and Phys.*, vol. xxiv. p. 127). In the unilateral condition it was found to be dextral in eight out of nine examples; and Cunningham suggests that this may be a reversionary feature, associated with the greater use of the right fore-limb.]

successive pieces. Its early condition is now most nearly retained for Mammals among the Edentata [i.e. in the Pangolin (*Manis*)], and even in the lower Apes extensive remnants of cartilage are occasionally present between the bony parts. In most other Mammals, the ossific nuclei which appear in the course of development of the sternum are the only indications of its former segmentation.[1] The fully-developed sternum of the Primates is practically a single broad and firm plate, the solidity of which compensates for its decrease in length.

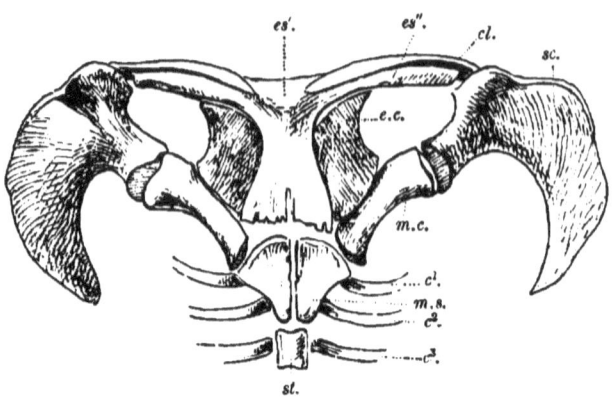

FIG. 28.—SHOULDER GIRDLE OF ORNITHORHYNCHUS.
m.s., manubrium sterni; $c^1., c^2., c^3.$, first, second, third ribs; *st.*, sternebra; *sc.*, scapula; *m.c.*, metacoracoid;[2] *e.c.*, epicoracoid; *cl*, clavicle; *es'.* and *es".*, interclavicle (episternum).

The origin of the Mammalian interclavicle (so-called episternum) is still somewhat undetermined; [but in its position beneath (ventrad of) the sternum proper in the young of the Mole (*es'.*, Fig. 29), in which its development has been most fully worked out, and in its relationships to the clavicles, it agrees with the interclavicle of Reptiles.]

In Monotremes (Fig. 28) the episternal apparatus (*es'. es".*) is triradiate, and disposed altogether cephalad of the sternum proper.

---

[1] [Approximation of more than one pair of ribs to the posterior end of the sternum is the rule in many of the lower Mammalia; in the Rabbit, where two pairs of ribs always have this relationship, it may or may not happen that a corresponding extra sternal segment is present in the adult. A careful study of the development of that animal's sternum has shown that this segment disappears by absorption where not retained—*i.e.* that a sternal segment may generally, though not invariably, be lost during ontogeny. This fact is of considerable interest in relation to the belief in a tendency towards abbreviation of the mammalian thorax postero-anteriorly (cf. Burne, *Proc. Zool. Soc.*, 1891, p. 159).]

[2] [Until recently known as the "coracoid"; cf., however, *infra*, p. 72.]

In the adults of the higher quadrupedal Mammals, the episternum is possibly for the most part represented by a couple of cartilaginous tracts, approximated to the sternal ends of the clavicles (*es.*, Fig. 30); and its body (*es.'*, Fig. 29), so far as is known, appears to become reduced, and either closely apposed to or fused with the anterior end of the sternum.

The following information concerning the human episternum is largely drawn from the admirable work of Ruge.

In an early embryonic stage, when the cartilaginous "sternal bands" have not yet united along their whole length, two independent masses, which soon become cartilaginous, appear at the upper end of the still forked manubrium sterni. At a later stage they fuse to form a single cartilaginous tract, which gradually interposes itself between the forks of the manubrium, until finally only the proximal surface of the cartilage projects from that structure.

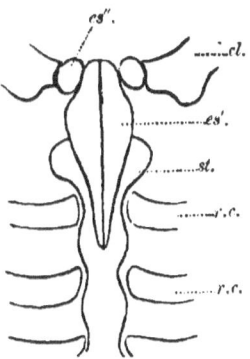

FIG. 29.—EPISTERNUM OF AN EMBRYO MOLE. (After A. Götte.) *st.*, sternum; *es'.*, central portion of the episternum; *es."*, lateral portion of the same; *cl.*, clavicle; *r.c.*, costal ribs. (The figure was constructed from two consecutive horizontal sections.)

As the two sternal ridges fuse completely, the boundary lines between the episternal cartilages and the manubrium become more and more indistinct, and finally altogether disappear, the former structure becoming incorporated in the latter. The manubrium of Man is thus a compound of two separate structures, one of which is certainly costal and derivative of the first pair of ribs. The homology of the other, *i.e.* of the suprasternal portion, cannot yet be decided with any certainty. There can be no doubt that we have in it the last vestiges of a skeletal structure, but whether they are those of a seventh pair of cervical ribs which once reached the manubrium, or of the central portion of the episternum of the Monotremes and lower Mammalia, must for the present remain undecided. If the latter supposition should prove correct, it would point to the originally paired nature of the Mammalian episternum, and support Götte's view of its origin from the median ends of the clavicles.

Brechet's cartilages, or bones, which occasionally appear at the antero-internal border of the sterno-clavicular articulation, and either become closely applied to the sternum or united with it, must not be confounded with the above-described skeletal structures, which are entirely incorporated into the manubrium. These "ossa suprasternalia" (*o.s.*, Fig. 30) may be derivatives of the episternal apparatus, as Gegenbaur has for years insisted, and probably of the central portion of the episternum. The lateral portions of this structure are usually homologised with the inter-articular cartilages that lie between the sternum and the ventral extremities of the clavicles (*e.s.*, Fig. 30). [There is, however,

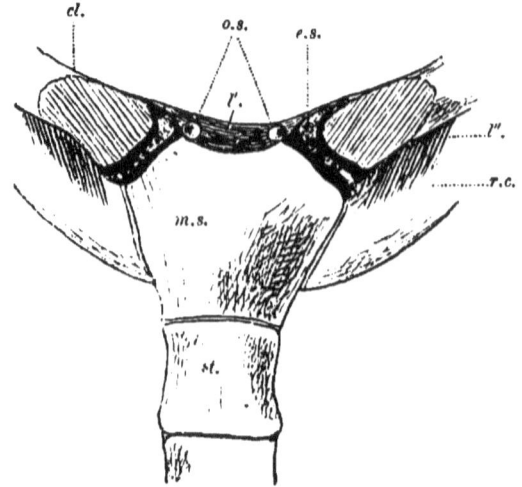

FIG. 30.—EPISTERNAL VESTIGES IN MAN.
e.s., "episternum" (sterno-clavicular cartilage); *o.s.*, ossa suprasternalia; *cl.*, clavicle, sawn through; *l'.*, inter-clavicular ligament; *l"*., costo-clavicular ligament; *m.s.*, manubrium sterni; *st.*, sternum; *r.c.*, first rib.

still considerable uncertainty about this; especially as Carwardine has recently shown [1] that the ligaments in which the "ossa suprasternalia" lie embedded when free, may or may not be continuous with an "inter-clavicular ligament" which, by its T-shaped character and detailed relationships, may suggest the inter-clavicle (episternum) of Monotremes and Reptiles.]

THE SKULL

In all Vertebrates the skull may be divided into two principal portions, the cranial and the facial. The cranial portion, or brain case, encloses the anterior part of the central nervous system, and is intimately associated with the higher

[1] *Jour. Anat. and Phys.*, vol. xxvii. p. 232.

sense organs and their investing capsules. In the embryo it is penetrated for some distance at its base by the forerunner of the backbone—the chorda dorsalis. For this reason it appears to be in a certain sense a prolongation of the axial skeleton of the trunk. The visceral or facial portion of the skull lies postero-ventrally to the cranial. It is closely connected with the pharyngeal section of the alimentary canal, the lateral walls of which

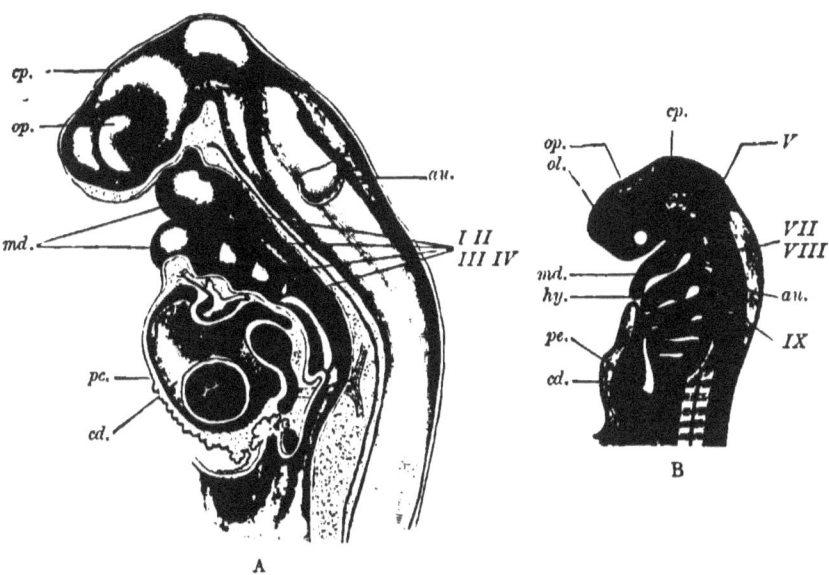

FIG. 31.—A, SLIGHTLY DIAGRAMMATIC MEDIAN LONGITUDINAL SECTION THROUGH THE HEAD AND ANTERIOR PORTION OF THE TRUNK OF A HUMAN EMBRYO, SEVENTEEN TO EIGHTEEN WEEKS OLD. (After W. His.)

cp., brain; *op.*, optic vesicle; *md.*, mandibular arch; *pc.*, pericardium; *cd.*, heart; *au.*, auditory vesicle; *I-IV*, branchial clefts.

B, EMBRYO TORPEDO, as seen by transmitted light. (After H. E. and F. Ziegler.) *ol.*, olfactory pit; *hy.*, hyoid arch; *V.*, trigeminal nerve; *cd.*, ventricle; *VII*, *VIII*, facial and auditory nerves; *IX*, glosso-pharyngeal nerve. Other references as for A.

are, in the embryo, perforated by "gill-clefts" (*I-IV*, Fig. 31, A), so called because their presence points back to a time in which this part of the alimentary canal served not only for taking in food, but for respiration, as is still the case in the lower Vertebrates. That the system of skeletal arches, which alternate with these clefts has, in man, undergone considerable modification and reduction (cf. Fig. 105) will not appear strange, when the biological conditions are taken into account. The only point of

E

essential importance for us here is the fact that the skull of Man and all Vertebrates is constructed on a common plan (cf. A and B, Fig. 31).

The fact that this ground plan is not so evident in the skull of the higher Vertebrata and Man as in that of the lower Vertebrates, is due to the progressive modification which the former have

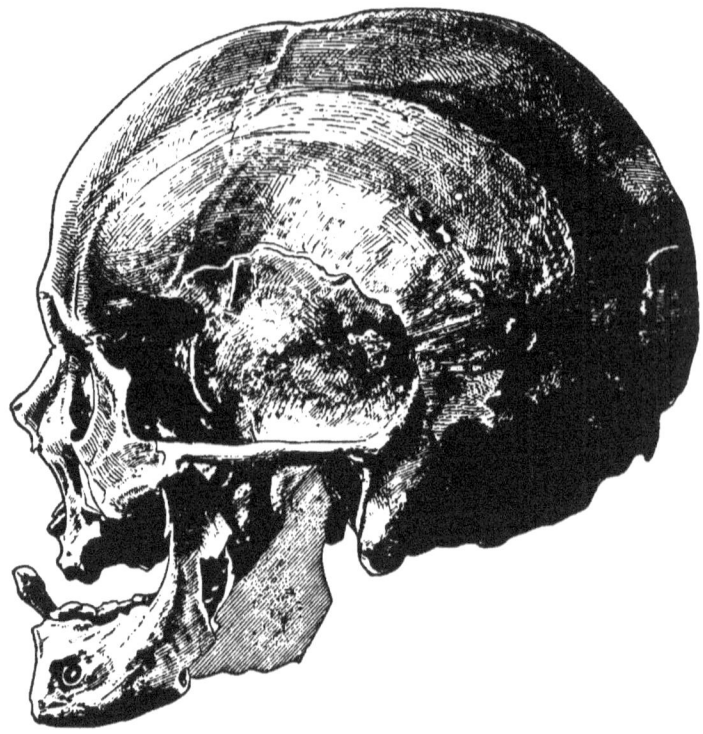

FIG. 32.—SKULL OF IMMANUEL KANT. (After C. von Kupffer.)
(The great size of the cranium is a noteworthy feature.)

undergone; and the final result has been that the human skull differs markedly not only from that of the lower Vertebrata, but also from that of the Anthropoid Apes, which in the rest of their skeleton agree so closely with Man. It will, therefore, be interesting to examine the two latter types of skull, in order to determine and, when possible, explain the differences between them.

On mere superficial examination, the proportionate difference in size between the cranium and the face of the two is most striking. In Man (Fig. 32) the cranium is a smooth and imposing

THE SKELETON

rounded or oval bony case, which contrasts strongly with the incomparably smaller one of the Orang (Fig. 36) and Gorilla, with their enormous external ridges and protuberances. These latter animals, like all the Anthropoids, differ from Man in the great development of the face, and especially of the jaws, which in Man are subordinate to the cranium. If, however, young stages of the Anthropoid are compared (Fig. 35), this distinction becomes less striking; for, as is well known, not only the whole head but the features of the young Ape bear a decided resemblance to those of the human fœtus. Indeed, it is certain that the divergence begins after birth, the characteristics of each type becoming more and more marked as age advances (cf. Figs. 35 and 36).

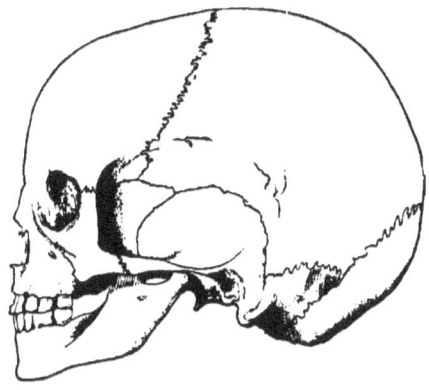

FIG. 33.—SKULL OF A CHILD SEVEN YEARS OLD. (One-third natural size.)

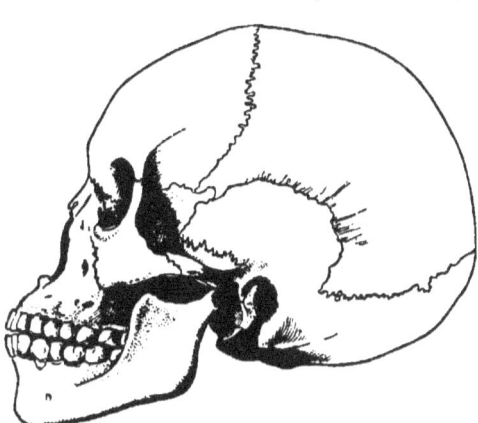

FIG. 34.—SKULL OF AN AUSTRALIAN FROM THE MURRAY RIVER. (One-third natural size.)

The chief cause of the distinction clearly lies in the greater development of the human brain. In the higher Vertebrates the brain must be regarded as the dominant organ of the head; and in Man it continues to grow even into the prime of life, the cranial capacity attained reaching in the male Caucasian an average of 1500 cubic cm., and the brain a weight of from 1375 to 1400 gr.

With regard to the cranial capacity of the lower races of mankind, observations made by the cousins Sarasin on the Veddahs of Ceylon are of special interest. In them, not merely the skull but the whole skeleton is remarkable for its delicacy, a character which, according to Virchow, distinguishes a number of the wild races inhabiting the islands of the East. The skull is on the average 200 gr. lighter than that of the European; it is very small, and the cranial capacity in the pure (unmixed) Veddah male is at most 1250 cubic cm., and in the female some 140 cubic cm. less than that.

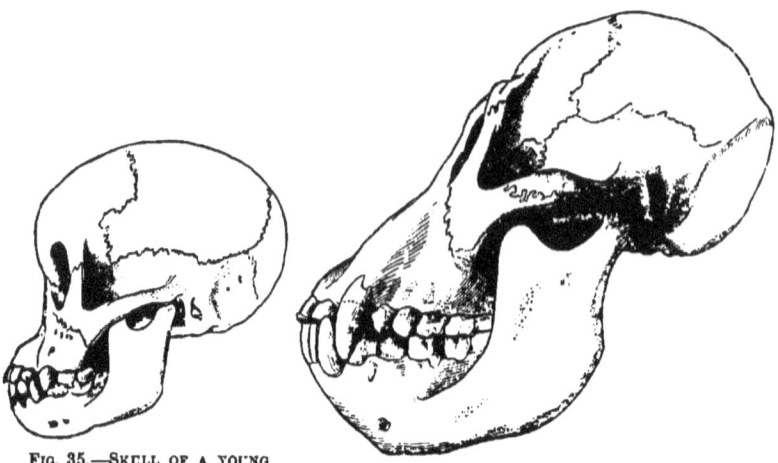

FIG. 35.—SKULL OF A YOUNG ORANG-UTAN. (One-third natural size.)

FIG. 36.—SKULL OF AN ADULT ORANG-UTAN. (One-third natural size.)

In cranial capacity the Veddahs are undoubtedly among the lowest of human beings, and this is quite in keeping with their low level of civilisation. The woolly-haired inhabitants of the Andaman islands are on approximately the same level, whereas the Bushmen and Australians rank somewhat higher.[1]

In shape the Veddah's skull is very long and narrow, *i.e.* strongly dolicocephalic. The cranium of the female is more rounded than that of the male—indeed, all the peculiarities which in the European distinguish the skull of the woman from that of the man are present in the Veddahs.

But while there is a difference of from 250 to more than 500 cubic cm. in the cranial capacity of the Veddah and the European, a far greater disparity occurs between the cranial

[1] [In the Akkas (the pygmy race of Central Africa), the cranial capacity of the skull of a male recently described by Sir W. Flower is 1102 cubic cm., and that of a female 1072 cubic cm. The same writer has, however, described the skull of a female Veddah, having a capacity of but 950 cubic cm., that being one of the smallest normal adult human skulls on record (cf. *Jour. of the Anthropological Instit.*, vol. xviii. p. 6).]

capacity of Man and that of the Anthropoid Apes, the latter ranging from about 427 cubic cm. (Chimpanzee) to 557 (Gorilla), *i.e.* averaging less than half that of the human races mentioned above. As yet no human skull has been discovered which bridges over this gap.

The cause of this great difference lies largely in the fact that the brain of the Ape makes no marked progress after birth, and this no doubt applies not only to its size, but also to its microscopic anatomy, *e.g.* to the differentiation of its gray cortex.

The Anthropoid skull is furnished with massive jaws controlled by powerful muscles and armed with formidable teeth. This extraordinary development of the facial portion of the skull which supports the entrance to the alimentary canal, is no doubt of compensatory value in the struggle for existence. We shall return to this subject in considering the dentition as a determining factor in the modification of the jaws.

The foregoing account of the changes undergone by the cranial skeleton has, I hope, shown that the human skull is subject to the same influences as that of the beasts, and that the two differ as divergent adaptive modifications of one and the same fundamental plan. This is not, however, an altogether satisfactory explanation, since the primary cause of this difference of modification (in Man in the psychic and brain-forming direction, in the Anthropoids in the vegetative direction) remains unknown.

That these divergent lines of modification from a common starting-point were entered upon very long ago is proved, not only by the sharply differentiated types of skull found both among Anthropoids and Men, but also by the fact that great and undoubtedly atavistic deviations from the general normal type of human skull are comparatively rare. The type appears complete, well established, and sharply individualised.

Exception must be made in the case of the dentition, to which the above is not applicable, and also in that of microcephalous and teratological conditions, although these are often enough utilised in building up the primitive history of the human skull. It is, however, possible, inasmuch as some of these cases certainly exhibit phenomena due to arrest of development, that an occasional indication of a former primitive condition may be revealed in them; but the pathological element is, as a rule, so strong that no certain morphological conclusions can be drawn— indeed, deceptive appearances may be expected at every step.

Gratiolet has established the fact that the higher races of

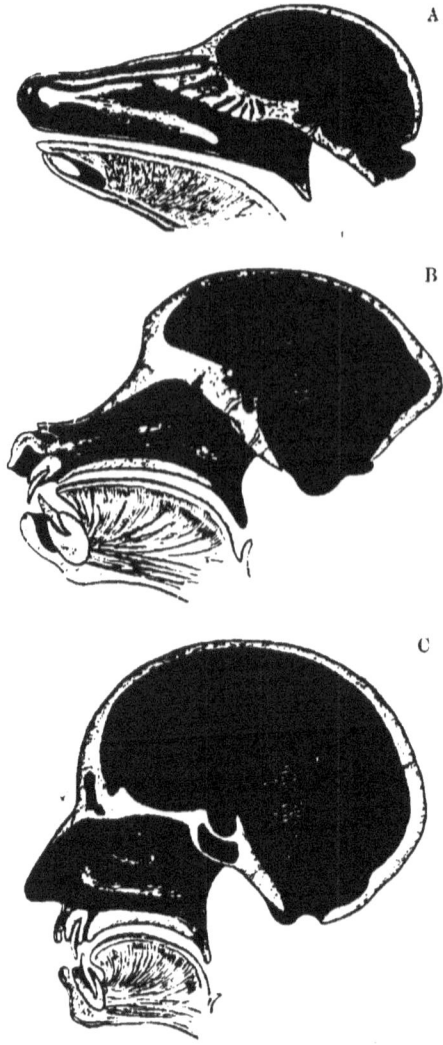

FIG. 37.—MEDIAN SECTIONS THROUGH THE HEAD OF A DEER (A), BABOON (B), AND MAN (C).
The relation of the cranium to the nasal cavity should be noted. The former, with gradual enlargement, comes to overlie the latter, thereby altering the facial angle (cf. with these Figs. 32-36).

men differ from the lower in the order of obliteration of the cranial sutures. In the lower races, as in the Apes, the process always begins anteriorly in the frontal region of the skull, i.e. at the fronto-parietal boundaries, and proceeds backwards. This naturally causes an earlier limitation in growth of the anterior lobes of the brain; whereas, in the higher (white) races, where the fronto-parietal suture disappears only after the obliteration of the parieto-occipital one, these lobes are capable of further development. This fact may well be closely connected with the intellectual difference between the races. It not infrequently happens that the frontal suture remains open;[1] but whether, as might suggest itself, this is to be regarded as indicative of a further development or, on the other hand, as a reversional feature, cannot yet be decided. On the latter assumption, the fact that fusion of the frontal bones occurs in many Mammals (Apes, Insectivora, Chiroptera, Monotremata, and others) is of interest, especially as reversion to the condition of the lower Vertebrates is a phenomenon, which, as we have already seen, is by no means unknown in Man. It appears to me that the two views may to a certain extent be harmonised, by considering that the original independence of the ossific centres inherited from lower ancestors may be sometimes retained and utilised in the interest of a progressive development of the anterior lobes of the brain.

Gegenbaur, in his *Lehrbuch der Anatomie des Menschen*, calls special attention to the independent ossification of that which becomes the postero-inferior angle of the frontal bone, i.e. that part of it which borders on the alisphenoid. Since, at birth, and even for some time after birth, traces of this division are evident, we are reminded of the post-frontal bone of the lower Vertebrates.[2]

On turning to that part of the skull where the parietals meet the occipital (the lambdoidal suture), an independent membrane bone is sometimes found, the so-called "interparietal,"[3]

---

[1] According to Welcker, the frontal suture often persists in Caucasians, less often in Malays, and very rarely in Americans, whereas the exact reverse is the case with the transverse occipital suture which divides the interparietal from the occipital bone proper. It often happens that the latter is found together with the frontal suture in one and the same skull. In the child the fusion of the frontal bones begins normally as early as the ninth month, and ends towards the close of the second year.

[2] This must not be confounded with the epipteric bone, which sometimes occupies approximately the same position (cf. *infra*, pp. 59 and 61).

[3] This is also known as the os transversum, triquetum, epactale, Goetheanum, and most commonly as the os Incae, because of its frequent occurrence in the skulls of the ancient Peruvians (i.e. 5 to 6 per cent, as compared with but 1 to 2 per cent in European skulls). A somewhat similar "præinterparietal" lying in front of this, and which will be described later, occurs in about 1 per cent of all cases.

between the parietals, assuming a markedly angular form (*i.p.* Fig. 38, A). Although this bone persists differently in different races, it is formed in the embryo from two distinct ossific centres,

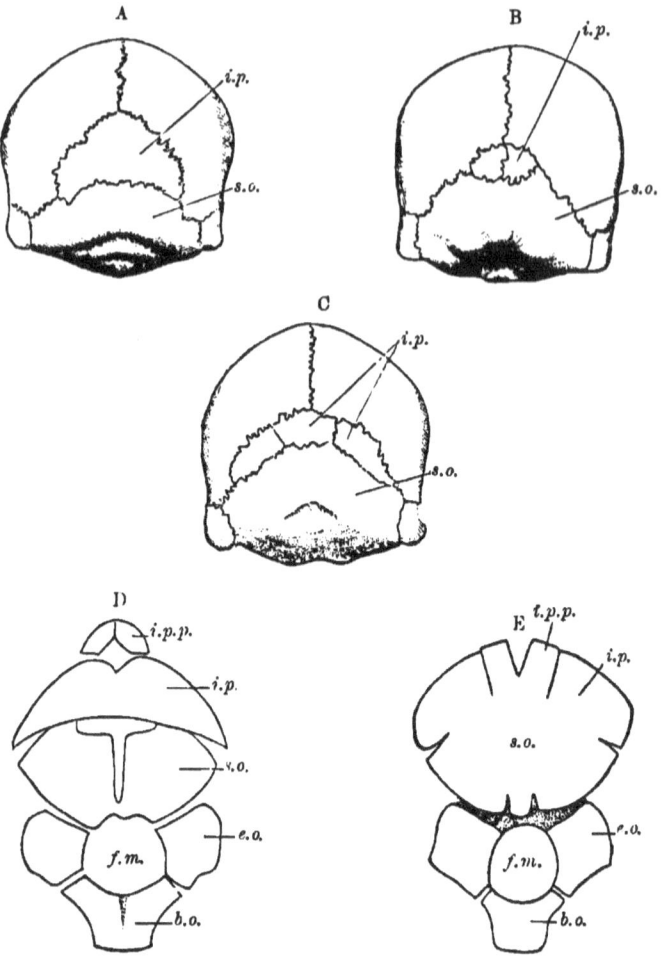

FIG. 38.—A to C, VARIOUS FORMS OF THE OS INCAE (interparietal bone). D, E, DIAGRAM OF THE BONES OF THE OCCIPITAL REGION IN THE EMBRYO.
(Partly after Ficalbi.)
i.p., interparietal ; *i.p.p.*, præinterparietal ; *e.o.*, exoccipital ; *s.o.*, supra-occipital ; *b.o.*, basioccipital ; *f.m.*, foramen magnum.

which, at a later stage, normally unite to form one mass with the supra-occipital. This fact testifies to its paired nature, and, as in the new-born child it is still separated by a cleft on each side of the median line from the adjacent and originally cartilaginous supra-occipital, it may perhaps have existed in the ancestors of man as an independent bone.[1]

The interparietals first appear in Mammals, but among the higher forms they are seen in a state of apparent degeneration, as would appear from their great variability in occurrence, form, and detailed relationships. They may, for example, remain either partly or wholly isolated; they may be either single, bilaterally symmetrical, or asymmetrical, or may be represented by but one lateral bone.

Other inconstant ossific nuclei of this region are the præinterparietalia. These may remain partly or wholly isolated, and show in form and position variations similar to those above described for the interparietals. The possible combinations of these anomalous bones cannot be discussed here (cf. Fig. 38).

The morphology of the præinterparietals is not clear, and it is by no means unlikely that, like the ossa Wormiana (o. suturaria), they fall under the category of accessory ossicles. The problem is rendered still more difficult by the fact that, so far as is known, they are constantly present only in the Horses, while in other Mammals they are of mere sporadic occurrence. In Man, as compared with the latter, they appear comparatively frequently (*i.e.* 1 per cent). Equally uncertain is the morphology of the os fronto-parietale [os antiepilepticum of the ancients], a bone which occurs very rarely in Man, in the neighbourhood of the fronto-parietal suture. This bone, which is more often found in the Cebidæ among Monkeys, and less frequently in Rodents, may be sometimes paired.

An atavistic significance may be probably attached to a bony process which occasionally appears in Man, behind and externally to the jugular foramen, and into which the rectus capitis lateralis muscle is inserted. This corresponds with the par-occipital or paramastoid processus of many Mammals, which attains its strongest development in Ungulates and Rodents.

There is one more point worth consideration in the occipital region, *i.e.* the median portion of the linea nuchæ superior.[2] A bony ridge (torus occipitalis), stretching at times as far as the linea nuchæ suprema, occasionally develops here. According to

[1] Welcker regards all the larger bones which are occasionally intercalated in the lambdoidal suture as fragments of the os Incae.

[2] It is difficult to decide whether the furrow or pit (fossette vermienne, Albrecht), sometimes formed for the reception of the vermis cerebelli, has any phylogenetic significance.

Ecker, this ridge is common in certain races, and it is said to be homologous with the massive occipital crest of the Apes.[1]

In the normal adult skull the sphenoid appears as a single mass, and at a certain age this fuses still further with the basioccipital bone. A comparative study of the Mammalian skull, as also an examination of the skull of the human embryo, however, shows that the apparently single sphenoid represents a series of fused bones. The basal elements of the skull are segmentally arranged; but comparison with the lower vertebrata shows that this is a secondary feature in no way indicative of original metamerism. The cranial "segments" are no part of a primordial segmentation corresponding with the embryonic somites, as has been clearly shown by Van Wijhe and Froriep from the study of development (cf. *infra*).

Comparative Anatomy shows us that the orbital and temporal fossæ were originally one (as they still are even among Lemurs). In the human embryo, and even in the new-born child, this fact is still indicated by the greater width of the spheno-maxillary fissure, the ultimate limitation of which, by extension and the final meeting of the alisphenoid and the zygoma (malar), is not then effected. Before this occurs the frontal and the malar have already come into close apposition, and in the double relation of the latter to the frontal bone on the one hand and the sphenoid on the other, we have a distinctive character of the Primates as opposed to all other Mammals. We find, accordingly, that these connections are formed very late in the development of Man, as compared with the relations of the malar to the maxillary and temporal bones, which are established much earlier ontogenetically, as they were phylogenetically.

Under ordinary circumstances, the upper edge of the ala magna of the sphenoid (alisphenoid) reaches the anterior lower angle of the parietal, but in rare cases (about 1 per cent of European skulls) this junction is prevented by the anterior edge of the temporal bone sending out a process to meet the frontal.

---

[1] [In the Gorilla the sagittal and lambdoidal crests attain so great a development in the male as to give the skull a carnivorous aspect. This feature is an accompaniment of the greater development of the temporal jaw-muscles; and it is not acquired by the female. So marked is this sexual difference between the skulls of these animals that had they been first found in the fossil state, they would in the highest degree of probability have been regarded as at least specifically distinct. We have here a most instructive example of an adaptive and secondarily acquired character.]

This so-called processus frontalis is remarkable on account of its more frequent occurrence in the lower races, such as Negroes, Australians, and Veddahs (according to the Sarasins it occurs in

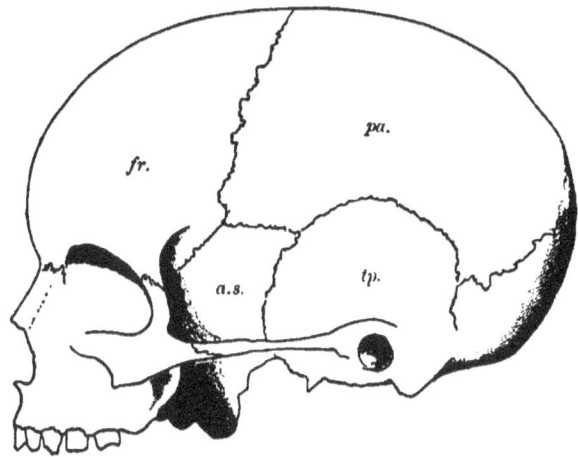

Fig. 39.—Skull of a Girl two years old, in which the temporal bone (*tp.*) is separated from the frontal (*fr.*) by the broad ala magna of the sphenoid (alisphenoid bone, *a.s.*) ; *pa.*, parietal.

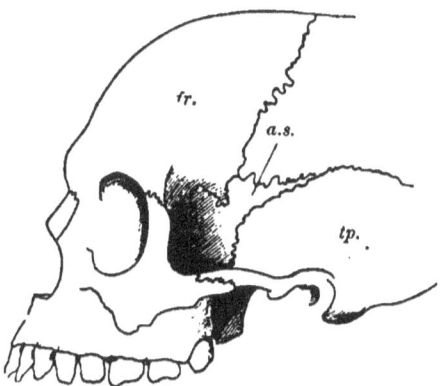

Fig. 40.—Skull of an Aboriginal Australian, in which the temporal bone is separated from the frontal merely by a long process of the alisphenoid (*a.s.*).

10 per cent of the last named). This process is also often found in the lower Mammals. [The upper edge of the alisphenoid, above alluded to, may be not infrequently replaced by a distinct bone (the epipteric of Flower before mentioned—cf. p. 55, footnote, and

Fig. 41, †). Thomson, from the study of a large series of skulls, has shown good reason for regarding this as one of the series of Wormian bones which so often occur in this region, and for believing it to arise by dismemberment from either the alisphenoid or parietal.][1]

The nasal bones which, as a rule, remain distinct, sometimes fuse to form one bone. This occurs far more frequently in the lower races (Patagonians and tribes of South Africa) than in the higher; and it is the more probably an atavism, since this fusion is normal in Apes. In the Chimpanzee it takes place as early as the second year.

The lachrymals are susceptible to not a few variations, and very rarely an abnormal enlargement of the hamular process causes these bones to appear at the surface of the face, as in many lower Mammals (Gegenbaur).

Many variations are to be found in the bones of the inner orbital wall. For example, the lachrymal bone may be altogether wanting, or only present in a vestigial form, so that the os planum (lamina papyracea) comes into direct contact with the ascending or nasal process of the upper jaw (premaxilla). In other cases the lachrymal bone may be divided into an upper and a lower portion by a suture, and there are other variations to which it and the development of the hamular process are susceptible; it may be occasionally replaced by a radially disposed series of small bones.

A similar division of the os planum of the ethmo-turbinal into several pieces has been observed (Turner, Macalister, Arthur Thomson); but it is questionable if any morphological significance is to be attached to these variations.

According to the cousins Sarasin, a lower stage of development is shown in the skulls of the Veddahs and others, in the downward prolongation of the nasal portion of the frontal bones into the orbits, which lie very close together and are spacious,

---

[1] [(*Jour. Anat. and Phys.*, vol. xxiv. p. 356). I have elsewhere pointed out (*ibid.*, vol. xxiv. p. *xviii.*) that the ossa præinterparietalia lie within the area normal to the parietals, and that therefore these, at least, among the intercalary elements of the cranium, may be similarly referred to an origin from those bones, by dismemberment, under the expansion of the brain case. The phenomenon appears to me akin to that of the well-known double ossification of the supra-occipital in its most expanded form (ex. Cetacea and some Insectivora), and of the occasional duplication of the lachrymal, and of the *os planum*, itself already intercalated in the orbital wall in the Primates. (My friend Dr. Forsyth Major has lately shown me that the Lemurs do not differ from the higher Primates in the absence of the latter character, as is generally believed).—G. B. H.]

with strong, over-arching, superciliary ridges. This may be carried so far that the fronto-nasal suture may lie almost on a level with the centre of the orbit, whereas, as a rule, it lies much higher. The arrangement manifestly involves the frontal in a far greater share of the orbital wall than is the case with Europeans; and, correlatively, the os planum is in this race somewhat more than 2 mm. narrower than that of the European.

The bridge of the nose in the Veddahs is not nearly so high as in Europeans, *i.e.* it remains sunk between the orbits. In other words, the two nasal bones do not slope outwards against one another as they do in Europeans (in profile, they together

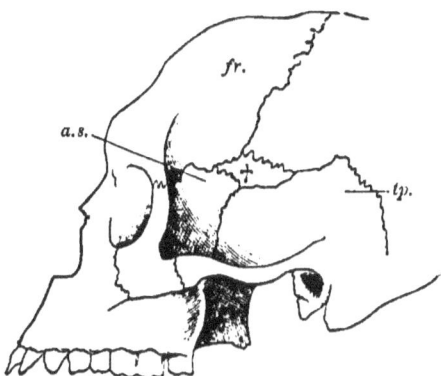

FIG. 41.—THE SKULL OF A NEGRO EUNUCH, in which the process of the alisphenoid (cf. Fig. 40) is represented by a distinct bone—the epipteric (†).

describe a curve slightly concave anteriorly), and this, in life, results in a flat nose. This condition is palingenetically reproduced in the European child, and finds its expression in the flatness of the nose, the bridge developing only in later years. The choanæ of the Veddah's skull are, on an average, half a centimetre lower than in the European.

Turning now to the facial portion of the skull the upper jaw first claims attention. That portion of it which carries the incisors is particularly interesting, because Ontogeny teaches that it was originally a separate bone, homologous with the pre- or intermaxillary of the lower Vertebrata. This bone is an inheritance which reappears with the greatest constancy from the bony Fishes upwards throughout the Vertebrata; but whereas in by far the greater number of these the premaxillary remains an independent bone, in Primates it early fuses with the adjacent elements of the upper jaw to form one mass. In Man this fusion usually occurs soon after birth; in most Apes, on the contrary, much later. In Man the fusion first involves the facial portion

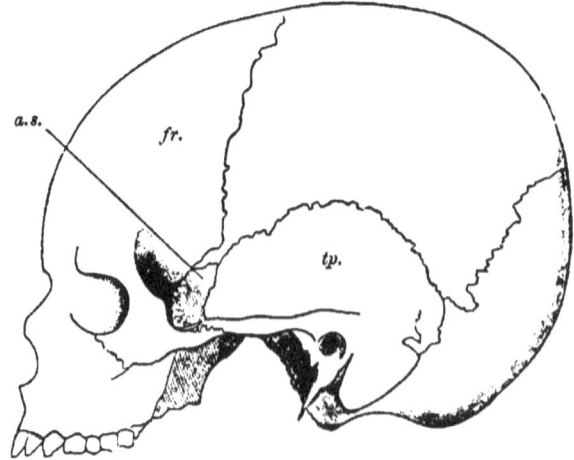

FIG. 42.—SKULL OF A TURCO, in which the temporal bone nearly reaches the frontal. Between the two a narrow process of the parietal is intercalcated.

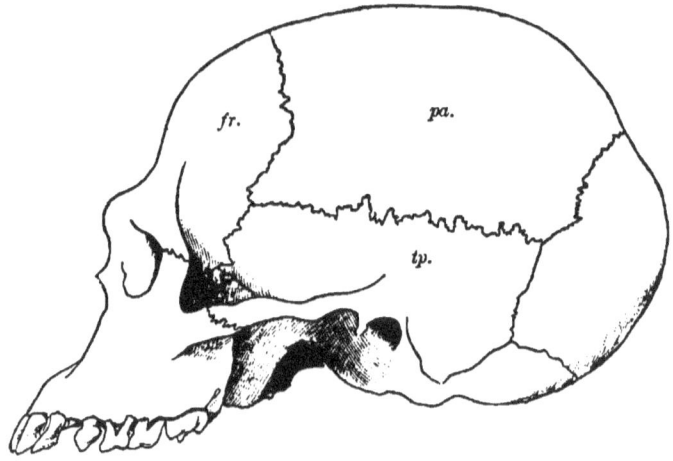

FIG. 43.—SKULL OF A TWO-YEAR-OLD CHIMPANZEE, in which the temporal bone is to a considerable extent in apposition with the frontal (*fr.*).

of the bone, its palatal part remaining for a long time, or even permanently, marked off from that of the maxillary by a suture or trace of a suture. The same is the case with the Anthropoids.

Only very rarely—and then, as a rule, in the lower races of mankind (Negroes and Australian aborigines)—does it remain distinct throughout its whole extent in later years, in otherwise normal skulls. The striking manner in which the original independence of the premaxillary bones is shown in people affected with the deformity known as hare-lip is well known.

The number of incisors connected with the premaxillary will be considered later in dealing with the buccal cavity. It may here, however, be remarked that Comparative Anatomy affords no explanation of the double nature ascribed by Albrecht to each half of the human intermaxillary bone.

Quite recently Waldeyer has drawn attention to certain peculiarities of the hard palate, *i.e.* variations in the posterior

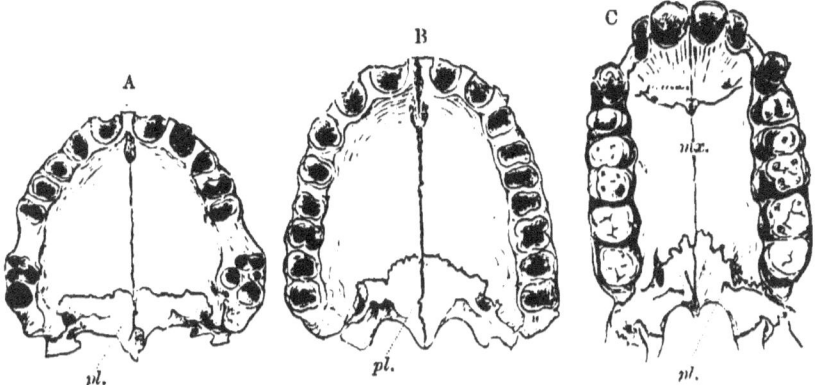

FIG. 44.—THE HARD PALATE, A, OF A CAUCASIAN; B, OF THE NEGRO; C, OF AN ADULT ORANG-UTAN. Showing the differences in shape of the bones. The palate of the Negro represents a type transitional between that of the Caucasian and that of the Orang.

nasal spine, which had previously escaped recognition, and I have confirmed his observations. This spine (Fig. 44) is derivative of the horizontal plates of the palatine bones (*pl.*), and is thus morphologically paired. Not infrequently a more or less marked double spine is found, and where this is most evident the horizontal plates of the palatines may sometimes not even meet in the middle line. In the latter case the palatine processes of the maxillæ may run back along opposite sides of the middle line, so as to take part in the formation of the posterior edge of the hard palate. These deviations from the normal arrangement have been observed in the skulls of Men and Gorillas.

There are further interesting variations in the relative positions of the palatine bone and the palatine process of the maxillary, and also in the relation of the former to the posterior edge of the hard palate.

As a rule, the transverse palatine suture runs right across the palate, *i.e.* the two horizontal plates of the palatine bones have a more or less straight anterior edge (Fig. 44, A). Not infrequently, however, the median portions of these plates are more prolonged anteriorly, the course of the transverse palatine suture being correspondingly irregularly oblique on either side, as depicted in Fig. 44, B.

I find the latter condition to be still more marked in the Orang-Utan (Fig. 44, C), and the same may be true, as Waldeyer has already shown, of other Mammals. [By analogy to the lower vertebrata] we have here an index of a low grade of organisation.

The proximal end of the first visceral skeletal arch (Meckel's cartilage) (I, *mk.*, Fig. 45), which developmentally precedes the bony lower jaw (*md.*),[1] is continued into the middle auditory chamber of the embryo as a cartilaginous enlargement. This becomes twice constricted to form the incus (*in.*) and the malleus (*ml.*) Some authorities homologise these with the quadrate and articular elements of the mandible of the lower Vertebrata, [but according to others they are structures *sui generis* distinct in origin from the embryonic lower jaw. The value of these elements is one of the most vexed problems in comparative morphology. All investigators are, however, agreed that they are the representatives of an apparatus, at least in part functional in lower Vertebrates, in effecting the indirect articulation of the jaw apparatus upon the skull, and that in Man and the Mammals, in which this articulation has become direct, this apparatus, under associated change of function, has entered secondarily into connection with the organ of hearing] (cf. Figs. 45 and 46).

A trace of the embryonic connection between the malleus and Meckel's cartilage is long retained, in the so-called processus gracilis of the malleus, which passes towards the lower jaw

---

[1] The prognathous type of skull has been assumed to be reversionary to a pithecoid condition ; but this consideration is by no means a simple one. The cousins Sarasin have pointed out that the lowest forms of human skulls, *e.g.* those of Veddahs, Andaman Islanders, and Bushmen, are of the orthognathous or (Andaman Islanders) mesognathous type. The orthognathous type may thus have been attained by human beings at a very early period, and subsequently lost. If this be the case (but it is doubtful) the prognathous condition of Negroes and Melanesians, and the great projection of the jaw in some woolly and straight-haired races, must be a secondary condition, which has been preceded by orthognathy. In this case the orthognathy once more attained by Europeans must be regarded as a third phylogenetic phase in the evolution of the skull (Sarasin).

through [an interspace between the elements of the auditory region of the skull, known as] the Glaserian fissure.

The second visceral or primitive skeletal arch (II, Fig. 45) becomes, in Man, proximally connected with the auditory capsule; distally it becomes related to the next arch behind (III of Fig.). Its intervening portion, which at first is cartilaginous, may become partly or altogether ossified, but it is usually transformed

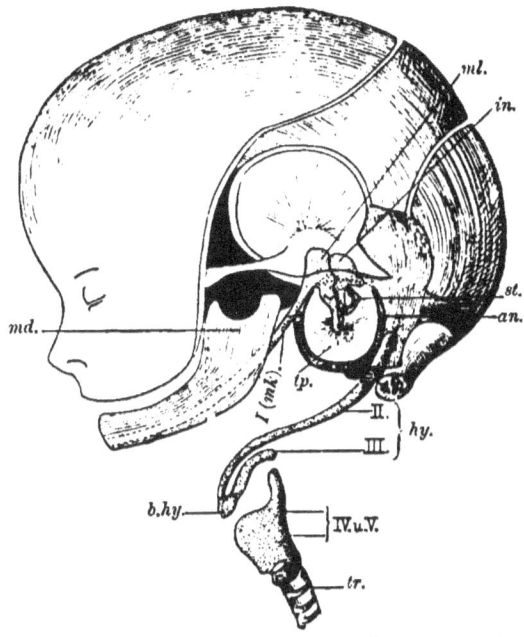

FIG. 45.—HEAD OF A HUMAN EMBRYO OF THE FOURTH MONTH. Dissected to show the auditory ossicles, tympanic ring, and Meckel's cartilage, with the hyoid and thyroid apparatus. All these parts are delineated on a larger scale than the rest of the skull.
ml., malleus; *in.*, incus; *st.*, stapes; *an.*, tympanic ring; *tp.*, tympanum; I (*mk.*), first skeletal (mandibular) arch (Meckel's cartilage); II, second skeletal (hyoid) arch; III, third (first branchial) arch; IV, V, fourth and fifth arches (thyroid cartilage); *b.hy.*, basihyal element; *tr.*, trachea; *md.*, bony mandible.

along the greater part of its length into a fibrous band. In other cases it is replaced by a series of small cartilaginous or osseous bodies which form a chain, recalling the arrangement existing in many lower Mammals. The proximal end of this arch becomes, in Man, the very variable styloid process of the temporal bone; the distal end, on the other hand, forms the lesser cornu of the hyoid. This latter bone (the hyoid) also consists of a central portion or body (*b.hy.*), and a larger or posterior

F

cornu (III), which is paired and projects therefrom backwards. The body may be regarded as the basal element of the second and third embryonic skeletal arches,[1] while the posterior cornua represent the lateral elements of the third (or first branchial) arch alone (cf. Figs. 45, 46, and 107).

In the earliest stages of the embryo, the ridge which will afterwards develop into the second or hyoid visceral arch, sends a process backwards, which covers a deep groove (the cervical groove) on the postero-lateral edge of the cephalic region. The third and fourth branchial arches lie in the hollow thus formed, and they gradually cease to be externally evident. The entrance to this cervical groove is bounded by the hyoid

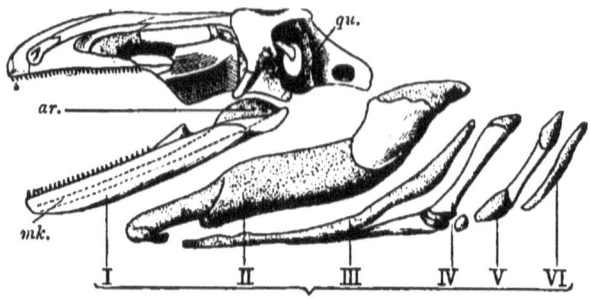

FIG. 46.—SKULL OF A TAILED AMPHIBIAN (*Menopoma*). The skeletal arches are lettered serially with those of Man, in Figs. 45 and 105.
qu., quadrate cartilage ; *ar.*, articular end of *mk.*, Meckel's cartilage ; I, mandibular arch ; II, hyoid arch ; III, IV, V, VI, branchial skeletal arches.

arch ; and there can be little doubt that we have in the above-mentioned ridge a feeble homologue of the gill-cover of fishes and metamorphosing Amphibia. It at a later stage fuses with the adjacent body wall, the cervical groove (branchial chamber of the Anamnia) becoming thus closed.

The hyoid apparatus, which is intimately connected with the cervical, lingual, and mandibular musculature, is in fibrous connection (thyro-hyoid ligament) with the upper edge of the laryngeal skeleton ; and of this skeleton the thyroid cartilage at least (IV, V, Fig. 45) arises from the fourth and fifth branchial arches (cf. Fig. 107 and p. 151).

[1] [It is usually stated to be ossified from a single centre in Mammals, but the fact, to which my friend Mr. M. F. Woodward has drawn my attention, that it may be occasionally subdivided by a transverse suture into two portions (ex. *Lepus*) indicative of its ossification from two recurrent centres, is of much interest in this connection.—G. B. H.]

THE SKELETON

SKELETON OF THE LIMBS

So far as their skeleton is concerned, the fore and hind limbs of Men and other Vertebrates, notwithstanding their various adaptive modifications, are unmistakably built on the same plan. This fact not only finds its expression in the strictly homologous segmentation of their free portions, but is confirmed by Comparative Anatomy and Ontogeny.

Without entering at length into the old controversy as to the phylogeny of the limbs, I would briefly define my own posi-

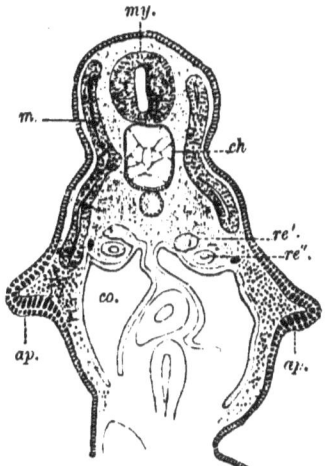

FIG. 47.—TRANSVERSE SECTION THROUGH THE EMBRYO OF A SHARK (*Pristiurus melanostomus*), 9 mm. long, showing the mode of origin of the Pectoral Limb Bud (*ap.*)
ch., notochord ; *co.*, cœlom ; *m.*, myomeres, seen to be growing ventrally ; *my.*, spinal cord.

tion with regard to this question. I agree with Balfour and Dohrn in regarding the limbs of the Vertebrates as outgrowths of the primitive body segments, and thus believe in their originally segmental nature; and I see in this an argument for the origin of existing Vertebrates from segmented Invertebrate ancestors. In other words, these limbs, which in origin are polymerous, involve phylogenetically a certain number of body segments with their muscles and nerves; and these, in consequence of functional adaptation, must necessarily undergo different modifications in the different groups of Vertebrates. Although this subject cannot be further discussed here, it may be remarked, in passing, that the differences between the anterior and posterior limbs, resulting from adaptive modification, become less marked the lower we descend in the vertebrate series; indeed, a starting-point of approximate structural uniformity is finally reached among the Fishes. In the higher types, and especially in Birds and Mammals, the limbs have greatly diverged. In the former, the whole weight of the body is thrown on to the posterior limbs, which are thus purely supporting organs; and the anterior limbs, relieved of their original supporting functions, have become transformed into organs of flight.

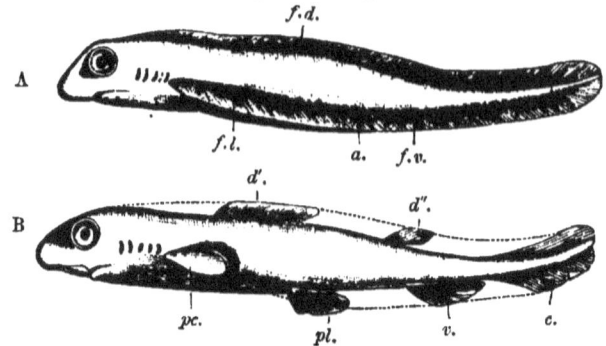

FIG. 48.—DIAGRAM ILLUSTRATING THE DEVELOPMENT OF THE FINS OF A FISH.
A, To show the first formed and originally continuous lateral ($f.l.$) and dorsal ($f.d.$) fin-folds; $f.v.$ indicates the point where the lateral folds are continued ventrally behind the anus ($a.$).
B, To show the definitive fins [which owe their independence to the absorption of the primarily continuous folds throughout the areas indicated by the dotted lines], $d'.$, $d''.$, dorsal fins; $pc.$, pectoral; $pl.$, ventral or pelvic fins; $v.$, anal; and $c.$, caudal fin.

An almost equally advanced modification is found in many Mammals, e.g. Man, in whom the anterior limbs have been transformed from ambulatory into prehensile organs, the "fore-feet" becoming hands.

A detailed comparison between the upper and lower limbs of Man will be instituted at the close of this section (*infra*, p. 91).

THE PECTORAL (SHOULDER) AND PELVIC (HIP) GIRDLES

That the limb-girdles were of later origin than the skeleton of the free limbs is rendered probable by the Ontogeny of all Vertebrates.

The following is the course of development in the embryo Shark:—

A number of originally separate skeletogenous rays ($rd.$, Fig. 49, A), develop in the dermal fin-folds [1]; and, by fusion at their proximal ends, even before they are at all chondrified, they give origin to a basal plate (bs). The anterior ends of the basal plates of opposite sides next approximate (*Fig. 49, B), and finally fuse in the middle line, leaving passages for their related

---

[1] [Great interest attaches to the recent discovery, that in the Palæozoic Selachian *Cladoselache*, these rays retained their primary independence in the adult pelvic fin. Cf. Dean, *Jour. Morph.*, vol. ix. p. 87.]

THE SKELETON

nerves. Of the cartilaginous arch thus formed, the middle portion becomes in the fore-limb the pectoral, and in the hind the pelvic girdle, and both of these must therefore be regarded as products of the skeletogenous blastema of the free limbs. The segmentation into a central girdle and lateral limb supports is effected by a process of resorption (cf. †Fig. 49, C), the points at which this is effected becoming the shoulder and hip-joints.

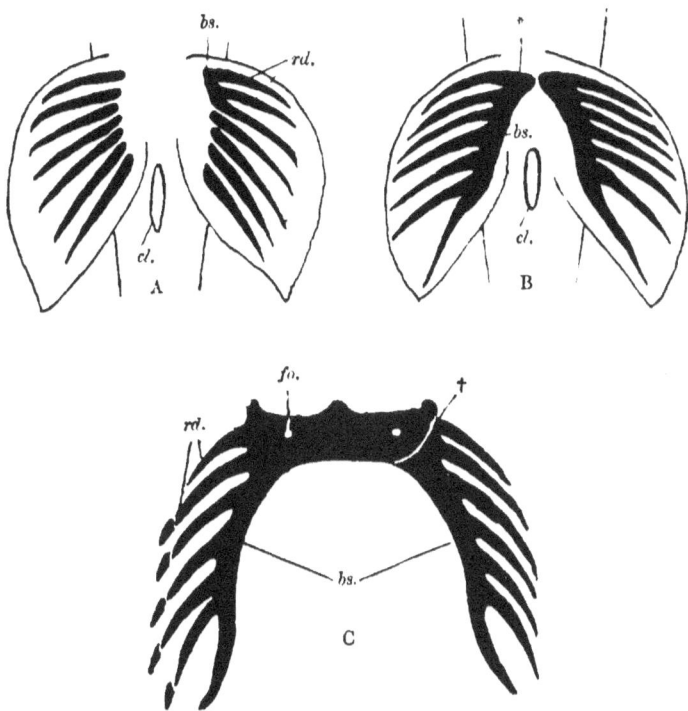

FIG. 49.—A, B, C, DIAGRAMMATIC REPRESENTATION OF THREE SUCCESSIVE STAGES IN THE DEVELOPMENT OF THE PELVIC FINS OF A SHARK.

rd., primitive skeletogenous rays; in A these are already commencing to grow together to form a basal plate (*bs.*); in B this fusion has taken place on both sides, and at the proximal ends of the basal plates are approximating to form the limb girdle; in C the process is completed, and at † the free limb skeleton is being constricted off. The formation of secondary rays at the periphery is delineated to the left of C; figure *fo.*, foramen obturatorium; *cl.*, cloacal aperture.

It would appear from the foregoing that not only the girdles, but also the basal limb supports which articulate with them (the later femur or humerus), were primarily the products of fusion of parallel rays. Inasmuch as this consideration, as will appear later, is of profound importance in dealing with the morphological significance of the limbs, this brief digression into Embryology has been unavoidable. Fig. 50 further illustrates the same subject, showing the probable manner in which the number of skeletal rays which unite to form the limbs of terrestrial Vertebrates is reduced.

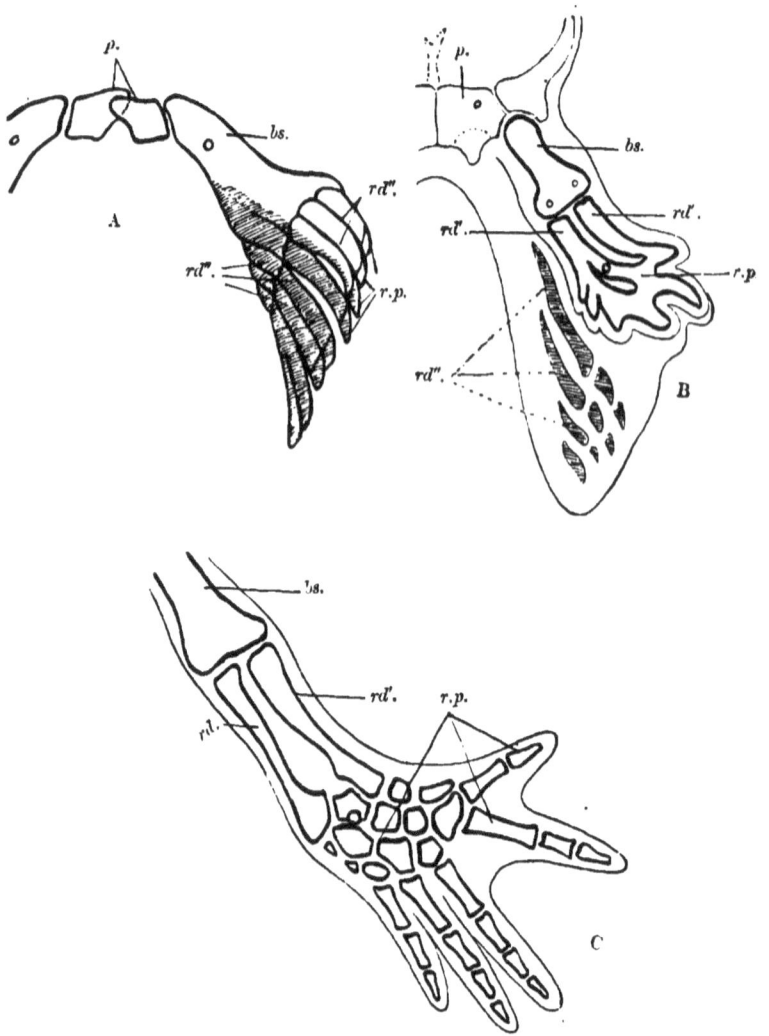

Fig. 50.—An Attempt to depict diagrammatically the Process by which, from the Study of Comparative Morphology, the Limbs of Terrestrial Vertebrata would appear to have been probably derived, by Modification, from the Fins of Fishes.

The shaded parts indicate rays which atrophy; A, pelvic fin of a Sturgeon; B, diagram of the posterior limb of a larval Salamander; C, the hind limb of an adult Urodele Amphibian (*Ranodon*); $p.$, pelvis; $bs.$, basale (femur); $rd'.$, proximal rays (tibia, fibula); $r.p.$, peripheral ray segments (tarsal and other elements of the pedal skeleton); $rd''.$, rays which atrophy and ultimately disappear.

Phylogenetically, the oldest elements of the pectoral girdle are the scapula and coracoid, and of the pelvic girdle the ischium and pubis; for though in certain Fishes the clavicle and the ilium are indicated, they are only fully developed from the Amphibia upwards.

Fig. 51 is the ventral view of the pectoral girdle of a tailed Amphibian. It shows that the clavicles (*cl.*) are directed forwards (*i.e.* towards the head), and that the coracoids (*co.*) overlap each other ventrally. The edges of the latter, which are connected by fibrous tissue, only loosely overlie the small so-called "sternum" (*st.*). The connection between the coracoids

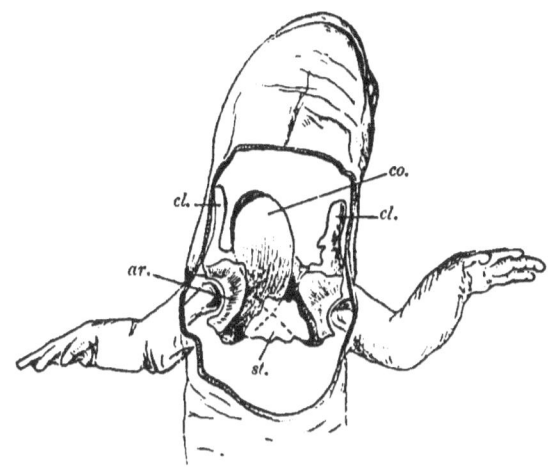

FIG. 51.—PECTORAL GIRDLE OF A TAILED AMPHIBIAN, FROM THE VENTRAL SIDE.
cl., clavicle ; *co.*, coracoid ; *ar.*, shoulder-joint ; *st.*, so-called "sternum."

and the sternum becomes much closer in Reptiles and Birds, and persists in the lowest Mammals. The withdrawal from this connection seen in the higher Mammalia is proportionate to the greater development of the antero-ventral element of the pectoral girdle, the clavicle. Through the mediation of this bone the scapula finds a new support upon the sternum, and thus the limb, being the farther removed from the trunk, attains far greater freedom of movement.

The expanded coracoid of the lower Vertebrata is, in Man, represented by an apparent process of the upper edge of the scapula, called the processus coracoideus (*co.*, Fig. 52). This serves as a point of origin and attachment for certain ligaments and muscles, but its original independence and greater significance is seen in the fact that it ossifies from two distinct centres, which in Man only completely fuse with one another and with the bony scapula after the sixteenth to the eighteenth year. [This double ossification of the coracoid occurs only in Mammals among living Vertebrates] The overhanging portion of the coracoidal region of the human blade-bone, which (*co.*, Fig. 52) from its suggestiveness of a bird's head has been termed the "coracoid process," answers in every detail of relationship to the epicoracoid of the lowest Mammals (*e.c.*, Fig. 28). The basal portion, or second coracoidal element (which does not appear in the human subject until the fourteenth or fifteenth year), represents, in a highly reduced and vestigial condition, the more robust element of the Ornithorhynchus coracoid (*m.c.*, Fig. 28). It was until recently known as the "coracoid"; but, as it and the epicoracoid together represent the entire coracoid of the lower Vertebrata, the term metacoracoid is now applied to it.][1]

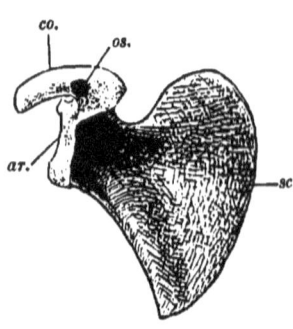

FIG. 52.—RIGHT BLADE-BONE OF A NEW-BORN CHILD, SEEN FROM THE INNER OR COSTAL SURFACE. *co.*, coracoid process; the dark spot at *os.* represents the first of its two centres of ossification; *ar.*, articular facet for humerus; *sc.*, scapula.

The scapula is in Man a broad bone, its form being doubtless attained in functional adaptation to a very strongly developed shoulder musculature. In those lower animals, in which the anterior limbs are simple ambulatory organs performing less complicated movements, the scapula is not so broad, especially at its median and hinder border—the so-called base. It is therefore very interesting to be able to prove, both by the Anatomy of the lower races (Negroes and aborigines of Australia) and by human Ontogeny, that the great breadth of the median part of the human scapula, and the sharper differentiation of its spine, may both be considered as secondarily acquired features, which stand in direct relation to the gradually increasing functional activity of the fore-limb.[2]

[1] [Cf. Lyndekker and Howes, *Proc. Zool. Soc.*, Lond. 1893, pp. 172 and 585.]
[2] [The scapula of the higher Mammalia differs most conspicuously from that of the lowest Mammals and all lower Vertebrates, in its expansion, cephalad of its spine, to form the so-called prescapular lamina. This is but feebly formed in Man. It attains its highest development in association with marked specialisation of the fore-limb—not, however, always for the same purpose. This is readily seen, for

The close connection between the increased efficiency of the fore-limbs and the stronger development of the clavicle has already been pointed out; and the great physiological significance of the clavicle is further shown by the fact, that at a certain stage in development it is the strongest portion of the whole human skeleton and the first to become ossified.[1]

One distinction between the shoulder and the pelvic girdle, evident even on superficial comparison, lies in the more limited capacity of movement of the latter, which is in turn associated with the more limited movements of the hind-limbs. But although mechanical causes, connected with the upright mode of progression, certainly play a great part in determining the condition of the latter, they do not furnish the complete explanation, as a similar immobility of the pelvis is found in the lowest terrestrial Vertebrates, Reptiles, and Amphibians. And further, as in both of these, and especially in the tailed Amphibians, no great distinction is found between the mobility of the anterior and the posterior limbs, the first cause of the distinction so marked in Man must therefore be sought elsewhere. It seems to me to lie, on the one hand, in functional adaptation of the pelvis to the requirements of reproduction, and on the other, in the fact that the distal part of the pelvis forms the functional posterior end of the trunk. At this part of the body, where the posterior apertures of the urinogenital and alimentary systems occur, a firm framework is needed for the related convergent viscera. Such a framework would be a predisposing factor in the development of the powerful sphincter and limb muscles, furnishing the latter with a more extensive and firmer surface of attachment, which could further be turned to account by the free posterior limbs.

The relationships of the pectoral and pelvic girdles to the vertebral column are essentially alike in principle. In neither case, among terrestrial Vertebrates, is the connection attained directly, but always through the intervention of ribs. The

example, on comparison of the Sea Lion (*Otaria*) and Great Ant-Eater (*Myrmecophaga*), in the former of which the prescapular lamina far exceeds in area the rest of the blade-bone. The Sea Lion uses its fore-limb as a swimming organ, the Ant-Eater for tearing up Termites' nests and digging.]

[1] In the scapula of the Veddahs, the greater slant of the spine towards the posterior edge, and the consequent greater development of the supraspinous fossa (prescapular lamina) as compared with that of Europeans, may be indicated as primitive features (Sarasins).

shoulder girdle is loosely attached to its ribs by muscles, the pelvic by firm ligaments and a definite articulation.[1]

In the human embryo, as in all living Reptiles, Birds, and Mammals, the embryonic pelvis is triradiate, its cellular blastema at first forming one mass with that of the developing femur: this condition I have traced through the whole series of Vertebrates.[2] After the pelvic blastema has, at a later stage, become differentiated from that of the femur, which is the first to become cartilaginous, the ilium, ischium, and pubis are laid down as distinct chondrifications. The fusion of the acetabular portion of these three pelvic cartilages takes place in the following order: first, the ischium alone unites with the ilium, and later, the ilium with the pubis. The ischium and the pubis do not send out acetabular processes towards one another, and for this reason a space is left at their point of apposition.

[The bone to which in the adult human subject the term pubis was first applied, is formed by the union of two distinct elements—a main one arising *in utero*, and a lesser, arising during the thirteenth year [3] within the acetabular region, and completely excluding its neighbour from that cavity. The latter element is of regular occurrence among the lower Mammalia, and being in them of considerable proportions has received the name "cotyloid bone" or "os acetabuli." In accordance, however, with its ultimate fate, it may be more appropriately termed the dorso-pubic element, and its neighbour the ventro-pubic.[4] Thus considered, comparison of the pubis with the coracoid (*ante*, p. 72) shows that in Mammals, and in them alone among living Vertebrates, each consists of two elements, of which one (epicoracoid and pre-pubic element) is excluded from the articular facet (glenoid cavity and acetabulum).]

In no other Mammals do the iliac bones diverge so greatly

[1] This difference appears less marked, and may altogether vanish, when we compare the [lower vertebrata. Among Chelonians the shoulder girdle very generally articulates upon the anterior thoracic vertebræ; and in] Fishes a firm connection is established between the shoulder girdle and the skull (Osteichthyes), or even between the former and the vertebral column (Rays), [such as is seen also in many Frogs and Toads, and may, under rare conditions, occur in Man himself.] In certain Salamanders we find, on the rib approximate to the inner border of the suprascapular, a plate-like cartilaginous expansion, which is fastened to the shoulder girdle by means of ligaments; [this, however, has probably to do with protection of an adjacent pulsatile "lymph-heart."]

[2] The author here refers in the original German to his "*Gliedmassen Skelet der Wirbelthiere*," Jena, 1892.

[3] [Cf. Krause, *Month. Internat. Jour. Anat. and Hist.*, vol. ii. p. 150.]

[4] [Cf. Howes, *Jour. Anat. and Phys.*, vol. xxvii. p. 550.]

as in the higher races of Men. This feature is not, however, marked during fœtal life, when the form of the pelvis recalls that found in the adults of the lower races of Men and in the Apes.[1] The whole embryonic pelvis is comparatively long and narrow; its angle of inclination is much greater than in the

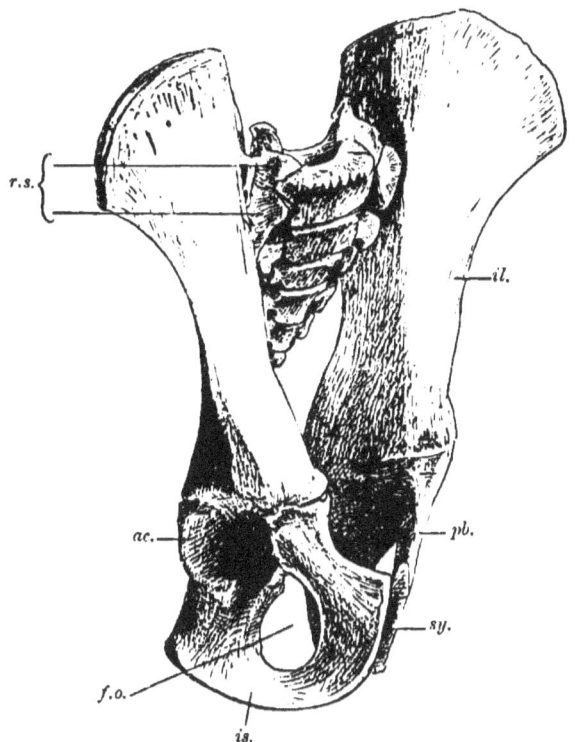

FIG. 53.—PELVIS OF A FEMALE CHIMPANZEE, TWO YEARS OLD.
r.s, sacral ribs; *ac.*, acetabulum; *f.o.*, obturator foramen; *is.*, ischium; *sy.*, symphysis pubis; *pb.*, pubis; *il.*, ilium.

adult, and the long axis of the symphysis pubis forms anteriorly with the axial line of the body a very acute angle. We herein meet with a form of sacrum resembling that of lower Mammals, and a promontory which only slightly projects (cf. Fig. 53). As a consequence, the entrance to the pelvis is also like that of the lower Mammals, and differs greatly from that of the later adult form.

[1] The pelvis of the Veddah, according to the Sarasins, differs from that of the European in its relative length and narrowness.

The close connection between the great expansion of the iliac bones and the upright gait of Man has already been pointed out (*ante*, p. 38).

The sexual dimorphism of the pelvis is more marked in Mankind than in any other Vertebrate; indeed, it may be considered as a characteristic of the human species, the rationale of which has still to be discussed.

If we consider the marked lateral projection of the iliac bones which is met with in both sexes, and has already been described and accounted for, it seems natural enough to regard their increased expansion in the female as an adaptation to sexual requirements. This increase of breadth is the more necessary, since the human embryo attains a higher development before birth than do the embryos of most Mammals, the skull and brain being incomparably larger in proportion to the size of the mother. So highly differentiated an embryo, again, must influence the pelvic aperture, and, indeed, the whole form of the lower parts, including the promontory, since the pressure of the pregnant uterus is not exerted ventrally as in Quadrupeds, but, on account of the upright gait, sagittally. The iliac wings thus play the chief part in carrying this weight, and naturally undergo a corresponding lateral plate-like expansion. Further investigation concerning the pelvis in relation to "labour" in the different races of Mankind would be of great interest. All that can now be stated with certainty is, that sexual differentiation of the pelvis, at least so far as the expansion of the iliac bones is concerned, is much less marked in the lower than in the higher races.

The Skeleton of the Free Limbs

As already indicated, the fore- and hind-limbs of Man conform to a single type; and any doubt which might exist as to the differences between the two having been secondarily acquired by functional adaptation, is dispelled by Comparative Anatomy and Ontogeny. As already pointed out (pp. 68, 69), a review of the various groups of Vertebrata shows that the farther we go back in the series the less marked are the differences between the fore- and hind-limbs; until at length, in the Fishes, we have an undifferentiated starting-point for the two. At the top of the scale we have the Birds with their fore-limbs metamorphosed into wings (under conditions by which the pelvis and vertebral column become correlatively modified with the hind-limbs, to support the weight of the body); and Man, with what was originally a forefoot turned into a hand.

Before trying to answer the question as to the mode of origin and progress of these important differentiations, let us consider the structural variations to which the free limbs are susceptible.

The free limbs undergo greater and more numerous modifications than their related girdles; and the probability that this may be perhaps connected with their exposed position and intimate contact with the environment, may be worth consideration.

THE SKELETON OF THE FORE-LIMB

The fore-limb of the Anthropoids is relatively longer than that of Man, and it is therefore specially interesting to note that in some of the lower races of Men the arms are relatively much longer than in Europeans. In the Veddahs this difference is even externally obvious, and when the skeleton is examined, is seen to be, as in the Anthropoids, chiefly due to the great length of the forearm (radius and ulna). If the length of the humerus be taken at 100, that of the radius is 73 in the male European, nearly 80 in the male Veddah, and 90 to 94 in the Chimpanzee (Sarasins). This great development of the forearm is distinctly a mark of low organisation, and it is a significant fact that it obtains in the European fœtus and child, only giving place to the definitive proportion with advancing age. (Similar variation with age is found in the fore-leg, cf. *infra*.)

The occasional perforation of the olecranon fossa of the humerus, to form what is known as the ent-epicondylar (supra-trochlear) foramen (Fig. 55), is undoubtedly to be regarded as atavistic. It is often found in the lower races of mankind, *e.g.* natives of South Africa, and has been observed in the Veddahs in as many as 58 per cent, in skeletons belonging to the stone-age, in the Anthropoids (Gorilla and Orang), and in the lower Apes.

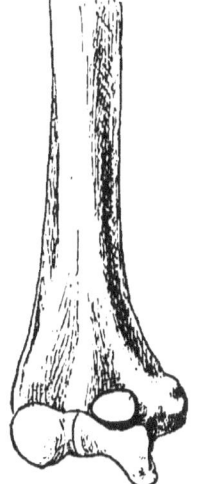

FIG. 54.—RIGHT HUMERUS OF A NEGRO, SHOWING PERFORATION OF THE OLECRANON FOSSA. (Anterior aspect.)

On the ulnar side of the lower end of the humerus, a few

centimetres above the internal condyle, a bony process (processus supra-condyloideus) (*pr.*, Fig. 55, D) sometimes projects in a hook-like manner, a fibrous band passing from it to the ent-epicondylar region. The Median Nerve runs through the foramen thus enclosed. This foramen is very common among the lower animals,

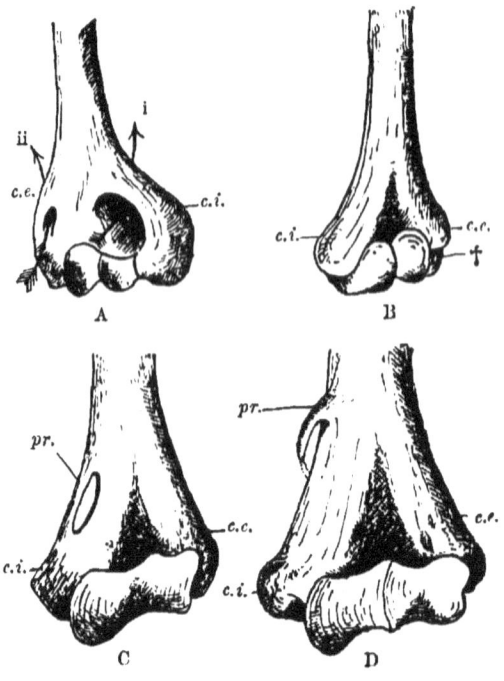

FIG. 55.—DISTAL EXTREMITY OF THE HUMERUS TO SHOW EPICONDYLAR FORAMINA.
A, in *Hatteria*; B, in a Lizard (*Lacerta ocellata*); C, in the domestic Cat; D, in Man; *c.e.*, external condyle; *c.i.*, internal condyle. In A the two foramina are developed (at i, the ent-epicondylar; at ii, the ect-epicondylar). The only canal (†) present in the Lizard (B) is on the external volar side, in the cartilaginous distal extremity. In Man (D) an ent-epicondylar process (*pr.*) is developed and continued as a fibrous band.

and is of very great antiquity. It is found not only in very many quadrupedal Mammals, but in Reptiles (Fig. 55, A and B), in fossil forms which skeletally combine Amphibian with Reptilian characters (*Palæohatteria, Homæosaurus*), and in fossil Amphibians (Stegocephala) of the Permian period (*Stereorhachis and Bothriops*).[1]

[1] [Struthers has recorded an interesting case of hereditary development of this supra-condyloid process (*Lancet*, 15th February 1873), and has specially advocated the view that the completion of the process in Man has a reversionary significance, and not that of mere overgrowth for protection, frequently occurrent in all parts

THE SKELETON

In the great majority of Reptiles a similar aperture (ectepicondylar foramen) is found on the outer side of the humerus, (Fig. 55, A ii), and in some both foramina are present. These are in both cases nerve canals, which fact suggests that they may not have arisen either among Amphibians or Reptiles, but rather among animal forms phylogenetically still older.

[In consideration of the facts already recapitulated (pp. 68-70) concerning the comparative anatomy and development of the vertebrate limb-skeleton, the probability that these condylar foramina may be indicative of a] polymeric origin of the basal segments of the limb-skeleton must not be overlooked, for, in the Ontogeny of the Sharks and Sturgeons, these latter can be traced to an origin by concrescence from parallel cartilaginous rays. If this be the meaning of the foramina, the fact that among living Reptiles they are most marked in the most primitive genus (*Hatteria*) is the more interesting.

I have elsewhere[1] raised the question whether the *foramina nutritia*, occurring in the long bones of the limbs, may not have had a similar origin. A wide field is here open for research, in which palæontology should play an important part.

Special interest attaches to the skeleton of the human hand, and there is still abundant room for further investigation concerning it.

Taking first the carpus, the resemblance of that of Man to the carpus and tarsus of the tailed Amphibians is most striking. In its proximal row there are the three well-known bones, the radiale (scaphoid = tibiale in the pes), the intermedium (lunar), and the ulnare (cuneiform = fibulare in the pes), cf. Figs. 56, 57, 59, 60. In the distal row, counting from the inner or radial face, lie the first carpale (trapezium = 1st tarsal or ento-cuneiform in the pes); the 2nd carpale (trapezoid = 2nd tarsale or meso-cuneiform in the pes); the 3rd carpale (magnum = 3rd tarsale or ecto-cuneiform in the pes); and the 4th carpale

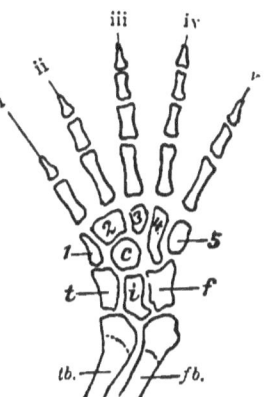

FIG. 56.—SKELETON OF THE HIND-LIMB OF A TAILED AMPHIBIAN (*Spelerpes fuscus*).
tb., tibia ; *fb.*, fibula ; *t.*, tibiale ; *i*, intermedium ; *f*, fibulare ; *c*, centrale ; 1-5, tarsalia ; i to v, digits.

of the skeleton (cf. *Rep. Internat. Medic. Congress*, Lond. 1881). A remarkable outcome of the latter tendency has been recently described by Grünbaum, in the discovery of a ligament which, bridging over the posterior condylar foramen, forms a tunnel for a branch of the occipital artery, and, by ossification, may form "a ring of bone projecting downwards from the lower surface of the occiput" (*Jour. Anat. and Phys.*, vol. xxv. p. 428, and Macalister, *ibid.* p. *iii.*).]

[1] Das Gliedmassen Skelet (see *ante*, p. 74, footnote).

(= cuboid in the pes). The last-named bone (4 and 5, Fig. 57) gives articulation to two metacarpals, viz. the 4th and 5th, and its originally double nature is thus indicated. This is shown (apart from comparison with the carpal skeleton of the lower Vertebrata) by the occasional division of this bone into two, not only in Man, but in the most varied Mammals (Marsupials, Rodents, Cetacea).

All who are in any degree acquainted with Comparative Osteology, know what a great part is played by the os centrale as a component of the carpus and tarsus. To Gegenbaur belongs the honour of having first recognised and appreciated this. All investigations made after the year 1864 had to start from

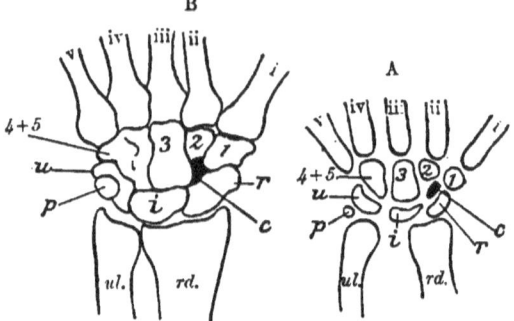

FIG. 57.—DIAGRAM OF THE HUMAN CARPUS. A, EMBRYO ; B, ADULT.
rd., radius ; ul., ulna ; u, ulnare (cuneiform) ; i, intermedium (lunar) ; r, radiale (scaphoid) ; p, pisiforme ; 1, 2, 3, carpalia (trapezium, trapezoid, and magnum) ; 4 + 5 = united 4th and 5th carpalia (represented in the adult by a single bone, the uneiform) ; c, centrale, which fuses later with the radiale (scaphoid) ; i to v, digits.

the broad basis laid down in his extensive researches into the limb-skeleton of representatives of the chief types of terrestrial Vertebrata. In only one of these was Gegenbaur unable to reach a perfectly satisfactory conclusion, and that was in Man himself. It was reserved for Rosenberg, ten years later, to establish the fact, that the centrale in an early stage of development (i.e. at the beginning of the second month of intra-uterine life) is a distinct carpal element. By this discovery the chain was completed, Man forming the last link.

Rosenberg's discoveries were soon confirmed and extended by other anatomists, among whom may be mentioned Leboucq and von Bardeleben. The former proved that the centrale did not vanish, as Rosenberg believed, i.e. it was not resorbed, but incorporated into the radiale (scaphoid) in the second half of the third month of fœtal life, giving rise to a prominence which can be recognised in the adult. This prominence is present also in the Chimpanzee, the Gorilla, and *Hylobates;* and as the centrale is most probably distinct in the embryo of these, it may well be that in them, as in Man, its independent existence has not long been suppressed. Further confirmation of this is afforded by the fact that it is still an independent bone in 0·4 per cent of even adult human beings, and that, normally, it retains its independence in the Orang and in most Monkeys.

In many Mammals (especially Marsupials, Rodents, and Insectivores) cartilaginous or bony skeletal elements occur on the outer and inner borders of both fore- and hind-limbs, which not only bear a superficial resemblance to the digital skeleton, but may in some cases be clad, like the true digits, in either a claw or a callous horny integument. Similar structures occur in many of the lower Vertebrates (Reptiles and Amphibians). These organs were formerly considered by both von Bardeleben and myself to be vestiges of now vanished digits, and were named by us "præpollex," "præhallux," and "postminimus."

I have, however, entirely changed my opinion as to the supposed atavistic nature of these structures, and now agree with others that these "supernumerary rays," whether they occur in the lower or the higher Vertebrata, are to be regarded rather as progressive structures of convergent and secondarily adaptive significance. Baur has contended, before all others, that the facts of palæontology favour the view that the terrestrial Vertebrata never possessed more than five rays in the skeleton of either fore- or hind-limb;[1] and my own recent investigations into the development of the limb-skeleton entirely confirm this conclusion.

From this point of view, the condition of "hyperdactyly," which not infrequently appears in Man and is often inherited for many generations, loses its supposed atavistic significance.

THE SKELETON OF THE HIND-LIMB

The human femur usually bears at its head two processes for muscular attachment, known as the trochanters, inasmuch as they give insertion to the rotator muscles of the limb. Special interest centres in the not infrequent presence of a third trochanter (*tc'''.*, Fig. 58), a development of the roughened area (tuberositas glutealis) which occurs on the external border of the bone

[1] [It is an interesting corollary to this, that the only fossilised limb in which anything comparable to a sixth digit has been found, is a fore-limb which, if not actually Mammalian, is that of a Reptile with Mammalian characters (*Theriodesmus*, from the Mesozoic beds of South Africa, cf. von Bardeleben, *Proc. Zool. Soc.*, Lond., 1889, p. 259; and Seeley, *Proc. Roy. Soc.*, Lond., vol. lv. p. 227). Nor must it be forgotten that the "præhallux" in its most highly differentiated and digit-like form (Frogs and Toads) is cartilaginous, *i.e.* so constituted that it would not be preserved in the fossil state.]

in question. This third, or gluteal trochanter, may be accompanied by a more or less extended ridge (*cr.*, Fig. 58) or by a pitlike depression. It is found in about 30 per cent of European skeletons;[1] in Negroes its occurrence is less frequent, and in the Anthropoids it is still rarer.

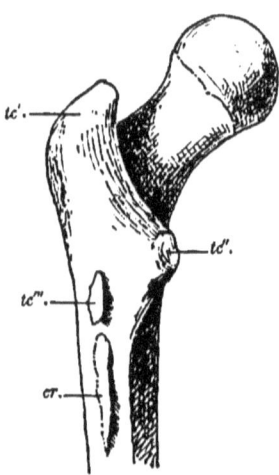

FIG. 58.—PROXIMAL HALF OF A LEFT HUMAN FEMUR POSSESSED OF THREE TROCHANTERS, POSTERIOR ASPECT.
tc'., greater; *tc''.*, lesser; and *tc'''.*, third or gluteal trochanter.

In the Lemuroidea, on the other hand, the third trochanter is almost always developed. Dollo attributes its gradual disappearance in Man to certain modifications which, in the course of time, have taken place in the gluteus maximus muscle. In the Lemuroids this muscle passes direct to the femur, and the development of a third trochanter is unquestionably an outcome of this association; but in Man, the gluteus maximus is partially inserted into the fascia lata investing the superficial parts of the limb; and this shifting of its attachment would appear to have led to an accompanying degeneration of the third trochanter.

In the Anthropoid Apes the insertion of the gluteus maximus into the fascia lata has gone much farther than in Man, *i.e.* this muscle has in them deviated farther from its original condition [in which we find it in many quadrupedal types], and the occurrence of the third trochanter is therefore much less frequent.

The lower part of the leg (fore-leg) has, like the lower part of the arm (forearm), but to a far higher degree, undergone great modifications in length in the races of mankind. The variations of the human tibia, indeed, are greater than those of any other bone in the skeleton. Apart altogether from variation in length, the term platyknemia is applied to a peculiar condition associated with great compression of the tibia. This is found in the lower races, accompanied by a strong development of the tibialis posticus muscle, and in skeletons belonging to prehistoric times.

[1] [Treves has recently called attention to a case in which it could be readily detected in the livin gperson (*Jour. Anat. and Phys.*, vol. xxi. p. 325).]

In the lower Mammals both tibia and fibula articulate with the femur, and contribute to the formation of the knee-joint. In Man, under advancing phylogenetic development, the weight of the body has come to rest on the tibia alone, and the proximal end of the fibula has become disconnected from the femur,[1] and has shortened and shifted downwards along the postero-external surface of the tibia.

The human fibula is now an appendage of the tibia, and the fact that its degeneration has not gone farther[2] is accounted for partly by its important connection with the heads of certain muscles of the leg (especially the peronei), and by the part which it plays in the formation of the ankle (external malleolus).

The external condyle of the tibia varies very much in different races. In the lower races it is much more convex than in the higher, and this is probably also the case in the oldest prehistoric men. This convexity is evidently connected with the frequent strong flexure of the knee-joint, such as occurs in squatting.

On the inner border of the distal extremity of the tibia (malleolus internus) there is, in the lower races, a special facet which articulates with the neck of the astragalus; and the presence of this may be also connected with the strong "dorsal flexion" consequent on the squatting posture. The astragalo-tibial articulation thus formed rarely occurs in the higher races; but parallel modifications of both the upper and lower ends of the tibia occur in the Anthropoids and among the lower Apes (Arthur Thomson).

Until approximately the seventh month of fœtal life, the tibial malleolus is larger than the fibular, projecting downwards farther than the latter. In the seventh month the two appear about equal, and then the fibular malleolus begins to take the lead. These phases of development are accompanied by corresponding modifications of the astragalus (Gegenbaur).

That the earlier condition of these bones is the inherited one seems probable from comparison of those of the Lemuroidea, Apes, and lower human races. Fig. 59 illustrates the manner in which the external or fibular malleolus ($c.f.$) gradually, in adaptation

---

[1] [The human fibula has been stated by Leboucq, Bernays, and others, to be during early development in contact with the femur, from which it would appear that the loss of connection between the two takes place ontogenetically. Grünbaum, examining the parts with extreme care, has lately shown (*Jour. Anat. and Phys.*, vol. xxvi. p. xx.) that this is not the case from the period of primary differentiation of the parts in cartilage onwards.]

[2] In many lower Mammals it has still further degenerated.

to the upright gait, becomes longer than the internal or tibial (*c.t.*); and also how the astragalus (*as.*) and calcaneum (*cl.*) which originally slope laterally outwards, shift inwards, *i.e.* towards the pre-axial side, so that they come more into a line with the long axis of the tibia.

The above-described modifications find a parallel in certain most important changes which the foot itself is even now undergoing. To understand these rightly we must enter somewhat into detail, in order to gain an insight into the primitive history of the human foot.

Thanks to Comparative Anatomy and Development, we have

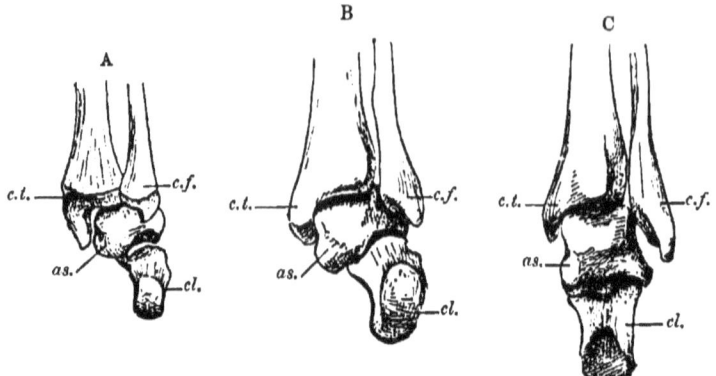

FIG. 59.—THE UPPER ANKLE-JOINT, POSTERIOR ASPECT.
A, adult Chimpanzee ; B, Australian native ; C, Caucasian, to show the increasing length of the malleolus fibularis (*c.f.*), and the difference in the position of the astragalus (*as.*) and calcaneum (*cl.*) in relation to the long axis of the tibia, in passing from the lower to the higher type.

obtained a sufficiently correct estimate of the skeleton of the limbs in general, to grasp the essential points in the plan of structure common to the hand and foot. The fact that there are obstacles in the way of obtaining a perfectly clear insight into this matter need not surprise us, when we take into account the long series of adaptations which have resulted in the human limbs ; indeed, we can no longer expect to find the primitive condition retained in either the fore- or the hind-limb. If the fore-limb has been transformed from an ambulatory to a prehensile organ, the hind-limb has already reached a third stage in progressive modification—as, having first served for support and locomotion, it next became transformed into a grasping organ (as is proved by the musculature of the sole of the foot, and by the Ape-like apposable condition of the great toe during fœtal life), and finally, on the assumption of the upright gait, it has changed back into an ambulatory appendage.

This ultimate modification has been accompanied by the greater development of the tarsus, and by the concomitant degeneration and decreasing mobility of the phalanges; and, correlatively, the foot has acquired a disposition at a wider angle to the fore-leg, and has become arched in adaptation to its supporting function.

These repeated changes of function may well have resulted in great structural changes, which we may now consider in some detail.

First, comparing the skeleton of the human foot with that of the Anthropoid Apes, we find the former distinguished by the following three points (cf. Figs. 60 and 62):—

(1) Stronger development of the great toe.[1]

(2) Greater development of the tarsal elements.

(3) Displacement of the great toe into a position of parallelism with the other toes.

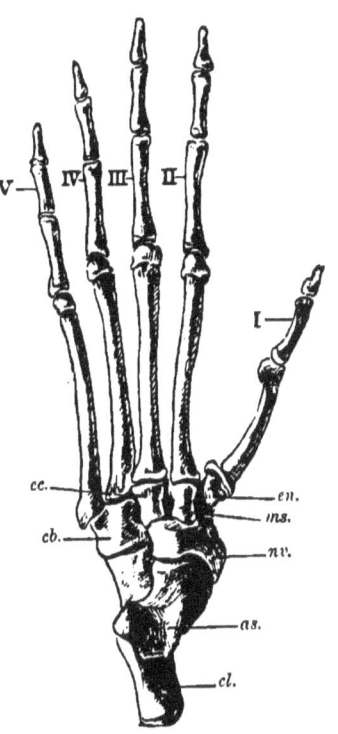

FIG. 60.—SKELETON OF THE LEFT PES OF A CHIMPANZEE, DORSAL ASPECT.
ec., ecto-cuneiform; *en.*, ento-cuneiform; *ms.*, meso-cuneiform; *cb.*, cuboid; *nv.*, navicular; *as.*, astragalus; *cl.*, calcaneum; I-V, digits.

If the foot of a second month's human fœtus be examined, with special regard to the last point, it will be seen (Fig. 63, B) that the position of the great toe almost entirely agrees with that of the thumb (63, A). When the limbs are laid against the trunk, both point towards the head in the position of abduction.

Whereas this is the normal lifelong position of the great toe of the Apes, and of the human thumb (cf. Figs. 60 and 61) in the human foot it is merely transitional, and is abandoned

---

[1] We have herein a noteworthy contrast to most of those lower Mammals in which the great toe is reduced, or has altogether disappeared. A claw may in the former case be found at its distal end (*e.g.* in the Dog), but even that may disappear.

as early as the eighth week of fœtal life. The definitive position (Fig 62) is, however, very gradually reached; for it is a well-known fact that the mobility of the great toe is far more marked in children at birth and in the earliest years of life than in adult Europeans.[1] In certain races (*e.g.* the Japanese)

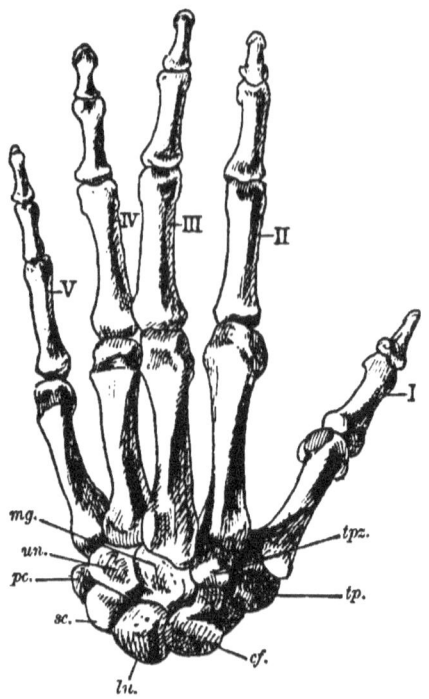

Fig. 61.—Skeleton of the Left Hand, Dorsal Aspect.
cf., cuneiform; *lu.*, lunar; *mg.*, magnum; *pc.*, pisiform; *sc.*, scaphoid; *tp.*, trapezium; *tpz.*, trapezoid; *un.*, uneiform. I-V, digits.

a considerable mobility is often retained throughout life; and the uses to which the great toe can be put fill a European with astonishment.

Bälz, in his work on *The Bodily Characteristics of the Japanese*, says: "The use made by the Japanese of the great toe as a kind of thumb is very remarkable; it can be independ-

[1] The foot of a child which has not yet learnt to stand or walk is a particularly interesting study. Not only are the toes capable of performing complex movements (the great toe being even utilisable for grasping purposes), but the sole or plantar surface of the foot, in its form and in certain of its furrows, resembles the palm of the hand far more than later, when socks and shoes have exercised an influence upon it.

ently moved, and so strongly pressed against the second toe that even small objects can be firmly held between them. A woman, when sewing, may hold the stuff with her toes, stretching it as she pleases; and it is asserted that Japanese women can pinch effectively with their toes. In general, the foot of the Japanese has retained much of its natural mobility. These people seem

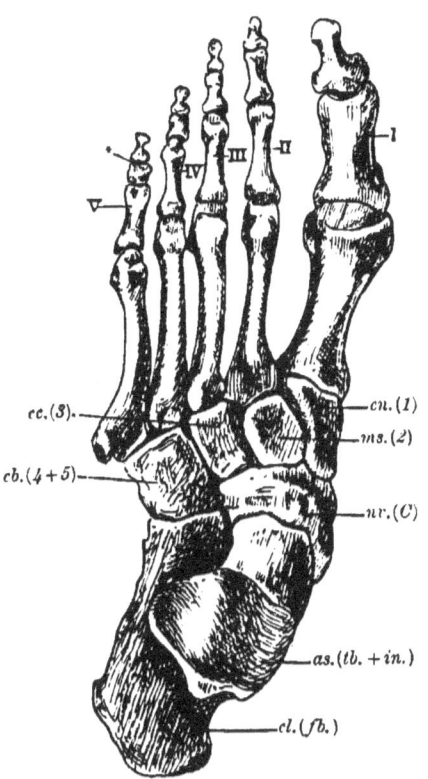

FIG. 62.—SKELETON OF LEFT FOOT, DORSAL ASPECT, FOR COMPARISON WITH FIGS. 60 AND 61.

as. (*tb.* + *in.*), astragalus (regarded as a product of fusion of the tibiale and intermedium of the lower vertebrata); *cb.*, cuboid; *cl.* (*fb.*), calcaneum (fibulare); *ec.*, ecto-cuneiform; *en.*, endo-cuneiform; *ms.*, meso-cuneiform; *nr.* (*C*), navicular (centrale); I-V, digits: 1-5, tarsalia.

to be able to hold on to the ground with the sole of the foot; and therefore when they need to stand firmly, as in fighting and wrestling, they are always barefooted. The first time one sees a Japanese man walking about with ease on a steep house-top as if on level ground, it makes one feel quite uncomfortable, but no fear of his falling need be entertained, for his foot accurately adapts itself to the surface of the roof!"

[Although the great toe of the adult human subject may be thus thumb-like in function, an important difference between the hallux and pollex exists, in the inconstancy in relation to the former of an opponens muscle, such as is present in the manus, and more generally in both manus and pes of the anthropoid Apes. The act of grasping by the human hallux differs from that by the pollex in being one of mere adduction and closer apposition of the first and second digits.]

The cousins Sarasin have pointed out, that in the Veddah's foot the great toe stands apart from the other toes, and that the last four metatarsals are turned towards the first one more than in a European foot. The whole foot is also flatter, as can be observed in the living state. [In dealing with this comparison allowance must be probably made for the use of the boot.] A more important distinction, from the comparative anatomical point of view, is that the tarsus is markedly shorter and narrower than that of the European. If 100 be taken as the length of the second metatarsal in a European, then 163 would represent the length of the tarsus; in the Veddah it is 152, in the Gorilla 145, and in the Chimpanzee 113, so that the tarsus is found to decrease in length as we descend in the series. A similar diminution in breadth is also recognisable.

According to Pfitzner, whose accurate observations on the variations in the human pedal skeleton are of special interest, the variations in the proportions of the foot, *e.g.* in the length of the metatarsals and phalanges, are far greater than those of the hand. This applies especially to the great toe and its metatarsal; and correlatively, the ento-cuneiform is much more liable to variation than are the meso- and ecto-cuneiform. The so-called Lisfranc's line is also liable to variation in its course, and this especially applies to the third tarso-metatarsal articulation. The latter does not as a rule continue the line of the fourth tarso-metatarsal articulation, but makes an angle with it, consequent upon the mode of articulation between the ecto-cuneiform and the fourth metatarsal, which is prolonged backwards. Here, as well as in the hallux, we have to deal with recent variation (Pfitzner). The great toe is in men not only absolutely but relatively longer than in women, and this is true of the thumb also,—a slight confirmation of the well-known saying that women represent the conservative and men the progressive element in human development—in other words, the greater development of the thumb and the great toe of the male must be considered as a recent acquirement. Accompanying this difference in the first toe, we note also the slighter reduction of the length of the other toes, and especially of the middle phalanges, in Man, as compared with woman. Man has, as a rule, the original elongated type of toe —woman the shortened and compressed type.

Further interesting results might be obtained by a careful comparison of the tarsometatarsal joint of the first toe in the various human races and in the Apes.

While, thus, progressive development takes place on the inner or tibial side of the foot as the result of functional adaptation, the following retrogressive processes take place on the outer or fibular side:—

The little toe is not infrequently two-jointed, the middle and terminal phalanges being synostotically confluent. Pfitzner found this to be the case in thirteen out of forty-seven examples. This fusion, which is, as a rule, found on both feet, is not due to the pressure of shoes or to any other mechanical causes,[1] but to the fact that the little toe and its metatarsus [2] are in process of degeneration. This process of reduction, which may end in the little toe becoming in a measure like the thumb and great toe, two-jointed, is particularly interesting, as it is taking place, so to speak, under our eyes. All stages from incomplete to complete fusion can be observed. Further, this degeneration of the little toe apparent in these facts can also be gathered from the condition of its muscles; [of these the flexor brevis often sends either but a very weak offshoot to the little toe, or, like the extensor brevis, none at all.]

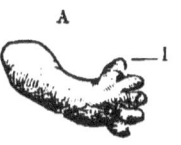
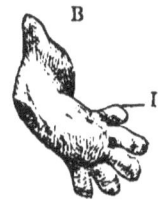

Fig. 63. A, right fore-limb; B, right hind-limb, of a human embryo in the second month of intrauterine life, to show the similarity in position and direction of the thumb and the great toe (I).

[1] I find this synostosis also present in the skeletons of Egyptian mummies of various ages, not excluding children. It may here be remarked that, according to Bälz, among the Japanese, who do not wear shoes, the little toe appears quite as reduced as in the European foot.

[2] We are at present unable to deal with the question of the significance of the independent origin of the fifth metatarsal tuberosity, which is the more surprising in consideration of the frequency of retrogressive processes on the fibular side of the foot.

It should, in passing, be noted that the mutual relationships between the muscles and bones are not absolutely similar in every single case, although a general agreement exists. The undeniably close connection between the modifications of two must not be regarded as that of cause and effect, but rather as the joint effect of a common cause.

Clear signs of degeneration are also to be found in the other toes, and especially their middle phalanges, while the terminal and

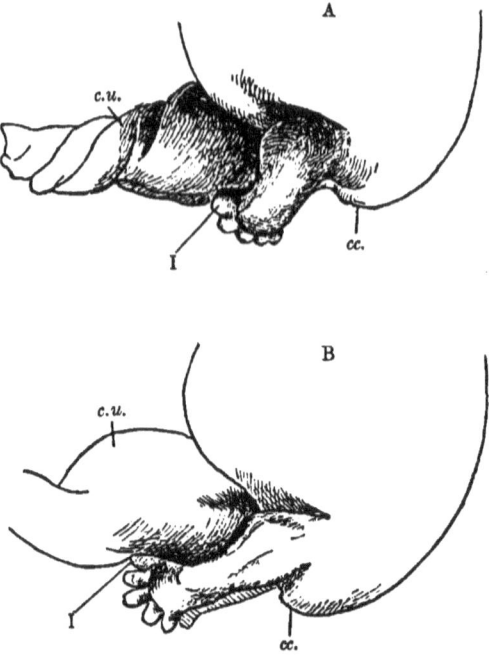

FIG. 64.—POSTERIOR END OF THE BODY OF TWO HUMAN EMBRYOS, WITH THE LEFT HIND-LIMB AND UMBILICAL CORD.
A, at the end of the seventh week ; B, in the middle of the eighth week. The position of the great toe (I) is noteworthy. *c.u.*, umbilical cord ; *cc.*, coccygeal eminence.

basal phalanges may be also affected. The second toe is mostly free from signs of degeneration: its middle phalanx shows a disposition to shorten, but it at the same time tends to become stronger rather than weaker. It might, therefore, be predicted of the human foot that it may end by possessing only two two-jointed toes, the great toe and its neighbour;[1] but the possibility of

[1] [It may be questioned whether it would not be more correct to predict, provided there is anything in this argument at all, that all the toes with the exception of the second may ultimately become two-jointed.]

development in other directions such as might counteract the present tendency must, however, be allowed for (Pfitzner).[1]

COMPARISON OF THE FORE- AND HIND-LIMBS OF MAN

In comparing the opposite extremities of the adult two difficulties have to be met, the first being that the knee and elbow-joint bend in exactly opposite directions, and the second that, owing to the inward rotation of the fore-limb, the homologous bones of the fore-arm and fore-leg (radius and tibia, ulna and fibula) are differently disposed.

Martins and Gegenbaur have endeavoured to explain these difficulties by spiral rotation of the humerus during development —said to be effected by alteration in growth of the epiphysial cartilage, with the addition of bony tissue at some points and its resorption at others. The distal end of this bone has its original ventral surface turned dorsally and *vice versâ*. By comparing the position of the humerus in embryos and adults it is found to rotate through an angle of about 35° (Gegenbaur).

Spiral rotation of the humerus actually takes place, not only in Man, but very commonly in other Vertebrates. It can further be proved that it progressively increases as we pass from the lower to the Caucasian races; and Broca affirms that an increase is to be found at different epochs within the same race.

But although the torsio humeri is an undoubted ontogenetic fact, according to more recent authors, it is questionable whether it affords any explanation of the difference between the fore- and hind-limbs. This subject is so important that we must enter into it at some length, referring especially to the works of Hatschek and Holl. The first of these investigators has rightly taken for comparison the lowest terrestrial Vertebrata, the tailed Amphibia, and he lays emphasis upon the fact that in these animals the position of the fore- and hind-limbs in relation to the trunk is almost identical. Both stand out at right angles to the long axis

[1] [It appears to me that the occasional longitudinal subdivision of the human hallux-tarsal (ento-cuneiform) into two distinct bones may be not improbably a phenomenon akin to that of the double ossification of the supra-occipital under expansion (cf. *ante*, p. 60), if not an actual index of progressive development now at work. My friend Professor Arthur Thomson informs me that, from a study of the articular surfaces of this bone, he believes the tendency towards duplication to be more general than is customarily assumed; and it would be most interesting to inquire whether among the Seals and Walruses, in which the inner and outer digits are one or both similarly dominant over the rest, indications of a corresponding variation might not be forthcoming in the fœtal state.—G. B. H.]

of the body. The elbow and knee joints are turned slightly outwards, the convexity of the former facing slightly backwards, that of the latter slightly forwards. The supporting portion of the limb looks in both cases outwards, and in each the anterior digit is rightly considered as the first of the series.

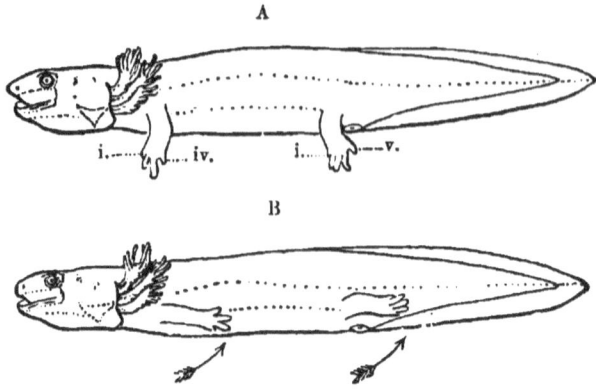

FIG. 65.—LARVAL SALAMANDER. (After Hatschek.)
A, with the limbs turned down ; B, with the limbs turned up.

In the higher Quadrupeds the anterior and posterior limbs undergo characteristic changes of position. First, the supporting segments of the two limbs (*i.e.* the manus and pes) are rotated inwards, so that their long axes, which were originally transverse to that of the body, come to be parallel with it [and their originally anterior borders become internal]; as a natural result of this, the first digit (pollex or hallux) becomes the innermost and the fifth the outermost. The rest of the limb, however, differs in its behaviour in the two members. In the fore-limb the humeral and radio-ulnar segments become flexed in such a way that the elbow is no longer directed outwards but backwards (cf. Fig. 65). In the hind-limb, on the contrary, the basal (femoral and tibio-fibular) segments are turned inwards, and so flexed that the knee is directed forwards. According to Hatschek the differences in position of the fore- and hind-limbs involve only their basal segments, their terminal segments (manus and pes) being displaced identically. It would follow from this that the changed position of the fore-limb has little if anything to do with the torsion of the humerus, which is very marked even in the Salamander, and must therefore be referred back to an early process antecedent to the changes under discussion.

Holl also repudiates the torsio humeri as the most important factor in effecting the torsion of the fore-limb. He, unlike others, considers that there is no very great difference between the position of the bones of the forearm and the fore-leg in Man. He rightly points out that the tibia and fibula do not lie parallel, but that the fibula lies external to and behind the tibia, and insists that it thus occupies, in relation to the tibia, a position similar to that of the ulna in relation to the radius.[1] In instituting these comparisons we ought to start with the hind-limb, which is simply so rotated at its base that the whole of its morphologically ventral surface becomes posterior in position, and not with the fore-limb, the torsion of which involves the independent segments individually, and should therefore be excluded in endeavouring to settle the question of homology.

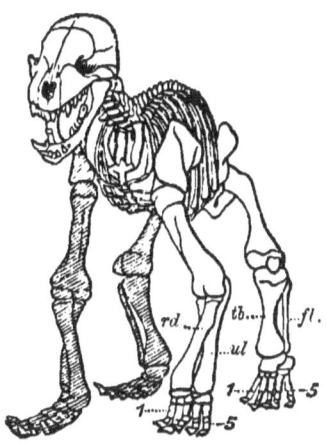

FIG. 66.—SKELETON OF A YOUNG BEAR ILLUSTRATING THE POSITIONS OF THE LIMBS. (After Hatschek.) *1-5*, digits ; *rd.*, radius ; *ul.*, ulna ; *tb.*, tibia ; *fb.*, fibula.

This consideration excepted, Holl agrees in the main with Hatschek as to the Quadrupeds; but he extends his observations to Man, and declares that if he be regarded as a Quadruped, the changes of position in the limbs are such that the homologising of them with those of Quadrupeds is not difficult, *i.e.* if a man goes on all fours the position of the shoulder girdle and with it that of the humerus is slightly altered. The head of the latter no longer points forwards, but backwards, and its great tuberosity comes to point forwards, just as in the quadrupedal Mammals, the distinction formerly established between them and Man in this particular thus disappearing.

[1] [Holl appears to have insufficiently appreciated the primary disposition of the limb-buds. The postero-internal displacement of the fibula upon which he lays such stress is well marked in the Marsupials, which, with the exception of the Dasyuridæ, have an opposable hallux. Detailed examination of the bones of the fore-leg of some of these animals and of the muscles which control their rotatory (so-called "pronator") movements, proves that the adaptive modification which the hind-limb has at any rate here undergone is of a distinct order from that of the fore-limb above described (cf. Young, *Jour. Anat. and Phys.*, vol. xv. p. 392). And it may be incidentally remarked that an opposable hallux appears independently among Rodents, in the common Dormouse.]

For the further study of the processes by which the limbs are displaced during development, I must refer the reader to the works of von Kölliker, Holl, and others. It should, however, be remarked once more that the twisting of the hind-limb occurs at the hip-joint merely, [and affects the limb as a whole, its originally ventral surface becoming posterior and its dorsal anterior in position, and that in the fore-limb the twisting most conspicuously affects the manus and the forearm, the radius undergoing a marked inward rotation upon the ulna. The humeral segment more nearly retains in the adult its original position], and the rotation and retroflexion which it ultimately exhibits chiefly result from a twisting of the shoulder girdle, with accompanying modifications of its articular head.

These changes in position of the shoulder girdle are connected with the development of the thorax. As long as the latter retains the laterally compressed form characteristic of most Mammals, and is not expanded dorsally, the scapula lies at its side. Later, when transverse enlargement and consequent dorsal expansion of the thorax are effected (cf. *ante*, p. 36), the scapula comes to lie upon (*i.e.* dorsad of) it. This change in the thorax plays a leading part in altering the position of the shoulder girdle as a whole, and of the limb attached to it.

If we wish to homologise the two pairs of limbs scientifically, we can only do so by tracing their displacements back towards their embryonic positions.

CHANGES OF POSITION OF THE LIMBS IN RELATION TO THE TRUNK

A comparison of the fore-limb of Man with that of the lower Vertebrates, and especially of the Fishes and Amphibians, and a careful analysis of the courses and relationships of its muscles and nerves with respect to the trunk and the spinal cord, lead us to the conclusion that the shoulder girdle and its associated limb originally lay farther forwards, *i.e.* nearer the head. The displacement backwards most probably took place, as has already been shown (*ante*, p. 44), simultaneously with the disappearance of the cervical ribs—indeed the loss of the latter certainly helped to bring this about, by compelling the scapula and clavicle to find points of attachment farther back on the thorax.

Whereas this shifting of the fore-limb takes place from before backwards, that undergone by the hind-limb is from behind forwards, *i.e.* towards the head. Both these alterations in position are most clearly reflected in the variations of the nerve plexuses of the limbs, the origin of which will be discussed later. We must, however, first ascertain what these variations are.

The lumbo-sacral plexus, as compared with the brachial, is the more subject to variation, and the less definitive. Even if the brachial plexus does show slight inconstancy, no such marked differences in the origin of its component nerve trunks occur as in the lumbo-sacral. In most cases, these variations in the limb plexuses are accompanied by variations in the vertebral column. For example, when the lumbo-sacral plexus has a markedly caudal origin, a supernumerary præsacral vertebra usually occurs; here we have an atavism, *i.e.* an indication of the primitive arrangement under which, as above described (*ante*, p. 33), the pelvis lay farther back. But we know that, during ontogeny, the pelvis undergoes a forward translocation. Correlatively, the lumbar plexus assimilates nerves lying farther forward than those which primarily formed it (the ileo-hypogastric, ileo-inguinal, and the genito-crural), while the posterior sacral nerves of the adult show signs of instability and degeneration, and may gradually altogether disappear.

The forward gathering of the nerves for the hind-limb is naturally accompanied by modification in the innervation of those parts of the urino-genital and alimentary systems which lie in the pelvis. These are obviously dependent on the pelvic girdle, and compelled to follow when it shifts along the vertebral column. The ischiadic and the pudendal plexuses are so closely connected that they could not in any case be separated; but the relationship between the pudendal and caudal plexuses is less intimate, and if the former shifts forwards with the crural plexus, its distal elements separate from it. These retrogressive nerves of the caudal region would necessarily increase in number in proportion to the forward translocation of the hind-limb, if the caudal region itself did not at the same time shorten (Eisler).

We thus have transition zones; and this becomes the more clear the farther the lumbo-sacral plexus shifts in a proximal direction. In extreme cases variation may extend as far forwards as the eleventh thoracic nerve, which then sends a loop to the twelfth.

Similar phenomena accompany the backward displacement of the fore-limb, but this, as already mentioned, appears to have nearly attained its definitive position.[1] The brachial transition zone is consequently more restricted and stable than the lumbosacral, rarely extending backwards beyond the second thoracic nerve. If, however, the upper limb preserves its original position (the seventh cervical rib persisting), the brachial plexus receives either no contribution or at best an insignificant one from the first thoracic nerve (Eisler).

Even if this conception of the "metameric transformation of nerves," deduced by Fürbringer, affords a partial explanation of the existence and present condition of the nerve plexuses, the actual causa movens lies deeper, *i.e.* in the original polymeric origin of the limbs. In the region from which they develop we meet with traces of a gradual fusion of originally distinct segments (somites), with further clear traces of the shifting which they have undergone during phylogeny. An excellent illustration of the commencement of fusion among the body segments is yielded by the transitional zones just defined. Quite apart from the already-mentioned variations of the nerves, the primitive segmentation of the ventro-lateral body muscles is gradually being obliterated, and the myocommata with the ribs are becoming vestigial— in fact the whole ventral body-wall is affected by this process of fusion (Eisler).

[1] That a further shifting of the human fore-limb in an antero-posterior direction may be expected is evident, firstly, from the varying relation of the brachial plexus to the anterior thoracic nerves ; and, secondly, from the very rare, yet occasional, retrogressive condition of the first thoracic rib before mentioned (*ante*, p. 43).

MUSCULAR SYSTEM

As might be expected, we find, in the 200 to 250 muscles which form the active motor apparatus of the human body, variations far greater and more numerous than any already described in the different parts of the skeleton.

It may confidently be asserted that hardly a single human subject has been examined which has not shown some variation or other in the muscular system; and in a great number of bodies new muscles are discovered which have not before been observed, and of which no mention can be found in text-books.

Considering this "embarras de richesse," we may be excused for entering in the following pages somewhat into detail; it is, in fact, absolutely necessary to do so in order to get a general idea of the immense mass of material available. Of the extent of this variation an approximate idea may be obtained from the fact that my French colleague Testut, in his work of 900 pages on the muscular anomalies in Man, has by no means exhausted the subject.

Examples will be considered in the following order:—
(1) Retrogressive or vestigial muscles.
(2) Muscles which, appearing only occasionally, are considered to be atavistic.
(3) Progressive muscles.

This order cannot be rigidly adhered to, inasmuch as both progressive and retrogressive development have been observed to take place, side by side, in one and the same muscular region. It is further to be noted that those muscles which are actually progressive as far as the genus Homo is concerned, are not recognisable as such in mere individuals; their anomalous conditions can only be considered as individual variations until traced through successive generations, *i.e.* until it is proved that they are inherited.

An accurate knowledge of Comparative Anatomy and Ontogeny

is necessary, to facilitate judgment and sharpen observation, in dealing with both progressive and retrogressive variations, which latter are the preliminary stages in degeneration. In the critical examination of the muscles, as pointed out by Fürbringer and Ruge, it is primarily important to ascertain their innervation. The nerve-supply is the safest criterion as to the morphological value of a muscle.

RETROGRESSIVE MUSCLES

OF THE TRUNK

The dorsal upper and lower serratus are, as is well known, connected together by a strong silvery aponeurosis. This is occasionally replaced by muscular tissue, which, in connection with the upper serratus—less frequently with the lower—may extend down as far as the sixth rib. This clearly points back to a primitive condition in which the two muscles were continuous. In contrast to this variation there occur others in which the two serrati are much less developed than usual, so much so that one or both of them may be entirely wanting. This is very important, as it leads to the conclusion that the serrati, like many other muscles, are being gradually transformed into tendinous tissue. The cause of this must be sought in the modification of the respiratory mechanism of the thorax, and the same would appear to be the rationale of the many variations of these same muscles observed in the Anthropoids (cf. *ante*, p. 45).

The degeneration of the caudal region in the human body has naturally been accompanied by a corresponding reduction of the related muscles, *i.e.* especially of those the homologues of which, in caudate Mammals, are strongly developed for moving the tail. These are serial with the musculature of the trunk, and can be divided into a ventral and a dorsal group. To the latter belong the extensor and levator coccygis, which lie along the posterior surface of the coccygeal vertebræ. This extraordinarily thin muscle bundle arises either from the great sacrosciatic ligament or from the lowest end of the sacrum, and sends out tendinous rays towards the apex of the coccyx.

To the ventral series belongs the coccygeus muscle, which arises from the spine of the ischium, runs along the lesser sacrosciatic ligament, and is inserted into the lateral edge of the coccyx. This muscle brings about the lateral movement (abduction) of the tail in the lower Mammals, and is therefore termed in them the abductor caudalis.

The curvator coccygis, which is met with on the anterior surface of the lower sacral and sometimes of the upper caudal vertebræ, belongs to this same category. It corresponds with the depressor caudæ of the lower Mammals.

The vestigial character of all these muscles is in several ways evident. They vary in form and size, and may be partly or wholly replaced by fibrous tissue, or, finally, one or other of them may be altogether wanting. This is also the case in the Anthropoids, where (*e.g.* in the Orang) their vestigial character is in some ways more pronounced than in Man.

Another caudal muscle may here be referred to, although morphologically it does not belong to the above-mentioned series. This is the caudo-femoralis (agitator caudæ) which, in a large number of Mammals (Monotremata, Marsupialia, most Carnivora, Lemuroidea, and tailed Monkeys) plays a great part, as flexor and abductor of the tail when the thigh is fixed, and which, in exceptional cases, appears in Man also. It lies at the lower edge of the gluteus maximus, being separated from it by only a small space. It arises from the lateral edge of the coccyx or of the last sacral vertebra, and is inserted into the femur below the point of attachment of the lowest bundle of the gluteus.

Normally, this muscle is wanting in Anthropoids, but it is not improbable that it may occasionally reappear in them as in Man.

In both the dorsal and ventral trunk muscles we find indications of original segmentation. In the intercostal muscles the segmentation is completely retained, and not infrequently tendons pass from the ends of the lower ribs into the broad abdominal muscles. Cartilaginous tracts are sometimes found persisting in a line with these tendons, but nearer the median plane, and they may be either free or connected with the tendons. Even in cases where all such indications are wanting, the innervation of these muscles points to a primitive metamerism.

In the same way, the rectus abdominis, by its "inscriptiones tendineæ," shows a more or less distinct segmentation.

This muscle in the lower Vertebrates (*e.g.* tailed Amphibians) extends from the pelvis to the head region; but in the higher Vertebrates, and particularly in Mammals, in accordance with advancing modification, and especially with the intervention of the sternal apparatus, it has become divided into a posterior and an anterior tract. The former arises from the pelvis, and is inserted anteriorly, as a rule, on a level with the fifth rib; the latter is represented by the ventral cervical muscles, viz. the sterno-hyoid and sterno-thyroid, which here and there bear inscriptiones tendineæ indicative of their former segmentation. To these must be added the almost constant omo-hyoid, which is provided with an inscriptio, and the thyro-hyoid. Farther forward these are joined by the hyo-glossus, genio-hyoid and genio-glossus, which belong to the same metameric series.[1]

In the lower Primates the rectus abdominis muscle still reaches to near the first rib, and thus recalls the connection with the cervical musculature mentioned above, which was first lost in the Reptiles. Even in Man it may sometimes run beyond the fifth rib and, under cover of the pectoralis major, pass as far up as the second. This is a striking case of atavism.

In the higher Primates the thoracic head of this muscle shifts back to the lower ribs, and this shifting towards the abdominal region is accompanied by an advancing loss of segmentation in both the Anthropoids and Man.[2] But even where this is most marked the muscle has not quite lost its thoracic character.

This retreat of the rectus muscle is intimately connected with the development of the great adductor of the fore-limb (the pectoralis major), since it is only when the upper parts of the rectus disappear that the muscular bundle forming the pectoralis major—and, indeed, that forming the pectoralis minor as well— is able to take possession of the firm anterior thoracic surface furnished by the ribs. Where, as in the lower Apes, the anterior end of the rectus muscle covers the thorax as far as the lateral edges of the sternum, a primitive condition being thus retained, those fasciculi of the pectoral muscles which arise from the skeleton come simply from the sternum. " We here have a conflict at close quarters between different parts of the organism" (Ruge).[3]

In connection with his studies of the abdominal musculature,

---

[1] [Cf. Albrecht. *Beitrag z. Morphologie des M. omo-hyoides u. d. ventr. inneren Interbranchialmusculatur i. d. Reihe d. Wirbelthiere.*—Inaug. Diss., Kiel., 1876.]

[2] In many cases the muscle withdraws in a distal direction even farther than the fifth rib, and derives its anterior (uppermost) slip from the sixth. A primitive slip from the eighth rib may also be retained (Ruge).

[3] Where, as a rare anomaly, the rectus abdominis is double on one or on both sides, a very low condition is indicated, this arrangement being typical in Amphibia and Saurians.

Ruge has called attention to a phylogenetic shifting of the navel. This occurs during the shortening of the thoraco-lumbar portion of the trunk (in relation to the segments of the rectus abdominis), and is accompanied by a gradual elimination of the posterior segments of the rectus. This process may not be yet finished; if, as has already been argued in dealing with the vertebral column (*ante*, p. 43), a progressive abbreviation of the thoracic region of the trunk is still taking place.

In front (ventrad) of the point of origin of the rectus abdominis, at the upper edge of the pelvis, there lies, in Man, the inconstant pyramidalis abdominis muscle. This is sometimes developed only on one side, and sometimes unrepresented, in which case it may be replaced by a tract of fibrous tissue. On the other hand, either one or both halves of this muscle may be double; and there are variations no less remarkable in its form and size. The pyramidalis usually runs either about half-way from the symphysis pubis to the navel, or only a third of that distance; it may sometimes, however, reach as far as the navel. In young children it is relatively larger than in adults. These facts may all be taken as evidence that the pyramidalis in Man (and the same applies to many Mammals, *e.g.* the Anthropoids) possesses all the peculiarities of an organ which has long been in a state of degeneration. It claims our attention principally as a striking example of the tenacity with which certain structures remain in the organism and are handed on, through inheritance, long after they have lost their specific significance. The reason for such continuance can only be that, in the course of phylogenetic development, the muscle has undergone a change of function, and has become associated with or subordinated to other muscles or groups of muscles. In this case the pyramidalis has been overmastered by the rectus abdominis.

In the non-placental Mammals (Monotremata and Marsupialia) the pyramidalis is powerfully developed in connection with the epipubes (so-called marsupial bones); and even in some Placentalia, such as the Insectivora (*e.g. Myogale pyrenaica*), it may almost reach the ensiform process of the sternum, thus playing an important part in strengthening the abdominal wall. The pyramidalis is undoubtedly an old muscle dating far back to pre-Mammalian times.

Both the abdominal oblique muscles may be considered as continuations of the intercostal muscles into the abdominal region, and, anteriorly, the scaleni muscles of the neck may be looked upon as forward extensions of the same. The neck, as has been seen from the study of the skeletal system (*ante*, p. 43), was formerly provided with free ribs; and hence this serial relationship of the cervical to the segmental thoracic muscles is easily understood. The degeneration of the cervical ribs has had (among other results) the effect of causing the short-fibred scaleni muscles, which once only stretched across the intercostal spaces, to unite and grow longer, so as finally to reach ribs which lie farther back. Further related modifications may be exemplified in the occurrence of supernumerary scaleni, such as the scalenus minimus (scalene intermédiaire, Testut), which is typically present in all Anthropoids, and by the numerous variations in origin and attachment of the three ordinary scaleni.

The transversus thoracis muscle (triangularis sterni) is clearly degenerating. This muscle, which lies on the inner side of the anterior wall of the thorax, arises from a variable number of slips. It arises, as a rule, from the cartilages of the third to the sixth ribs, and occasionally receives a slip from the seventh rib also. This fact helps us in homologising it as a continuation of the transversalis abdominis. These two muscles are separated by one of the bundles which give rise to the diaphragm.

THE MUSCLES OF THE CERVICAL AND CEPHALIC REGIONS

In addition to the structural changes going on in the scaleni, which have been already mentioned, the following facts are worth recording:—

The original community of the trapezius and the sterno-cleido-mastoid muscles is indicated by their common innervation, and further by the fact that the interval between them is still not infrequently occupied by the cleido-occipitalis which runs from the clavicle to the occipital bone. This muscle thus forms a link between the trapezius and the sterno-cleido-mastoid, and when strongly developed brings about a more or less complete fusion of these two muscles, *i.e.* reinstates the original condition.

These facts might have been included in the remarks on muscles which occasionally appear and may be considered atavistic, but they are here dealt with as they indicate a gradual disappearance of certain fibrous areas in the region of these muscles, *i.e.* they point to a retrogressive condition.

A similar relationship exists between the anterior belly of

the biventer maxillæ (digastricus) and the mylohyoid (as may be gathered from their innervation), while the posterior belly of the former may sometimes fuse with the stylohyoid.

Undoubtedly the most interesting of all the retrogressive muscles of the cervical region is the so-called platysma myoides (subcutaneus colli). This muscle is also related, as will be shown later, to certain cephalic muscles, and requires a more detailed description (cf. *infra*, pp. 104 and 114).

Whereas most muscles are closely connected with the skeleton, there are, in the Vertebrates, certain muscles which both arise from and are inserted into the integument or the subcutaneous tissues. These are the cutaneous muscles (panniculus carnosus of the lower Mammalia).

These cutaneous muscles are [with rare exceptions] only feebly developed among Fishes and Amphibia, but in Reptiles and Birds they play a great part in connection with the scutes, scales, and feathers. They are, however, most developed in Mammals, in which they may spread like a mantle over the back, head, neck, and flanks (*e.g. Echidna, Dasypus*, Pinnipedia, *Erinaceus*, and others).

In Man and the Anthropoids only feeble traces of this musculature are found, such as the platysma-myoides already mentioned, which spreads over the upper part of the thorax and the neck and partly over the face (cf. Fig. 67). Other slight traces are found in the shoulders, back, abdomen, axilla, forearm, hand, and buttocks.

Among the lower Mammalia the panniculus carnosus functions as a protective against injury to the skin. The reaction of the skin of horses when stung by insects may be given as an example of this.

The mimetic musculature is very closely connected with the cutaneous, and is at least partly to be derived from it phylogenetically. In a general sense, the differentiation of the mimetic musculature may be said to advance with advancing intelligence; and we may therefore expect to find it most highly developed in the Primates.

The phylogenetic development of this system has been studied by Gegenbaur and Ruge. According to Gegenbaur, the human platysma appears to be the remnant of a musculature which was continued on to the head, but which has only retained its primitive undifferentiated condition on the neck. The chief reason of this is that the platysma, even in Man, is sometimes directly connected with the zygomaticus minor, the orbicularis palpebrarum, the auricularis anterior, and the transversus nuchæ. On the other hand, however, the fact that the mimetic musculature is innervated by the facialis (*n.fc.*, Fig. 69), a nerve which, by location and distribution, is connected with certain muscles of the visceral skeleton, compels us to conclude that this (the mimetic) musculature has to some extent wandered from its original

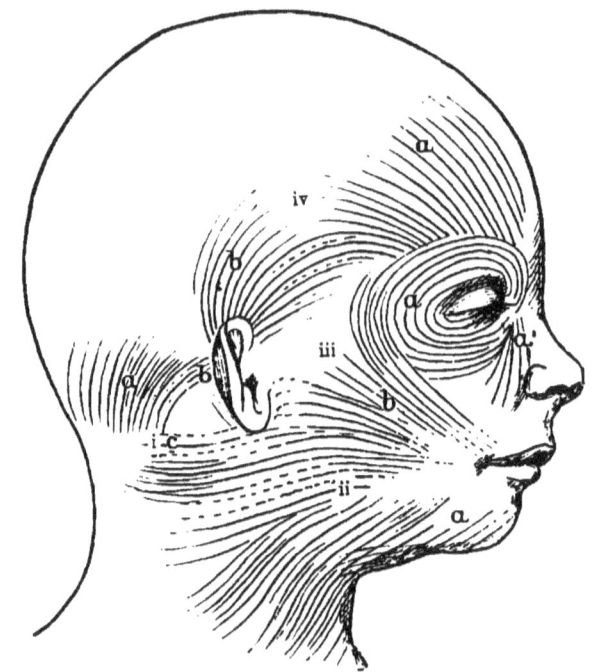

Fig. 67.—Diagram of the Distribution of the Platysma over the Head. (After Gegenbaur.) The larger areas are marked with Roman figures, the smaller with letters (cf. with Fig. 70).

position. It would appear to have moved up from the region of the lower jaw,[1] and to have entered into close connection with the soft parts surrounding the auditory and buccal apertures, *i.e.* with the lips and with the pinna, which are themselves of secondary

[1] According to Killian, it is more than doubtful whether Ruge is right in assuming a post-auricular upward wandering of the platysma. Killian holds that the pars occipitalis of the platysma had from the beginning a dorsal position, and that it is nothing more than the posterior superficial layer of the dorsal portion of the musculature of the hyoid arch, as it appears not only in most Mammalian groups, but also in many species of Birds, *e.g.* Owls, in which even external auditory

origin. In time the eyes, forehead, temples, and the parietal region were reached.

In the Lemuroidea the mimetic muscles, instead of being sharply individualised as in Man, are not anatomically distinct, *i.e.* they are merely parts of a great muscular tract, in which a superficial and a deeper layer can be distinguished (cf. Figs. 68

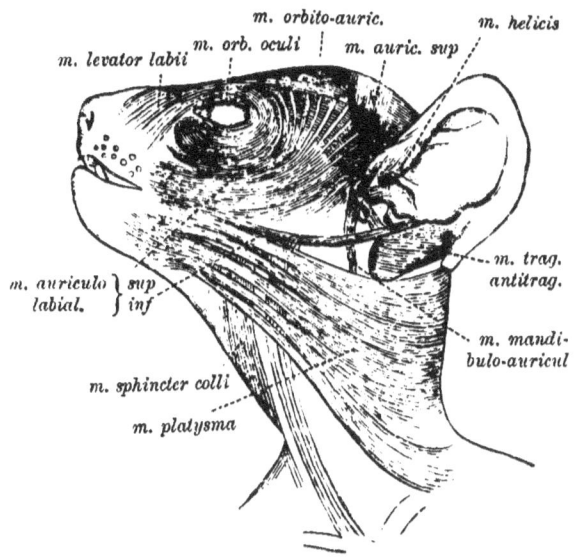

FIG. 68.—SUPERFICIAL MUSCULATURE OF THE FACE IN *Lepilemur mustelinus*. (After Ruge.) The deeper layer (*m. sphincter colli*) is visible in the neck.

and 69). The superficial layer is the platysma, the deeper the so-called sphincter colli.

In those exceptional cases in Man, in which the cervical portion of the platysma is developed, it is called the transversus nuchæ. Schultze found this in eighteen out of twenty-five bodies, Macalister in 35 per cent; others, however, have been less fortunate. It was always found to be symmetrical, *i.e.* developed on both sides. This muscle, which is almost always present in the human embryo, corresponds in position with the protuberantia occipitalis; from this it radiates outwards along the linea semicircularis, towards the tendon of the sterno-cleido-muscles split off from it. It is also found in Reptiles (Saurians and Chelonia). In Crocodiles a vestige of it is found in the powerful levator auriculæ. Even in Amphibians and Sharks this muscular tract is already developed, and from it can be derived those human muscles which are innervated by the ramus auricularis posterior nervi facialis.

mastoid, or even as far as the posterior edge of the auricularis posticus. It may even completely fuse with the latter, which thus appears to arise from the protuberantia occipitalis, as seems to be the case with many lower Mammals.

The second and deeper layer of this cervical muscle, the

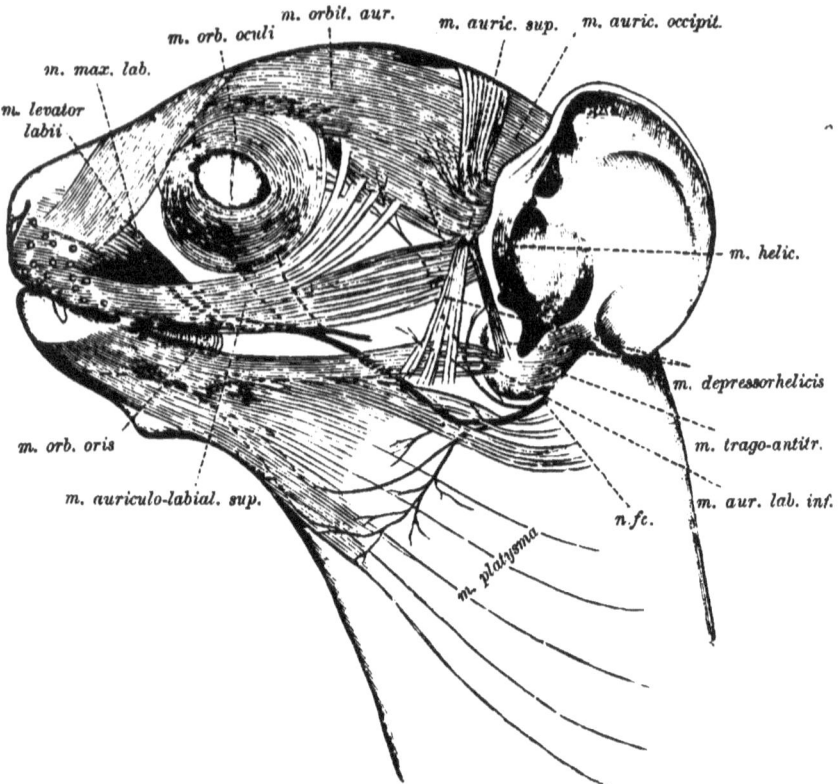

Fig. 69.—Facial Muscles and Nerves of the *Lemuroid propithecus*. (After Ruge.) Superficial muscles with the branchings of the facial nerve (*n.fc.*).

sphincter colli, runs from the occipital region over the edge of the jaw to the regio parotideo-masseterica, the lip and adjacent parts. We shall consider later which of the human facial muscles are derived from this, and which from the platysma; at present we need only deal with the vestiges, often very slight, of this musculature which was probably incomparably more developed in the ancestors of Man. Those mimetic muscles which are found partly near the ear and partly on the cranium, show great individual variation, those on the right sometimes differing from those on the left in one and the same person. By taking their physiological activities into account we can establish three or four stages in their degeneration.

These muscles may be dealt with in four series, as under :—

1. Muscles of the cranium, known collectively as the epicranius. Of this the frontal portion (frontalis) is still under

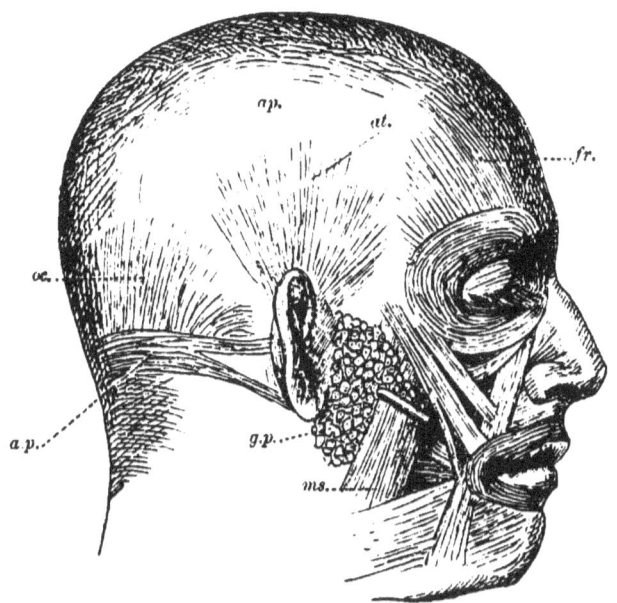

Fig. 70.—Muscles of the Epicranial Region in Man, with certain of the Facial Muscles. (After Gegenbaur.)

ap., epicranial aponeurosis ; *a.p.*, posterior auricular muscle ; *at.*, attollens auriculam ; *fr.*, frontalis muscle ; *g.p.*, parotid gland ; *ms.*, masseter ; *oc.*, m. occipitalis.

control of the will, as is seen in frowning; but the power of throwing the entire epicranius into contraction, as in moving the scalp, is possessed by but few individuals.

2. Muscles round the pinna : attrahens, retrahens, and attollens auriculam (cf. Figs. 70 and 71). The capacity for moving these muscles varies greatly in individuals. In most people it is entirely wanting; and the retrogressive character of these muscles is due to the degeneration of the pinna (cf. *infra*).

3. Intrinsic muscles of the pinna (derivatives of the muscles mentioned under 2, which have become exclusively related to the

pinna, and there again further differentiated). Among these may be mentioned certain bundles which separate off from the

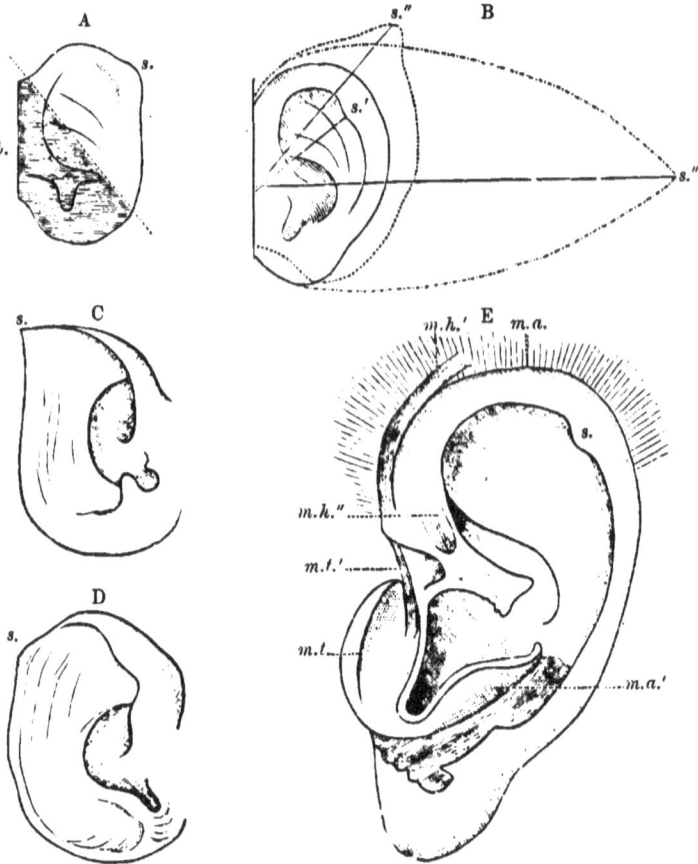

FIG. 71.—A, PINNA OF A PRIMATE DIVIDED INTO ZONES, THE SHADED PORTION BEING THAT OF THE AUDITORY EMINENCES OF THE EMBRYO, THE UNSHADED THAT OF THE LATER FORMED AUDITORY FOLD ; b, ITS BASE.
B, pinna of Man, of a Baboon and of an Ox, drawn to the same scale and superposed, s'., spina or tip of the ear in Man ; s"., the same of the Baboon ; and s"'., the same of the Ox (homologous points) ; C, pinna of *Macacus rhesus*, with the tip (s.) pointing upwards ; D, pinna of *Cercopithecus*, with the tip pointing backwards ; E, pinna of Man, with its muscles ; m.a., attollens auriculam ; m.a'., antitragicus ; m.t., tragicus ; m.t'., inconstant muscle bundle, stretching from the tragicus to the edge of the helix ; m.h'., helicis major ; m.h"., helicis minor ; s., tip of the ear (spina) rolled over ; A-D, after Schwalbe ; E, after Henle.

retrahens auriculam, chief of which are the transversus and obliquus auriculam (auricularis proprius, Ruge) which, belonging to the most folded part of the pinna, are very small.

The helicis major (Fig. 71, $m.h'.$) and the tragicus ($m.t.$) (the second of which is often wanting), are to be derived from the scutulo-auriculare (a portion of the depressor helicis, Ruge), found in those Mammals which still possess a free and movable scutulum. The helicis minor ($m.h''.$), antitragicus ($m.a'.$), and the incisuræ Santorini, which belong to the cartilaginous wall of the external auditory meatus, are the proper ear muscles (auriculares proprii), and related to the principal cartilages and the pinna alone.

Taking all the facts into consideration, this intrinsic musculature of the pinna, which is no longer under the control of the will, must be considered as the vestige of a primitive apparatus functional either for the opening and closing, or for the widening and narrowing of the auditory funnel and the external auditory passage (cf. chapter on the auditory organ, *infra*).

4. To the fourth class belong those mimetic muscles which have undergone the greatest degeneration, *i.e.* those which have become transformed into tendinous or membranous structures (fasciæ). For example, the auriculo- (temporo-) labialis muscle of the Lemuroids (cf. Figs. 68 and 69) has, in Man, been replaced by the fascia temporalis superficialis, and the sphincter colli muscle by the fascia parotideo-masseterica. A great part of the human epicranial aponeurosis (galea aponeurotica), further, consists of muscle bundles of the occipitalis transformed into tendons.

[It is interesting to note that the power of contracting the platysma, the ear muscles, and others not normally under the control of the will, has been observed in a few cases to go hand in hand with that of a voluntary control of the heart's action.][1]

MUSCLES OF THE LIMBS

The palmaris (= p. longus) and its homologue in the hindlimb, the plantaris, are time honoured (and certainly among the best) examples of the gradual degeneration of a muscle. The degeneration of the former has not yet proceeded as far as that of the latter, as is most evident in the fact that while the palmaris still reaches the palmar fascia of the hand, the plantaris only in exceptional cases becomes connected with the homologous plantar fascia of the foot, and in doing so regains its former significance as a flexor of that organ.

The plantaris must therefore, as an original flexor, have

[1] [Cf. E. A. Pease, *Boston Med. and Surg. Jour.*, 30th May 1889.]

begun to degenerate from the time that the plantar fascia became secondarily attached to the calcaneum, and helped in the formation of the arch of the foot, as the latter became transformed into a supporting organ.

But why are the palmaris and plantaris of Anthropoids, in which such transformations do not take place, also in a degenerate condition? It does not appear difficult to answer this question if we consider that these muscles originally extended, as do their homologues in the lower Mammals,[1] through the mediation of the palmar or plantar fascia to the phalanges, and acted as common flexors of the fingers and toes. If so, in the course of time—to confine our attention to the hand—as the flexores digitorum communis superficialis and profundus became more extensively and more subtly differentiated from the primitive "pronato-flexor mass" (Humphry), the fibrous terminal expansions of the palmaris withdrew more and more from the fingers, and found points of attachment in the palm of the hand and in the ligamentum carpi transversum. Thus would the finger flexor appear to have become a hand flexor. As such, however, it could not, on account of its attachments, develop the same strength as the proper hand flexors,[2] which are directly attached to the skeleton, and which, as we see where the palmaris is wanting, are competent alone to bend the hand. The palmaris becoming thus superfluous, is variable and occasionally absent.

A further consequence of the transformation of the hind-limb into a supporting and ambulatory organ, is that some of the flexor muscles which originally ran down without interruption to the sole of the foot have become interrupted at the protuberantia calcanei by the dorsal flexion entailed. Another muscle of this flexor series, *e.g.* the short flexor, which corresponds with the flexor digitorum communis superficialis of the hand, has shifted its point of origin farther and farther down, till at last, on the acquisition of the upright gait, it has reached the calcaneal tuberosity. In doing so this muscle has become more and more closely connected with the plantar fascia; and at present it shows in many ways, *e.g.* in the variation of its terminal tendons

---

[1] It is said that in Negroes the palmaris is still not infrequently inserted into the metacarpals.

[2] That it is still functional in the hand is shown by its occurrence, which must still be considered normal. It is absent on one or both sides in about one in every ten bodies.

and the frequent absence of that to the fifth toe, evidences of a retrogressive tendency.

The special extensors of the fingers undergo similar variations, being now as a rule restricted to the thumb, the index, and the little fingers. Occasionally, however, the third and fourth fingers also receive tendons from the extensor minimi digiti, and the middle finger may receive a tendon from the extensor indicis proprius.

The changes brought about in the sole of the foot naturally affect the dorsum as well. There can indeed be no doubt that changes have taken place in the extensor brevis digitorum of the foot (*e.br.*, Fig. 72) complementary to those above described in the flexor digitorum communis brevis. The extensor brevis digitorum must formerly have arisen higher up the fore-leg, and have secondarily shifted downwards to the dorsum pedis. The connection demonstrated by Ruge between the short common flexor of the toes and the interossei pedis undoubtedly indicates the "extreme limit of the distal wandering of the extensor brevis."

Ruge has further proved the interesting fact that all the seven interossei pedis at a certain stage in the human embryo have a plantar disposition, and that they shift at a later stage to a position between the metatarsals, there to divide into the plantar and dorsal series. An exact parallel to this is found in certain Apes (*Cebus*, *Cercopithecus*) and in most of the lower Mammals, in which the interossei have a plantar position throughout life. In the

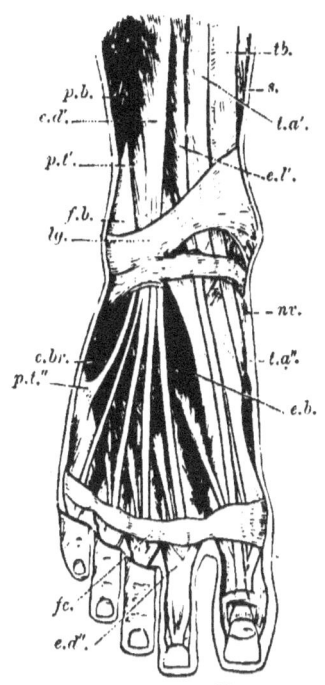

FIG. 72.—SUPERFICIAL MUSCLES AND TENDONS OF THE DORSUM OF THE RIGHT FOOT. One-third natural size. (After Rauber.)

a, tibia; *b*, fibula; *c*, navicular; *t.a'.*, tibialis anticus muscle; *t.a".*, its tendon of insertion; *e.l'.*, M. extensor proprius hallucis (e. hall. long.); *e.d'.*, M. extensor communis digitorum (e. digit. longus); *e.d".*, its expansion and insertion on the second toe; *p.t'.*, peroneus tertius; *p.t".*, its insertion on the fifth metatarsal bone; *s.*, M. soleus; *p.b.*, M. peroneus brevis; *e.b.*, M. extensor hallucis brevis; *e.br.*, extensor brevis digitorum; *lg.* anterior annular ligament; *fc.*, transverse band of the dorsal fascia of the foot.

Chimpanzee and Gorilla they are not so markedly dorsal in position as in *Ateles, Inuus*, and the Orang; the latter therefore are, in this respect, the nearest to Man.

The adductor hallucis with its caput obliquum and transversum [usually described as a distinct muscle, the transversus pedis] originally forms one mass; this points back to the time when it was more strongly developed, and when the great toe was capable of more extensive movement (cf. *ante*, p. 85). The fifth toe also once moved more freely, as is indicated by the opponens minimi digiti, which is only secondarily differentiated during embryonic life from the mass of the flexor brevis minimi digiti. The former muscle is, comparatively speaking, much stronger in embryonic life than later, when it may entirely disappear.[1]

MUSCLES WHICH APPEAR OCCASIONALLY, AND MAY BE CONSIDERED ATAVISTIC

In dealing with this group of muscles, we may confine ourselves to those which point back to lower grades of organisation, through which the ancestors of Man may have passed phylogenetically. I wish to insist on this, since nothing is gained by simply labelling muscles "theromorphic," and since, in my opinion, in dealing with such muscles, Testut and certain other authors have exceeded the bounds of moderation.

One of these apparently atavistic muscles, the cleido-occipitalis, which forms a connecting tract between the trapezius and the sterno-cleido-mastoid, has already been mentioned (*ante*, p. 102). To the same category belong certain muscle bundles which here and there partly fill up the interval between the pectoralis major and the latissimus dorsi. A typical example of these has been lately described by my pupil Endres (*Anat. Anzeiger*, Bd. viii. p. 387), the morphological significance of the so-called Langer's arch being incidentally discussed.

A muscle which very rarely occurs in Man is the latissimo-condyloideus (dorso-épitrochlearis of French authors), an appendage of the latissimus dorsi, branching off from the latter shortly before it is inserted into the humerus. From

---

[1] The opponens minimi digiti seems to attain development only in the Chimpanzee among Anthropoids. [Incidentally to this topic and to that of the reduction and co-ossification of the penultimate and terminal phalanges of the little toe (cf. *ante*, p. 89), it is interesting to observe that the muscles of the little toe are more reduced in the higher Apes than in Man.]

this point the muscle runs perpendicularly along the triceps (radiating out into the surrounding fasciæ) to the condylus internus humeri, into which it is inserted. This muscle is present in all Anthropoids, and is either directly inserted into the olecranon or contributes to the triceps.

Near the sternal line the so-called "sternalis" muscle is sometimes found. This is a small bundle, which varies in form and in the direction of its fibres, lying ventrad of the pectoralis major. It may either be bilaterally symmetrical or present only on one side. In the former case, the two muscles may cross one another and be continued direct into the sterno-cleido-mastoid.

[Considerable controversy has from time to time arisen concerning this sternalis. It occurs in some 3 to 5 per cent of subjects, and is invariably innervated by the anterior thoracic or intercostal nerves. While it has by some been referred to a possible origin from the pectoralis major, the rectus abdominis, and other muscles, it has by others been regarded as a vestige of the panniculus. One interesting variation to which it is liable is that of forming a connection between the external oblique of the abdominal region and the sterno-mastoid. Parsons has recently shown that in Rodents the abdominal panniculus, on reaching the axillary border of the pectoralis, divides into a superficial and a deep stratum; and from a very careful analysis of the detailed relationships of the panniculus in these animals, he has adduced strong reason for regarding the fascial sheath of the human external oblique as its modified deep abdominal portion. He further gives reasons for believing that the deep part of the cervical panniculus has become incorporated in the sterno-mastoid, and ultimately regards the sternalis as a vestige of that portion of the panniculus which originally connected its deep cervical and deep abdominal sections.][1]

Between the internal condyle of the humerus and the olecranon, in Man, a fibrous band always runs, transversely, below the superficial fascia which bounds posteriorly the deep indentation in which the ulnar nerve lies. This band corresponds with the epitrochleo-anconæus muscle, which is constant in many Mammals; it is only occasionally muscular in Man and the Anthropoids, and then varies greatly in form and size. It

---

[1] [Parsons has further simplified matters by suggesting that the pectoralis major may be itself a derivation of the panniculus. Cf. *Jour. Anat. and Phys.*, vol. xxvii. p. 505.]

is always innervated by the ulnar nerve. According to W. Gruber (St. Petersburg), it was found in about 34 per cent, but, according to Wood (London), in only 8 per cent, of bodies examined—a want of agreement which may perhaps be indicative of a racial difference. This muscle must be referred back to a time when a transverse shifting of the ulna was possible in the ancestors of Man, as it now is, to some extent, in many lower animals; and it would appear that after the movements of this bone had become limited almost entirely to flexion and extension, the muscle gradually degenerated and disappeared.

Finally must be mentioned the levator claviculæ and the ischio-femoralis or glutæus quartus, which occasionally occur in Man. The latter muscle is constantly present in Anthropoids [as the so-called scansorius].

3. Progressive Muscles

Attention has already been drawn to the fact (*ante*, p. 97) that in certain regions progressive and retrogressive variations may occur simultaneously; and this is nowhere so conspicuous as with the facial muscles. Some of these which are in various stages of degeneration have already been referred to (*ante*, p. 109). All the other mimetic muscles (*i.e.* by far the greater number) appear to be progressively developing, in correlation with the increase of the intellect and the correspondingly advanced functional activity of their associated nerves. This advancing specialisation is indicated in the aberration of certain parts, and the formation of new layers of muscle. These changes have brought about striking differences between these muscles in Man and the homologous tracts in the Lemuroidea, where they are simple and comparatively easy to understand. We are thus able to demonstrate for the mimetic musculature very great variations of form and size in both a progressive and retrogressive direction, as indeed is the case in all organs which are in the act either of suppression or of differentiation, *i.e.* are not in a definitive state.

Progressive development is especially shown in the muscles round the eyes, the mouth, and the nose, and also in those of the sub-zygomatic region.

Ruge expresses himself upon the tendency to further development and completion of the human facial muscles, very aptly, as follows:—

"A free subcutaneous position, slight relations to the skeleton, and the absence of definite fasciæ, offer most favourable conditions for the initiation of new combinations. The muscular elements can naturally only enter upon new departures in various directions for the attainment of a greater functional activity, as the result of very definite causes. These causes are undoubtedly present in Man, and lie in his mental qualities and in the faculty of speech. The latter calls the muscles around the mouth into activity, and the former seek expression in the play of the features. These causes of the differentiation of new facial muscles hardly exist in the lower animals, which fact accounts, it appears to me, for the absence among them of those signs of progressive variation with which we shall become acquainted in the musculature of the human face. It may be different, however, in the case of variations due to quite other causes. The possibility of great variability in the facial musculature of the lower animals cannot be denied à priori; nor can we dismiss the objection that the few observations which have been made on animals have by no means settled what must be considered as the normal condition for them. In answer to this, I would, however, emphasise (1) the fact that variation in the muscles of animals is rarer in the wild state than under domestication; and (2) the consideration (to which Dobson has rightly called attention) that variation in that most domesticated of all animals, Man, ought to be far greater than in animals, which, being subject to natural selection, in which the fittest survives, have, in some respects, a narrower field allotted to them for modification."

"The chief factor in the transformation and diversity of form of the facial muscles in Man, as opposed to the other Primates, is the extensive development of the brain-case. This transformation alone is enough to account for changes in those muscles which lie upon it. But the development of the brain is closely connected with the acquisition of mental powers in Man. The development of language has necessarily determined a corresponding development of the muscles round the mouth and nose. If we can only demonstrate some slight progressive development in these parts something will be gained, for we shall be able to say that where the higher development of Man leads us to expect more complicated anatomical arrangements, these are actually found. Vivacity and diversity of expression of the mouth and eye are a peculiarity of Man; they mirror forth the higher psychical activity, and can only be acquired by the perfecting of

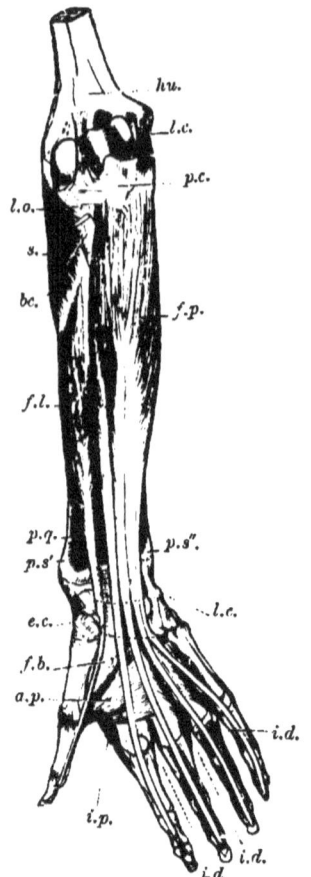

Fig. 73.—DEEP MUSCLES ON THE FLEXOR SIDE OF THE FOREARM. One-fifth natural size. (After Rauber.)
The muscles of the upper arm, and the superficial muscles of the forearm and hand, with the lumbricales, are removed. The position of the anterior annular ligament is indicated by two dotted lines. $hu.$, humerus; $p.c.$, processus coronoideus ulnæ; $l.o.$, the orbicular ligament; $p.s'.$, proc. styloideus radii; $p.s".$, proc. styloideus ulnæ; $e.c.$, eminentia carpi ulnaris; $l.c.$, lig. accessorium cubiti mediale; $s.$, M. supinator; $f.l.$, M. flexor longus pollicis; $f.p.$, M. flexor profundus digitorum; $p.q.$, M. pronator quadratus; $f.b.$, deep head of the flexor brevis pollicis; $a.p.$, M. adductor pollicis; $i.p.$, M. interosseus dorsalis primus; $i.d.$, Mm. interossei dorsales et volares; $bc.$, bicipital tendon.

the muscles round these organs. It is, therefore, a fact of the greatest importance that, while many variations are found in the muscles near the mouth and the eyelids of Man, indicative of new possibilities of development, in the other Primates these muscles show a monotonous constancy. May it not also be possible that still more subtle differences occur between the various human races in the detailed arrangement of the facial muscles? In such a question, however, a trustworthy decision can of course only be arrived at after extended comparative inquiry."

In addition to the facial region, there are three others in which progressive muscular variations are to be found. Taking first the hand, we may select for special consideration the thumb. We are immediately struck by its apparent superfluity of muscles.[1] Our attention is specially arrested by the long flexor of the thumb

[1] For instance, the abductor pollicis has often a double or even triple tendon, and supernumerary tendons of the most various muscles, as if attracted by a magnet, often become inserted into the thumb (e.g. tendons from the brachio radialis, extensor pollicis longus and brevis, extensor longus radialis and extensor digitorum communis). In all these we probably have to do with the beginnings of secondary processes of differentiation, which have already been indicated in connection with the skeleton of the hand (ante, p. 77).

(fl. longus pollicis) (*f.l.*, Fig. 73), the differentiation of which out of the common mass of the flexor profundus digitorum (*f.p.*) commences in Anthropoids, but is first carried out in Man. Not infrequently, however, more often in the lower than in the higher races, we find reversions to the primitive condition, *i.e.* a more or less extensive inter-communication of fibres of, or even a fusion between, the flexor pollicis and the flexor profundus.

This differentiation of the flexor longus pollicis, which finds its highest expression in the attainment of independent movement and in the greatest possible play of the thumb, has its parallel in that of the flexor longus hallucis (*f.h.*, Fig. 74), which is derived from the flexor digitorum communis pedis.[1] The interchange between the fibres of these two muscles is so very frequent that it is hardly ever wanting. Further, all the variations observed in them are normally met with in Apes, even to the different radiations from the tendinous anastomosis to the toes.[2]

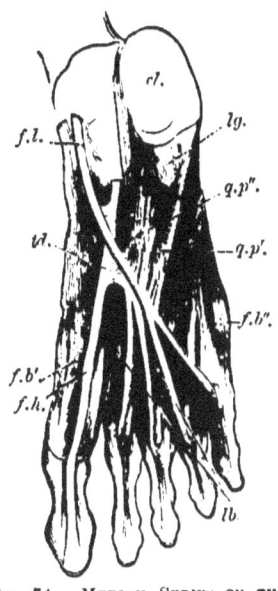

FIG. 74.—MEDIAN SERIES OF THE PLANTAR MUSCLES, IN THEIR CONNECTION WITH THE FLEXOR TENDONS. One-third natural size. (After Rauber.) *cl.*, tuber calcanei; *lg.*, ligam. calcaneo-cuboideum plantare; *f.l.*, tendon of flexor longus digitorum; *f.h.*, tendon of flexor longus hallucis; *td.*, tendinous connection between flexor longus and adjacent tendons; *q.p'.*, lateral head of the M. quadrati plantæ flexor accessorius; *q.p".*, its median head; *lb.*, Mm. lumbricales; *f.b'.*, M. flexor brevis hallucis; *f.b".*, M. flexor brevis minimi digiti.

[1] In the Gorilla the flexor digitorum communis profundus is subdivided into two portions. The ulnar portion is inserted into the fifth, the fourth, and the middle fingers, the radial one into the index finger and the pollex. Testut has proved that this condition may rarely occur in Man, and that it sometimes occurs on both sides in the same individual. In the Orang there is only a simple undivided flexor digitorum communis profundus without any tendon for the thumb. This arrangement also has been four times observed in Man—in one case in a microcephalous individual.

[2] The frequent variations in the development of the caro quadrata Sylvii, and its occasional entire absence, find a parallel in Anthropoids. In the Chimpanzee, for example, the muscle is often reduced to a single little fleshy bundle, or may be altogether wanting, as appears to be the case in the Orang, Gibbon, and Gorilla. In all cases, however, the numerous variations indicate that the caro quadrata attained its present position secondarily, *i.e.* that it must formerly have lain higher up on the calcaneus and the fore-leg; and, indeed, an extension of the muscle in this direction has been observed.

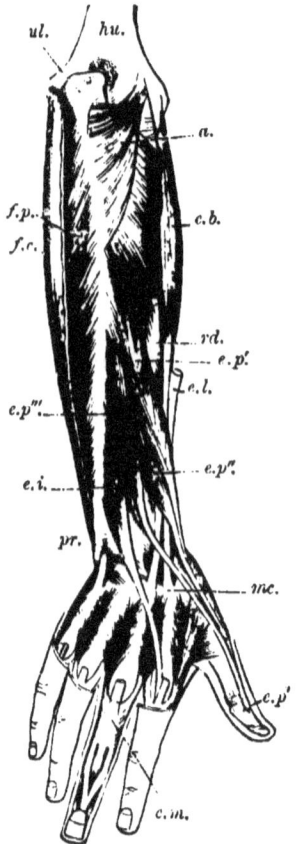

FIG. 75.—DEEP DORSAL MUSCLES OF THE FOREARM. One-fifth natural size. (After Rauber.)

hu, humerus; *ul.*, olecranon process of ulna; *rd.*, radius; *pr.*, processus styloideus ulnæ; *mc.*, os metacarpeum secundum. *a.*, M. anconæus; *f.p.*, M. flexor profundus digitorum; *f.c.*, flexor carpi ulnaris, separated from the fascia of the forearm; *e.b.*, extensor carpi radialis brevior; *e.l.*, the tendon of the extensor carpi radialis longior; *e.p'.*, M. ext. metacarpi pollicis ossis; *e.p".* M. ext. primi internodii pollicis; *e.p'".*, M. ext. secundi internodii pollicis; *e.i.*, M. ext. indicis; *e.m.*, insertion of the extensor tendon into the middle finger, and its connection with the second and third dorsal interossei.

We saw above that a number of muscles and tendons meet in the thumb; and the same applies, though to a lesser degree, to the great toe. To it offshoots of the extensor hallucis longior and the tibialis anticus or their tendons pass; these, however, do not indicate the commencement of a new development, but rather a reversion to a former condition, in which the great toe was capable of freer movement.

It would be difficult to decide to what extent the variations which occur on the ulnar border of the forearm and hand, in the region of the extensor and flexor carpi ulnaris and the extensor digiti quinti proprius, may be the beginnings of a progressive development. On the other hand, there can be no doubt that the changes at the fibular border of the foot, which have already been mentioned (*ante*, p. 112), are degenerations.

The already described differentiation of a flexor longus pollicis and a flexor longus hallucis out of the original simple flexor masses, finds a parallel in the Ontogeny and Phylogeny of the superficial and deep common flexors of the fingers. The two latter are connected by an interchange of fibres which may amount to complete fusion; and in many of the lower Vertebrates these muscles may not only be connected with one another, but also with neighbouring muscles, such as the pronator teres, palmaris longus, flexor carpi radialis and ulnaris. The two flexors originally formed (as in the lower Mammals) one mass; and in the human embryo they still arise as a single blastema, which is only at a later stage of development split up by ingrowing partition walls of connective tissue.

In Anthropoids these muscles are throughout life connected by anastomosing strands, which clearly indicate their former union, and to this cause, and the lack of a distinct flexor pollicis proprius, is due the less marked specialisation of the Anthropoid hand as compared with that of Man. In Man, the flexores digitorum communes, superficial and deep, are, as a rule, distinct; but the more or less complete fusion often found between them points to the fact that their separation is (geologically speaking) not of long standing, and has not yet become stereotyped.

The same is the case with the not infrequent fusions involving the two radial extensors of the hand, which must also be regarded as reversionary. Indeed, these two muscles may fuse completely, and, in such a case, we have a realisation of that lower condition in which only one single extensor carpi radialis externus is present.

A further instance of progressive development in muscles is exemplified by the glutei. These, including the adductors of the thigh, show their original unity by frequent blending; and very often a more or less complete fusion takes place between them and the pyriformis, or between the latter and the gemellus superior. Further, the frequent absence of the gemellus superior in Man deserves mention, because this muscle is also often wanting in the Anthropoids.

The special development of the gluteus maximus is a characteristic peculiarity of Man. This muscle has a humble origin among the lower Vertebrates, and even in the Anthropoids there is nothing comparable in size and strength with its excessive development in Man, which is a direct accompaniment of the upright gait. The muscle fixes and steadies the pelvis, or rather, the whole trunk, on the heads of the femora, and through them on the lower limbs, as on a support or stand.

Closely connected with the assumption of the upright gait by Man, which involves the transformation of the former prehensile feet into ambulatory and supporting organs, is the development of the superficial muscles of the posterior surface of the fore-leg, *i.e.* of the calf. The gastrocnemius and soleus were formerly as directly connected with the sole of the foot or with its fascia as was the plantaris. The terminal tendons of these muscles have alike shifted back to the calcaneal tuberosity; but while the plantaris very soon began to degenerate, the soleus and gastrocnemius [1] have attained an excessive development specifically characteristic of Man. We have here another instance of retrogressive and progressive changes taking place side by side in one and the same region.[2]

Retrospect

Gathering together the conclusions which follow from the above review of the musculature, we find first that age seems to have no influence on the frequency of variation and reversionary phenomena. We must, however, except fœtal life, since, during that period, certain muscles may appear which afterwards suffer more or less complete degeneration.

No definite laws can be framed either as to the disposition or division, the symmetry or asymmetry, of the muscles, or as to the general condition of the body to which they belong, *e.g.* the strength or weakness of the individual. Correlative changes counteracting those due to variation are not observed. It is the exception to find that anomalies extend to the homologous muscles of the fore- and hind-limbs of the same side.

Examination of eighteen male and eighteen female bodies by Professor Wood at King's College, London (in 1867-68), led to the conclusion that anomalies are more frequent in the musculature of the limbs than in that of the rest of the body, and that the fore-limb is in particular distinguished by their occurrence (292 variations were found in the fore as against 119 in the hind-limb). It has further been ascertained that variations become more frequent as examination proceeds in a distal direction, *i.e.* as those peripheral parts of the body are reached which are more directly exposed to the modifying influences of the environment.

[1] A sesamoid bone sometimes occurs near the lateral point of origin of the gastrocnemius. In Anthropoids and many other Mammals several such bones (fabellæ) are found, one, for instance, at the median point of origin of the muscle.

[2] Various circumstances point to the fact that the biceps femoris, semitendinosus and semimembranosus, originally arose higher up than at present, viz. from the ilium, and the sacral, or caudal vertebræ. The fact that they have wandered on to the ischial tuberosity would appear to be connected with the forward translocation of the pelvic girdle already discussed (*ante*, p. 33).

In general, the principle holds good that those muscles are most subject to variation which can be dispensed with without disturbance or disadvantage to the organism as a whole, either because they can be easily replaced by other muscles, or because they have only a subordinate part to play. In illustration of this I would merely refer to the pyramidalis, the abortive caudal muscles, the muscles of the pinna, the palmaris and the plantaris, the vestigial character of which clearly points to their ultimate complete suppression.

Research has shown, however, that it is not only to the retrogressive tendency of the muscles that variation is due, but that variation may in some cases indicate a tendency to progressive development. The best example of this is afforded by certain flexor muscles, and by the flexor longus pollicis, and the gluteus magnus.

A third kind of variation occurs, in those cases in which a tendon may return to former points of insertion on neighbouring bones, *e.g.* the rectus abdominis is occasionally inserted on to the more anterior ribs. And to the same category belong the splitting off of the abductor hallucis from the tibialis anticus, which occurs in very varying degrees.

All these cases, which must be denominated reversionary, indicate the extraordinary tenacity with which certain peculiarities persist and are repeatedly passed on from one generation to another. This power of reproduction must, however, necessarily grow weaker, as an organ in course of time loses its original functions in adaptation to new ones. As a consequence of this, attempts at reconstruction necessarily become more and more imperfect.

The same is the case with many other muscles (*e.g.* the sternalis, levator claviculæ, latissimo-condyloideus, and epitrochleo-anconæus) which now only rarely occur in Man, and which, when they are present, furnish important indications of a long-past period in the development of the human race.

There is no good ground for doubting the possibility of the hereditary transmission of muscular anomalies, although, as Testut rightly remarks, the difficulty of obtaining material for a direct proof is evident. The difficulty in this case is greater than in that of mere external variation, such as pigmentation, different coloration of the opposite eyes, abnormal hairiness, birth-marking, polydactyly, and others akin to these.

It is reserved for future investigators to add to our as yet scanty knowledge on this subject, by using more fully the material which the different human families and races could afford us. It is not impossible that some of the views till now held, *e.g.* that Negroes and other low races do not differ specifically in their myology from the Caucasians, and do not show more frequent variations, may have to be modified.

Anthropotomy has here a great field. On the other hand, the mass of recorded observations upon muscular anomalies in general is so great, and the agreement of many of these with the condition normal in Apes is so marked, that the gap which usually separates the muscular system of Man from that of the Anthropoids appears to be completely bridged over (Testut).

THE NERVOUS SYSTEM

THROUGHOUT the animal kingdom the nervous system is more conservative in character than any other, and it thus offers a more limited field for the study of vestigial structures. The latter, however, as we shall see, are not altogether wanting; indeed, they may be here of special interest, as they afford the best proof of the extreme tenacity with which an organ, or some part of an organ, may persist and be transmitted through an immense period of time, when its functional activity is to a marked degree reduced, or even no longer evident.

The central nervous system of the Vertebrata, as is well known, arises from the so-called medullary folds of the outer germinal layer, and is thus essentially a modified derivative of the epiblast—the so-called "sensory layer." The latter, in the lower animals, *e.g.* certain Cœlenterates, in which there is no sharp differentiation into a central and a peripheral nervous system, remains superficial in position and is directly the medium of communication with the external world. This, combined with the fact that, in Vertebrates, the brain and spinal cord are among the first differentiated organs, is a distinct proof of the great age and physiological importance of the nervous system.

THE SPINAL CORD

When first differentiated, the nervous axis, as already mentioned, corresponds in extent with the axial skeleton; but it soon appears to shorten, partly from inequality of growth, and partly in consequence of modification taking place in the posterior portion of the vertebral column. The spinal cord no longer extends throughout the whole length of the vertebral canal, its posterior tapering extremity [*i.e.* the portion caudad of the spinal nerve-roots, where the filum terminale begins] reaches no farther down [in Man] than to about the boundary between the

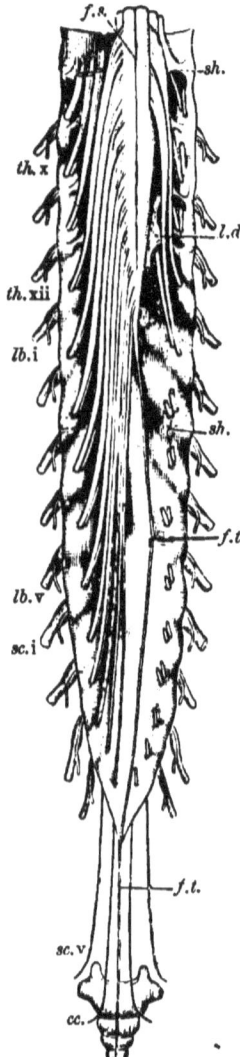

thoracic and lumbar portions of the column. This shortening, as above said, is more apparent than real, for the vertebral column [growing the more rapidly] extends farther and farther back beyond the posterior limit of the spinal cord. [It is worthy of remark that this inequality of growth, so marked in Man, is still more conspicuous among certain lower Mammals—*e.g.* the Hedgehog, in which the filum terminale commences in the anterior thoracic region.]

The filum terminale (*f.t.*, Fig. 76) runs through the lumbar and sacral regions of the vertebral column into the caudal; and this terminal filament, which grows with the growing vertebral column, is the vestigial homologue of the posterior portion of a spinal cord which, in the ancestors of Man, may have run evenly throughout the whole length of the vertebral column, as it now does in many lower Vertebrates. This process of reduction, which sets in at the posterior end of the spinal cord, is profoundly significant, as we have already had to describe a similar process of reduction going on at the posterior end of the axial skeleton itself (*ante*, pp. 28 *et seq.*).

I should like to suggest the consideration whether certain pathological conditions may not be traced to this source, if only indirectly? I refer to those frequent diseases of the spinal cord known as tabetic, which in by far the greater number of cases arise at its posterior end. May not the above described condition of the lumbar

FIG 76.—LOWER PORTION OF THE SPINAL CORD, WITH THE CAUDA EQUINA AND THE ENVELOPING DURA MATER. (Dorsal aspect.) One-half natural size. (After Schwalbe.)

The dura matral sheath has been opened up from behind and laid back; on the left side the roots of the nerves are represented entire; on the right, the lower of these are shown removed above their passage through the sheath, and the bones of the coccyx are delineated in their natural relative positions, in order to show the relations of the filum terminale and the coccygeal nerves.

cc., coccygeal nerves; *f.s.*, dorsal longitudinal fissure; *f.t.*, filum terminale, slightly displaced to the right side; *lb.* i and v, first and fifth lumbar nerves; *l.d.*, ligamentum denticulatum; *sc.* i and v, first and fifth sacral nerves; *sh.*, the dura matral sheath; *th.* x and xii, tenth and twelfth thoracic nerves.

portion of the myelon be considered as a predisposing factor in the degenerative processes apparent in such cases? A parallel to this occurs, it seems to me, in the processes of reduction at the upper part of the thorax already mentioned (*ante*, p. 43), and in the pathological processes which set in at the tips of the lungs, perhaps connected therewith.

That there are also *progressive* processes going on in the human spinal cord is probable, from the following observations made by Lenhossék on Mice, Guinea-pigs, Rabbits, and Cats. In these animals the pyramidal tracts are much more feebly developed than in Man (in whom they attain their highest differentiation), and their position in the spinal cord varies greatly. In the Guinea-pig, Mouse, and Rat, they run in the dorsal columns, in the Rabbit, the Cat, and other Carnivora, in the lateral, and in Man, partly in the lateral and partly in the ventral columns. This may perhaps be indicative of a gradual shifting of these tracts from the dorsal to the ventral columns, as we pass from the lower to the higher Mammalia; and it would be interesting to investigate this point in the Apes. Even in Man the definitive condition is not reached, for the fact that the pyramidal tracts may run either along the ventral or the lateral columns is evidence that they are still subject to variation.

Since the pyramidal tracts cross one another completely in all animals which have been examined, it seems likely that their alleged semi-decussation in Man is only apparent, as the elements of the ventral tracts do eventually cross one another. And further, since these ventral tracts are wanting in Man in fifteen cases per cent, it would be necessary, if belief in semi-decussation is to be persisted in, to consider that a certain number of individuals were remarkable exceptions in that important character. Inasmuch as this supposed variation is unaccompanied by exceptional conditions of other parts of the organism, it is altogether improbable that it exists.

I must refer the reader to the works of Waldeyer for an account of the differences to be found between the human spinal cord and that of the Gorilla.

Before turning to the condition of the brain, attention may be drawn to a small body which lies beneath the last coccygeal vertebra, known as the coccygeal gland. This, on account of its close relation to the arteria sacralis media, is usually, but, it seems to me, incorrectly, relegated in text-books of human anatomy to a connection with the vascular system. Considering the established fact that the caudal end of the spinal cord, at an early period of development, reached exactly to that point at which the coccygeal gland is found later, and that, as already

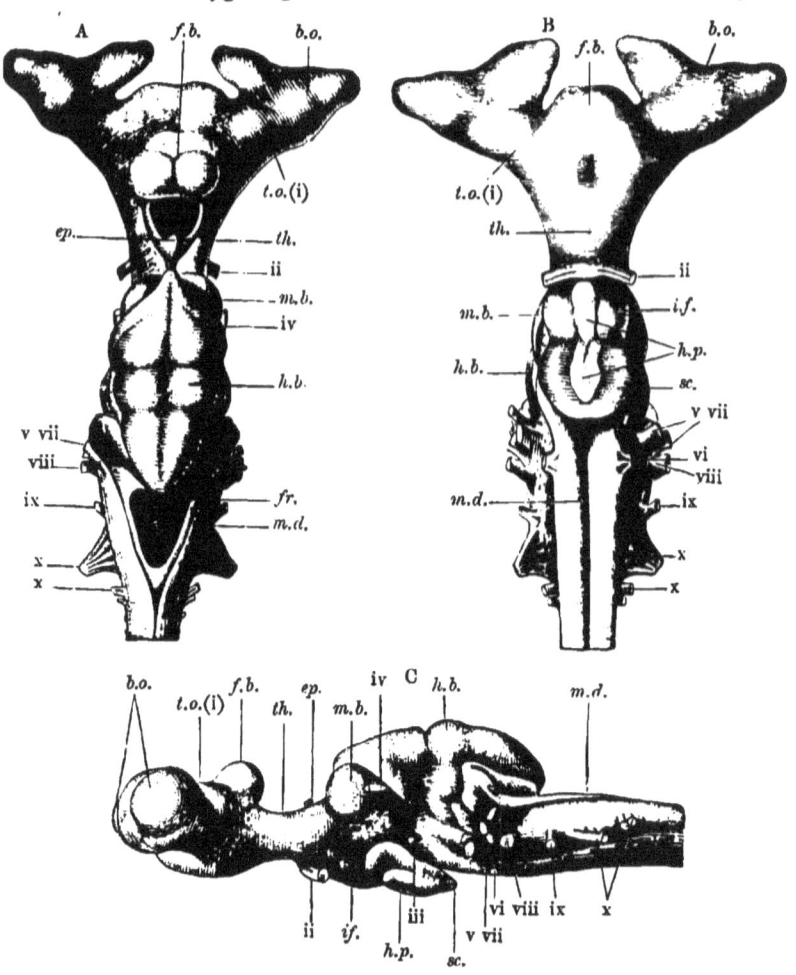

FIG. 77.—BRAIN OF A DOG-FISH (*Scyllum canicula*).
A, dorsal ; B, ventral ; C, side view ; *b.o.*, bulbus olfactorius ; *ep.*, pineal gland cut short ; *f.b.*, fore-brain ; *f.r.*, fossa rhomboidalis ; *h.b.*, hind-brain (cerebellum) ; *hp.*, hypophysis ; *i.f.*, infundibulum ; i to x, first to the tenth cranial nerves (the thalamencephalon and the fossa rhomboidalis are in life covered by epithelium (plexus chorioidei), not delineated ; the ventral vagus roots are omitted from Fig. B) ; *m.d.*, medulla oblongata ; *m.h.*, mid-brain (optic lobes) ; *sc.*, saccus vasculosus ; *t.o.*, tractus olfactorius.

mentioned, all the important variations at the caudal end of the trunk are primarily associated with degeneration of the spinal cord at that region, I am inclined to think that some connection exists between the latter and the coccygeal gland. This gland is undeniably a vestigial organ, but we have as yet no certain knowledge of either its significance or its primitive history.

BRAIN

The human brain, in the course of its development, passes in regular order through conditions characteristic of certain of the lower Vertebrata (ex. disposition of the cerebral vesicles, smooth surface of the hemispheres), and these lower conditions are in rare cases retained, as in many microcephalous individuals, as the probable result of arrested development. There are not infrequent deviations from the normal arrangement of the cerebral furrows and convolutions, which are closely connected with the development of the gray matter. These deviations can be best studied by the aid of Comparative Anatomy and Ontogeny, and the same may be said of the posterior cornu of the lateral ventricle, the calcar avis, and the eminentia collateralis Meckelii. Conspicuous among variable cerebral furrows we note the parieto-occipital fissure (*f.po.*, Fig. 78), which is occasionally very pronounced. This fissure runs out laterally, and may probably be a reversion to the pithecoid type (it is called in German the "Affenspalte"). In its normal condition it seems almost to be vanishing, as compared with its supposed homologue in the brain of the Ape.[1]

In spite of difference in detail, there is a closer general resemblance between the human and the Anthropoid brains than between the brains of any other two Vertebrate groups.

With regard to the weight of the brain in Anthropoids generally, the material as yet examined is not sufficient for the determination of averages and formulation of general conclusions. With the Chimpanzee, however, this is not the case, as a rela-

[1] [The term parieto-occipital fissure insufficiently defines this supposed homologue of the "Affenspalte." Cunningham in a recent elaborate treatise (*Cunningham Memoirs*, vii. *R. Irish Acad.*, 1892) has devoted much attention to this topic. He and other leading authorities are agreed that, whether the "Affenspalte" of the Ape is present in the human adult or not, the "fissura perpendicularis externa" of the fœtus is its homologue. During the passage of these pages through the press, Benham, in a very careful study of the Chimpanzee's brain, has shown (*Qu. Jour. Micr. Sci.*, vol. xxxvii. p. 47) that the transverse occipital fissure which replaces this external perpendicular may be genetically related to it, and that therefore Ecker's original view that the "Affenspalte" of the Ape is represented in the adult human brain by that which he termed the "sulcus occipitalis transversus" may be correct.]

128   THE STRUCTURE OF MAN

tively large number of specimens have been examined; and

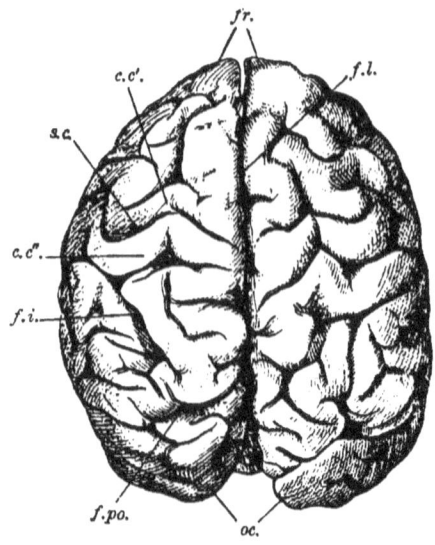

FIG. 78.—CEREBRUM OF A FEMALE CHIMPANZEE TWO YEARS OLD. (Dorsal aspect.) (Showing Asymmetrical Development.) *c.c'., c.c".*, anterior and posterior central convolutious ; *f.i.*, interparietal fissure ; *f.l.*, the longitudinal fissure ; *f.p.o.*, parieto-occipital fissure ; *fr.*, frontal lobes ; *oc.*, occipital lobes ; *s.c.*, sulcus centralis.

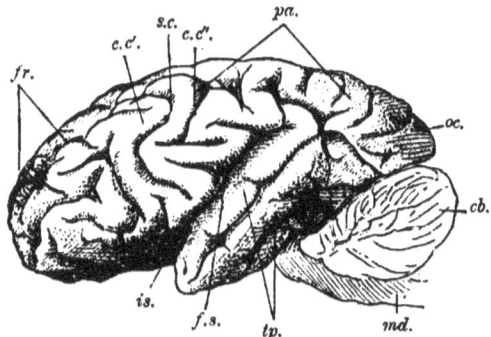

FIG. 79.—BRAIN OF A FEMALE CHIMPANZEE TWO YEARS OLD. (Lateral aspect.) *cb.*, cerebellum ; *c.c'., c.c".*, anterior and posterior central convolutions ; *fr.*, frontal lobe ; *f.s.*, fissura Sylvii ; *is.*, island of Reil ; *md.*, medulla oblongata ; *oc.*, occipital lobe ; *pa.*, parietal lobe ; *s.c.*, sulcus centralis ; *tp.*, temporal lobe.

further, a review of the facts known concerning the Gorilla and Orang reveals statistics which may be of use to future investigators. For details on this subject I must, however, refer the reader to the works of Möller and others.[1]

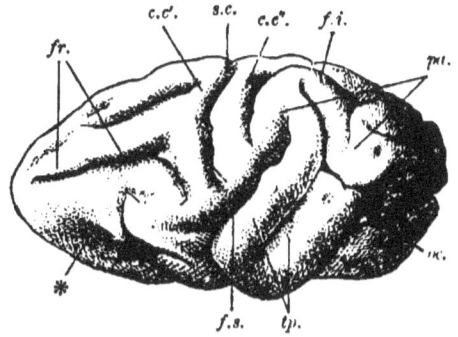

FIG. 80.—CEREBRUM OF THE GIBBON (HYLOBATES). (Lateral Aspect.)
References as for Fig. 79.

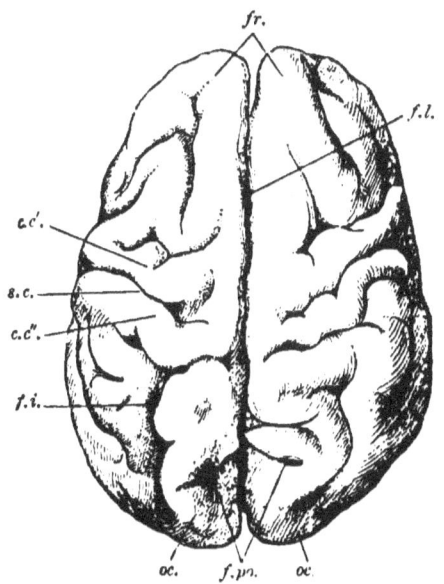

FIG. 81.—CEREBRUM OF A HUMAN EMBRYO IN THE SEVENTH TO THE EIGHTH MONTH.
(Dorsal Aspect.)
References as for Fig. 78.

---

[1] Joh. Möller, *Abhandlg. d. Zool. u. Anthrop. Ethnol. Museums zu Dresden*, 1890-1891. [Cf. also D. J. Cunningham, *Cunningham Memoirs, R. Irish Acad.*, No. II., 1886; No. VII., 1892; and Benham, *op. cit.* In these works the literature of the subject will be found.]

K

If we take the average weight of the body of a Chimpanzee from two to four years old as 8½ kilogrs., and the average weight of brain as 343 grs., we shall have 1 : 24·7 as the relative weight of the latter. An Orang of the same age appears to possess a rather heavier brain (1 : 22·3 or 340 : 7600). A comparison of these two Anthropoids with Man, the ratio of whose brain weight to his body weight between the second and fourth years ranges from 1 : 18 to 1 : 16, shows that the difference at this age is not great, as would seem natural when we recall the greater similarity to human beings shown by young Anthropoids. In older Chimpanzees (90-106,6 cm. long)

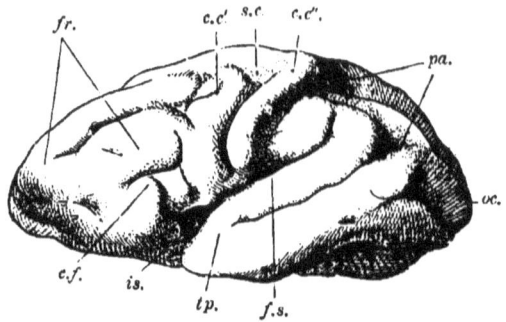

FIG. 82.—CEREBRUM OF A HUMAN EMBRYO SEVEN TO EIGHT MONTHS OLD.
(Lateral View.)
References as for Fig. 79.

the relative brain weight is markedly lower, viz. 1 : 42,5 (391 : 16650) or 1 : 52 (375,6 : 19500). It is probable, however, that the average brain weight in older Chimpanzees is considerably lower, as in a body weighing 28 kilogrs. it scaled 1 : 75. If this is the case, a comparison with an adult human being, in whom the average brain weight is 1 : 40-35, shows that the brain of Man is relatively at least twice as heavy as that of the Chimpanzee, and absolutely three or four times as heavy. We learn from this that the brain of the Ape, unlike that of Man, develops little with age, and attains its definitive condition far sooner.

The Chimpanzee and the Orang appear to have approximately the same brain weights, but the Gorilla stands markedly distinct from them, its body being far larger, while its brain does not correspondingly increase in size. The weight of the body of an adult Gorilla being taken at 94-95 kilogrs., and the brain weight at 425,25 grs., the relative weight of the latter would be 1 : 220 (Möller). A comparison of the cerebral surface shows that Man differs from the Anthropoids in the preponderance of the frontal lobe (*fr.*, Figs. 78-82) and, to a lesser degree, of the occipital lobe (*oc.*), and in a corresponding backward extension of the temporal lobe (*tp.*). The parietal lobe (*pa.*) is about equally developed in the brains of Man and of Anthropoids (Möller).

Since this subject has so far been, comparatively speaking, little investigated, and since our knowledge of the functional

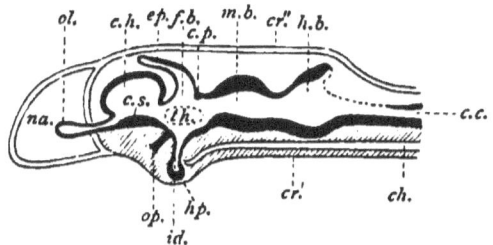

FIG. 83.—HYPOTHETICAL MEDIAN-LONGITUDINAL SECTION THROUGH THE SKULL AND BRAIN OF A VERTEBRATE EMBRYO. (Partly after Huxley.)
cr'., basis cranii ; *ch.*, chorda dorsalis ; *cr''.*, roof of the skull ; *na.*, nasal cavity ; *c.h.*, cerebral hemisphere, with the corpus striatum (*c.s.*) lying basally, and the olfactory lobe (*ol.*) anteriorly ; *f.b.*, thalamencephalon (fore-brain), which has been produced dorsally into the pineal gland (*ep.*), and basally into the infundibulum (*if.*), *hp.*, the hypophysis. Anteriorly, the base of the optic nerve (*op.*) is seen, and in the lateral wall the position of the optic thalamus is indicated (*th.*) ; *c.p.*, posterior commissure ; *m.b.*, mid-brain ; *h.b.*, hind-brain ; *c.c.*, canalis centralis.

significance of the different regions of the brain is still far from complete, no general conclusions as to the possible correlation of these differences with mental peculiarities can be drawn.

The slight projection of the cerebellum from below the edges of the occipital lobes in Anthropoids, is due less to the narrowness of the latter than to the striking breadth of the cerebellum itself (Möller). Even in man the occipital lobes do not always completely cover the cerebellum, but in this matter considerable variation occurs.[1]

Special interest attaches to the pineal gland (epiphysis cerebri) (*ep.*, Figs. 84 and 86) which arises in the region of the roof of the fore-brain.

In the lower Vertebrates this organ either lies free or is embedded in a depression or foramen (parietal foramen) of the

[1] It must be left to future investigators to prove whether the topography of the course of the fibres in the optic chiasma given by Joh. Möller for Anthropoids, *i.e.* the constant occurrence at the surface of certain groups of fibres, has a parallel in Man (perhaps in embryos or the lower races).

skull roof. In Man and Mammals the pineal gland is pushed away from the free surface of the brain by the growth of the hemispheres, and it is thus shifted back till it comes to lie in a depression between the corpora quadrigemina (nates). It is in

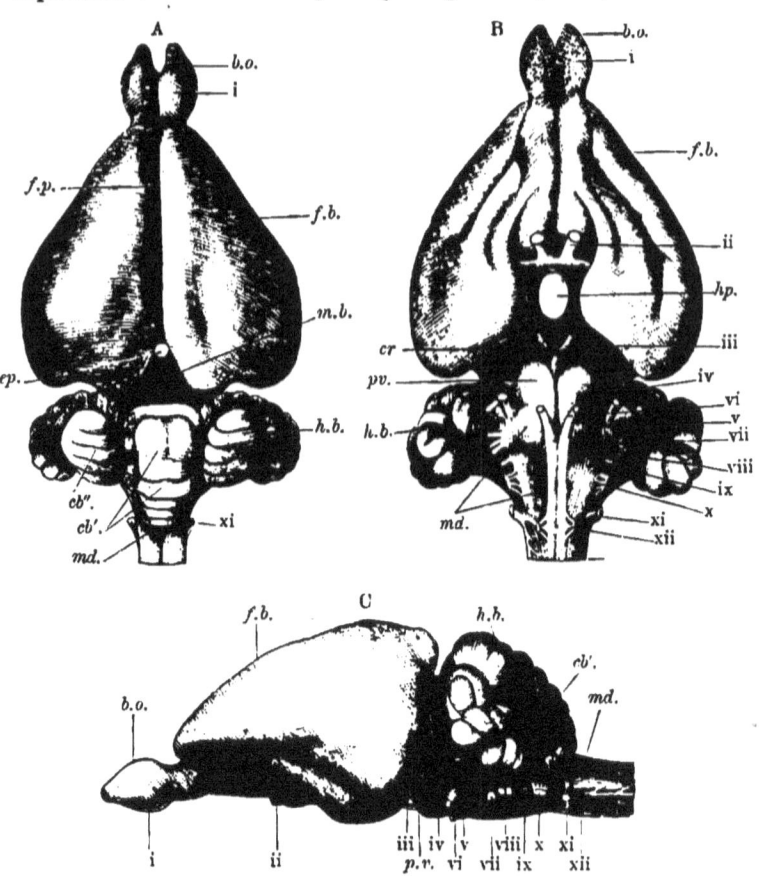

FIG. 84.—BRAIN OF A RABBIT.

A, dorsal; B, ventral; C, lateral view; *b.o.*, bulbus olfactorius; *cb'.*, median lobe of the cerebellum (superior vermis); *cb".*, its lateral lobe; *cr.*, crura cerebri; *ep.*, glandula pinealis; *f.b.*, fore-brain; *f.p.*, fissura pallii; *h.b.*, hind-brain; *h.p.*, hypophysis; i to xii, first to the twelfth cranial nerves; *m.b.*, mid-brain; *md.*, medulla oblongata; *p.v.*, region of the pons.

this position recognisable, in Man, as the well known dorso-ventrally compressed pine- or cone-shaped organ. Into it the lumen of the third ventricle frequently extends; and its base divides into two stalks, which pass directly into the tæniæ medullares and thalami

THE NERVOUS SYSTEM

optici. The pineal gland of Anthropoids is identical in appearance with that of Man.

The pineal gland in Man is remarkable for its rich vascularity and for its cellular follicles, in which concretions (brain sand) may develop.

This "gland" has all along claimed the special attention of morphologists; and as great difficulty has been found in under-

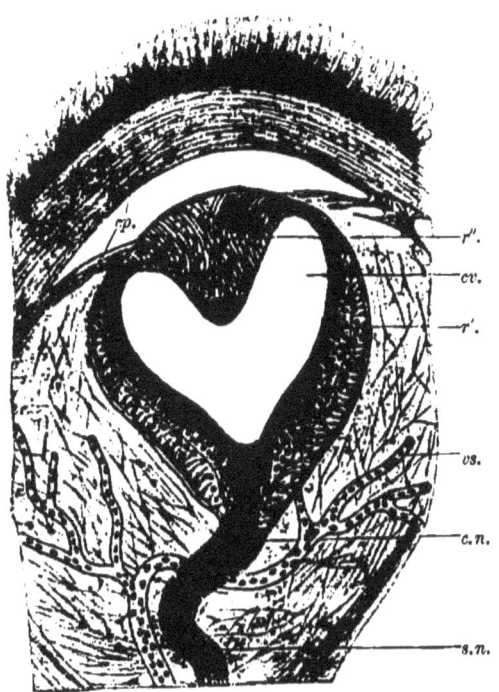

FIG. 85.—LONGITUDINAL SECTION THROUGH THE PINEAL ORGAN OF A REPTILE (*Hatteria punctata*). (Slightly magnified.) (After Baldwin Spencer.) *cp.*, connective tissue capsule ; *r″.*, "lens"; *cv.*, cavity of the organ filled with fluid; *r′.*, retina-like portion of the vesicle ; *vs.*, blood-vessels ; *c.n.*, cells in the nerve stalk (*s.n.*).

standing it, it has received very different explanations. It is only in recent years that light has been thrown upon it by numerous works devoted to its comparative anatomy and ontogeny. It has been proved that, in close connection with the actual stalk of the gland, there is a second vesicular outgrowth, which, in certain Vertebrates, shows undeniable traces of being a rudimentary unpaired organ of sight. [This organ is now known to arise during development in all classes of Vertebrates], and to have undergone degeneration in the course of Phylogeny, as the roof of the skull became more and more solid. The nerve belonging to it is, so far as is known, most fully retained in certain Reptiles. In some animals this organ only occurs in the embryo, and altogether disappears at a later stage.

In examining the finer histological structure of the pineal or parietal organ in the Lizard-like Reptiles and the Slow-worms, we find the upper wall may in many cases become thickened to form a transparent epithelial plate (r''., Fig. 85), which is often lens-shaped, while the rest of the epiphysial vesicle (r'.), which is often flattened, is differentiated into a multilaminar "retina." "Lens" and "retina" thus arise in complete continuity out of one and the same structure; and it is only at a late stage in development that a more or less distinct demarcation between them is effected (Béraneck). The organ is invested by a capsule of connective tissue (cp.).

In many cases the skin which overlies the parietal organ, as well as the connective and dural tissues below it, remain free from pigment, indeed they are sometimes so clear and transparent that they might be considered as a kind of cornea. This justifies the assumption that the function of the organ may not be altogether lost even now.[1] Owsiannikow claims to have found traces of a vitreous body within it.

According to Leydig, Selenka, and others, there is found in the embryos of various Vertebrates (Selachians, Reptiles, Marsupials, and probably in others) another unpaired dorsal appendage of the fore-brain, for which Selenka has suggested the name "frontal organ" or "paraphysis."

Whereas the epiphysis grows forward, the paraphysis, which arises much later ontogenetically, grows backward and, when the epiphysis is once fixed in the epidermis, pushes itself in under that organ, so that the parietal eye comes to rest on the paraphysis as on a cushion. Until the embryo is mature, the epithelial tube of the paraphysis remains hollow and in open communication with the cavity of the brain.

If it be established that the pineal organ and gland are really *sui generis*, distinct in origin, there is evidence of three out-

---

[1] [In view of the intimate relationship between birds and reptiles, it is an interesting circumstance that Klinckowström has discovered in embryos of certain of the former (*Anser, Larus*.) a "brow spot," which in its structural differentiation suggests not only the last trace of a pineal organ, but a pineal scale like that of living lizards. Spengel's *Zoolog. Jahrb., Anat. Abth.* Bd. v. p. 177.]

growths from the roof of the brain, of which one, the pineal organ, can with certainty be regarded as originally a sense organ.

[Locy, from the study of young shark embryos, has adduced reason for believing[1] that, at an early stage in development, two pairs of accessory optic vesicles appear, concurrently with those giving rise to the retinæ of the paired eyes. The ultimate fate of the former has yet to be fully worked out, and nothing is as yet known concerning the post-embryonic development of the paraphysis. There is, however, reason for thinking that the latter probably takes part in the formation of the choroid plexus; but whether this is the case or not, Locy's observation seems to indicate that the pineal organ at least may have been originally paired.]

At the under surface of the thalamencephalon, and connected with the infundibulum, there lies an appendage of the brain called the hypophysis or pituitary body.

Two distinct structures enter into the formation of this organ, one glandular and the other nervous. The former arises in Man and the higher Vertebrates by a constriction from the primitive mouth sac (stomodæum) of the embryo, and the latter is, as a rule, assigned genetically to the floor of the thalamencephalon. Future research must show how far this is the primary origin of at least the glandular portion of the organ, and this is the more desirable since some very interesting results recently obtained by von Kupffer, from the study of Lamprey and Sturgeon embryos, have given new zest to the inquiry into the primitive history of this enigmatical structure. The subject cannot be dealt with in detail here, but mention may be made of at least a few of the chief points concerning it.

According to von Kupffer, the hypophysis arises in the above-named Fishes in the manner described by Scott for the Amphibia (*Amblystoma*). At a very early embryonic stage an ectodermal cell-strand grows in from the anterior region of the head. This cell-strand in the Sturgeon consists of two closely applied epithelial plates which form a fold, and at the point at which it arises the antero-dorsal border of the fore-brain is connected with a thickened portion of the ectoderm by an originally hollow and subsequently solid tract. This ectodermal thickening is termed by von Kupffer the median olfactory plate, and the corresponding cerebral outgrowth the lobus olfactorius impar: in fact, according to this author, the Sturgeon,

[1] [*Anat. Anzeiger*, vol. ix. p. 169.]

during its earliest development, passes through a monorhinal stage, and probably more or less distinct traces of this can be discovered in the embryos of all Vertebrates.

From this median or unpaired olfactory plate, therefore, which may be homologous with the anterior neuropore of embryologists, and with the "olfactory organ" of *Amphioxus*, the hypophysial tube arises, prior to the formation of the mouth, and, growing down gradually, approaches the base of the brain till it reaches the neighbourhood of the infundibulum. The epithelial strand later separates off from the ectoderm, and finally to a great

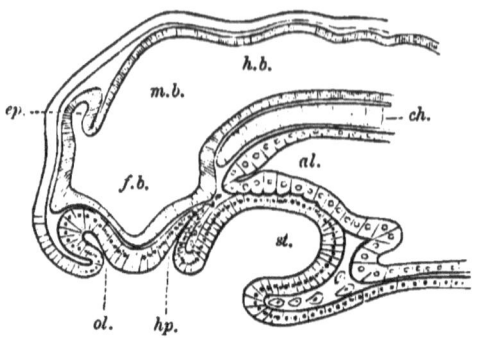

FIG. 86.—MEDIAN LONGITUDINAL SECTION THROUGH THE HEAD OF A NEWLY-HATCHED LARVA OF THE SMALL LAMPREY (*Petromyzon planeri*).
f.b., fore-brain; *m.b.*, mid-brain; *h.b.*, hind-brain; *ep.*, glandula pinealis; *ol.*, olfactory organ; *hp.*, hypophysis; *st.*, buccal sac (stomodæum); *al.*, endodermal cavity (mid-gut); *ch.*, chorda dorsalis.

extent degenerates, so that at last nothing remains of it but its constricted, swollen end—the glandular hypophysis of adult anatomy. A somewhat similar arrangement is seen, as has already been said, in Ammocœtes and certain tailed Amphibians.

The facts appear to me strongly to confirm the view that the hypophysis corresponds with the primitive mouth (archistoma) of the ancestors of the Vertebrata.

The present vertebrate mouth (neostoma) is by some considered to have arisen by the running together of a pair of branchial clefts; but this is by no means definitely proved.

According to Scott, the close connection between the hypophysis and the oral invagination (stomodæum) of the higher Vertebrates was developed secondarily in consequence of cephalic flexure, due to the preponderating development of the fore-brain. If so, the hypophysis had originally no relation either to the mouth or the nose, but is to be regarded as an organ (? sensory), inherited from a supposed invertebrate ancestor, which originally had the form of a blind sac on the free surface of the head, close to the olfactory organ. Scott and von Kupffer thus differ considerably in their views; [but whatever the original significance of the hypophysis, all observers are agreed that it is the vestige of an organ originally distinct from the present vertebrate mouth and from the nose of at least the gnathostomata. With respect to it, the Vertebrata collectively fall into two distinct and diversely modified assemblages, viz. (i.) the *Epicraniata* (Lampreys and Hags), in which it is carried up with the nose and perforates the basis cranii from above; and (ii.) the *Hypocraniata* (Fishes proper, Amphibians, and Amniota), in which it is carried down and inwards with the mouth, and perforates the basis cranii from beneath.]

We still have to consider those cases in which degeneration of the brain is either beginning or has made some progress. We find an instance of commencing degeneration in the lobus olfactorius, to which we shall have to return when considering the olfactory organs. A case of advanced degeneration is seen in the roof of the fourth ventricle. This, in Man, as in all Vertebrates, becomes almost entirely transformed in the course of Ontogeny into a vascular membrane, overlying a simple epithelium, and continuous laterally and anteriorly with the pia-mater. The lining epithelium is continuous laterally and posteriorly with the delicate structures bordering on the calamus scriptorius known as the obex, ponticulus, and ligula (tænia). These all consist of nervous tissue, and are to be classed · morphologically with the epithelial layer just mentioned. The rudimentary character of the series is evident, and the same applies to the velum medullare posterius.

In contrast to the degenerate portions of the brain, other parts are found to be in course of progressive development; these more than compensate for the loss not only of the above mentioned, but of all other degenerating parts. We have only to mention the cerebrum, with its continually developing complexity of the nerve tracts, especially the complex components of the gray cortex, which, as the organs of the mental faculties, are kept in constant touch with the surrounding world by means of the centripetal and centrifugal tracts of the peripheral nervous system.

To this topic we shall have to return. It will here suffice to mention one more portion of the brain in which variation in form and size are evident to the naked eye, and are, I consider, to be interpreted as progressive. This is the lobus occipitalis of the cerebral hemisphere, in which we find great variation in the extent of the calcar avis, and the posterior cornu of the lateral ventricle. Exact statistics on this subject are a desideratum.

[In connection with the question of structural degeneration of the brain, certain recent observations of Forsyth-Major are of especial interest. It has been generally assumed that the smooth cerebrum and exposed cerebellum of the Lemurs, which are placed at the root of the order Primates of which Man is the highest member, are primitive characters, indicative of a relationship with and origin from a lowly order of Mammals. Forsyth-Major has discovered evidence of structural simplification and degeneration, during Ontogeny, of the brain of certain Lemurs (apparently in correlation with preponderating development of the face and nose) which points to the conclusion that the supposed primitive characters named may be secondary and retrogressive— a welcome suggestion, in view of Cope's discovery that the oldest known Lemurs (Anaptomorphidæ) had large and highly-organised brains. The brain of the human fœtus, at from three to five months, develops certain convolutions which are early lost and have nothing to do with those of the adult. Kölliker, Beer, Cunningham, and others have investigated them, and the latter, suggesting that they may be the expression of mechanical effects consequent on a "quadrupedal growth pause" in development, has proposed to term them "transitory fissures" (microgyri of Beer). Considerable interest attaches to the occasional appearance of convolutions upon the surface of the hemispheres in normally smooth-brained Mammals ; as also to the question whether these are progressive structures, or conversely, whether they, and the convolutions which seem to disappear during Ontogeny among the Lemuroidea, may have anything to do with the "transitory fissures" above-named. A wide field of inquiry is here opened up, which gives promise of most important results.][1]

PERIPHERAL NERVOUS SYSTEM

But few retrogressive phenomena are here met with ; among these are the present condition of the rami recurrentes of the three branches of the trigeminus and of the vagus, which run to the dura mater, and further, of the ramus auricularis of the latter nerve. The fact that in the region of the hypoglossus vestiges of the posterior roots with their ganglia have been found in human embryos, as they were long since in certain lower Mammals, indicates that assimilation of spinal or vertebral elements may be going on in the occipital region of the skull. Certain delicate nerve loops which lie in the region of the trigeminus, facialis

---

[1] [Cf. Forsyth-Major in Rothschild's *Novitates Zoologicæ*, vol. i. p. 35 ; and Cunningham, *Cunningham Memoirs, R. Irish Acad.*, No. VII. p. 30.]

and glossopharyngeus nerves, or are connected with their ganglia, may possibly be retrogressive in nature; but we cannot enter further into their study here, as to do so would lead us too far into Comparative Anatomy, and be beyond the purpose of this work.

The variations which are continually taking place in the brachial and lumbo-sacral nerve plexuses, in connection with the shifting of the limbs and their girdles during development, have been already considered in detail (*ante*, pp. 95 and 96).

THE SYMPATHETIC SYSTEM

Here also extraordinary variations are to be found in the form, number, and size of the ganglia of the main trunks, in the peripheral plexuses, and in the connections between the two chief trunks; but, except in the caudal portion of this system, we are not justified in assuming that we have to do with retrogressive phenomena.

THE SENSE ORGANS

THE sense organs have always been classified into lower and higher, and that not without justification. Conspicuous among the lower sense organs are those of the tactile sense lying in the integument; and by the higher sense organs are understood the olfactory, visual, auditory, and gustatory apparatus, which are located in special depressions or cavities of the head.

It may now be considered as certainly established that all the latter may be traced back phylogenetically to tegumental sense organs, and that their sensory epithelia are to be regarded as modified epidermal derivatives.

INTEGUMENTAL SENSE ORGANS

It appears to me not improbable that the tactile bodies which are profusely scattered throughout the integument of man are genetically closely connected with his gradual loss of hair. I am led to this conclusion by the fact that tactile bodies appear in the lower Mammals principally, indeed, perhaps exclusively, in places where there is no hair (proboscis, entrance to the mouth, plantar surface of the paw). They appear unnecessary in hairy parts of the body, because the hairs themselves, being richly provided with nerves, are capable of exercising a delicate tactile function.

How far certain epithelial structures proved by Maurer to exist in the hair germs are to be deduced from phylogenetically older tegumental sense organs like those of the Anamnia, must be established by further investigation (compare also the already-mentioned temporary appearance of sense organs in the cephalic region in embryos, *ante*, p. 133).

THE OLFACTORY ORGAN

The Number and Structure of the Olfactory Ridges and the Turbinals

Following Broca and Turner, we may divide Mammals, according to the development of their olfactory apparatus, with especial reference to its cerebral portion ["rhinencephalon," "lobe limbique"] into series, viz.:

[i. Osmatic series, turbinals present and usually five in number.]

(a) Macrosmatic [organs of smell largely developed], (most Mammals, e.g. Edentata, Ungulata, Carnivora, Rodentia, Marsupialia, and Lemuroidea).

(b) Microsmatic [olfactory apparatus relatively feeble] (Pinnipedia, Whalebone - Whales, Apes, Man, and Monotremata).

[ii. Anosmatic series, organs of smell, apparently absent in the adult]—(Dolphins and Toothed - Whales generally, although many of these require further investigation with regard to this point).[1]

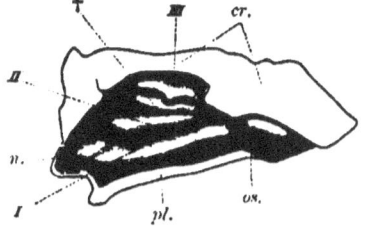

FIG. 87.—LATERAL VIEW OF THE NASAL CHAMBER OF A HUMAN EMBRYO.

I, II, III, the three olfactory ridges; †, supernumerary ridge which occurs in the embryo; *n.*, tip of the nose; *pl.*, hard palate; *cr.*, base of the skull; *os.*, ostium of the Eustachian tube.

The first point to be established is the primitive number of the olfactory ridges. The investigations of Zuckerkandl lead to the conclusion that the original number of these ridges was comparatively small, and that where, among Mammals, we have a large number or a more complicated form of turbinal, they have been secondarily acquired in the interest of a greater physiological efficiency.

Most orders of Mammals, e.g. the greater number of Carnivora, Rodentia, Insectivora, Lemuroidea, Marsupialia, with *Ornithorhynchus* (*Echidna ?*), have five olfactory ridges; but the Ungulata

---

[1] [Kükenthal has recently worked out the development of the olfactory organ in the Delphinidæ, and has proved (i) that the union of the external nasal apertures is a secondary process occurring during Ontogeny, and (ii) that in the young embryo well-developed olfactory lobes and bulbs are present which disappear in the adult.— *Denksch. d. medic.-natur-wiss. Gesellsch.*, Jena, Bd. iii. pp. 326 *et seq.*]

have, as a rule, more than five, and sometimes as many as eight. The Edentata possess from six to eleven (*Orycteropus* has eleven, *Dasypus* nine, *Bradypus* and *Manis* seven, *Myrmecophaga* six), and the Primates from one to three.

At a late embryonic period three olfactory ridges are often present in Man, inasmuch as between the superior and inferior a third projects into the lumen of the nose (cf. Fig. 87). This last, when present, is more or less distinct at birth, but it becomes reduced later, the superior ethmo-turbinal, as a rule, growing over it like a cover. With this superior ethmo-turbinal, which must be considered as primary, the rudiment of a fourth is found (cf. Fig.); but this is further differentiated only in exceptional cases. We thus have at least four ethmo-turbinals represented in the developing human nose, with three olfactory meatuses; and this arrangement recalls those Mammals in which there are four corresponding ridges present in the adult.

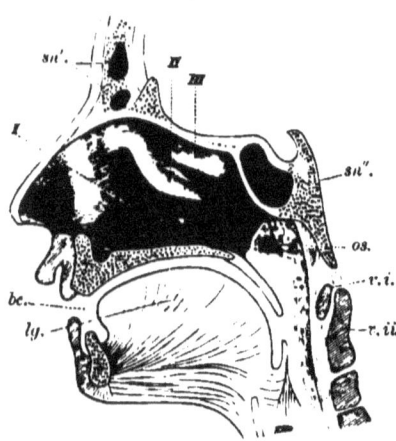

FIG. 88.—SAGITTAL SECTION THROUGH THE NASAL AND BUCCAL CAVITIES OF THE HUMAN HEAD.

I, II, III, the three olfactory ridges; *sn'.*, frontal sinus; *sn".*, sphenoidal sinus; *os.*, opening of Eustachian tube; *bc.*, entrance to the mouth; *lg.*, tongue; *v.i.*, atlas vertebra; *v.ii.*, axis vertebra.

[Concerning variation of the olfactory meatuses of the human adult, on recent examination of 152 individuals,[1] the dominant condition—presence of three—was observed in 56 per cent; four were noted in 41 per cent, and five in 1·3 per cent. In three instances (*i.e.* approximately in 2 per cent) only two were found, the superior turbinated bone being absent; and in one of these "there was a horizontal plate of cartilage projecting into the nasal fossa from the septum on a level with the inferior turbinated bone."]

When it is further remembered that the maxillary, frontal, and sphenoidal sinuses (*sn'.*, *sn".*, Fig. 88) are also lined by olfactory mucous membrane,

[1] [Made under the auspices of the Collective Investigation Committee of the Anatomical Society of Great Britain and Ireland. See *Jour. Anat. and Phys.*, vol. xxviii. p. 73.]

and that in the sinus frontalis of the embryo (as Professor Killian, who has paid especial attention to this subject, has kindly informed me) even now ridge-like structures sometimes occur, reminding one in the manner of their origin of the ethmoidal system, it seems probable that there was once a still more highly specialised development of the olfactory organ.

The above remarks apply to the olfactory region proper, *i.e.* to the ethmoidal labyrinth with its olfactory ridges. I have so far purposely avoided the term turbinal, and have always used instead the word ethmo-turbinal, or Schwalbe's term "olfactory ridge," in order to exclude any suggestion of parallelism with the "turbinal" of the lower Vertebrata. But we now come to the question of the persistence of the latter among the Mammalia. To these animals it has been handed down as the "inferior turbinal," but it now possesses no olfactory epithelium, having evidently undergone a change of function. In animals in which smell is acute, it is folded or more or less branched, *i.e.* is much more complicated than in animals with less keen scent, in which it is merely singly or doubly scrolled. The latter must be considered as the more primitive condition, from which the former was secondarily developed.

The conditions which have led up to reduction of the olfactory organ in the vertebrate series are very various. In Man its degeneration is due to the subordinate part played by it. The olfactory apparatus is here, as Broca has rightly remarked, but a modest vassal of the brain, which does not reach the perfection of the other higher sense organs.

JACOBSON'S ORGAN

The first indications of this organ appear to occur among the tailed Amphibia,[1] in the form of a small ventral diverticulum of the nasal cavity (*jc.*, Fig. 89, A, B), which either retains its original position throughout life, or in the course of development becomes shifted so as to lie in the maxillary sinus (Fig. 89, E).

At exactly the same point near the nasal septum, where, in the Amphibia, this organ arises, in the Amniota Jacobson's organ is found, in the form of a diverticulum of the principal nasal

[1] Apparent indications of this apparatus are forthcoming in certain fishes (*Polypterus*).

144 THE STRUCTURE OF MAN

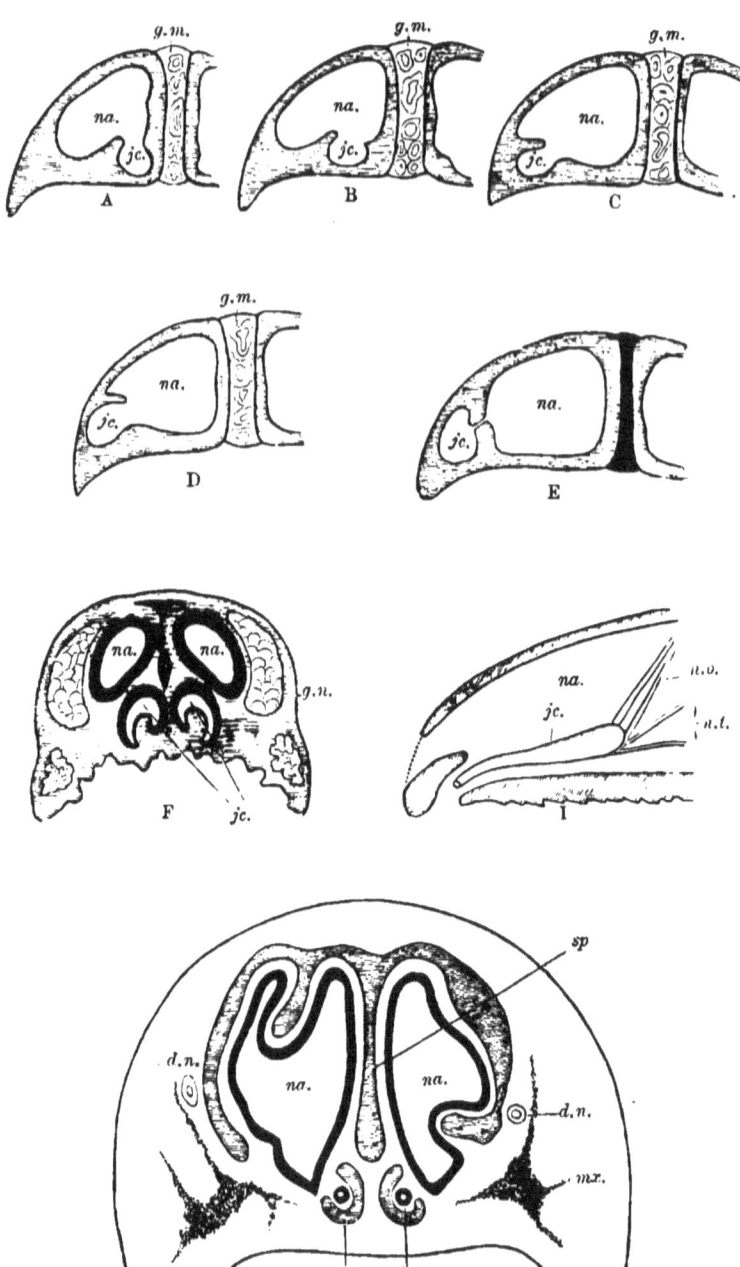

THE SENSE ORGANS

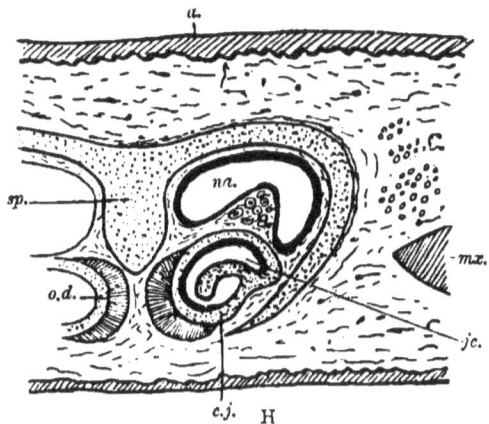

FIG. 89.—A-D, VARIOUS STAGES OF DEVELOPMENT OF [THE SO-CALLED] JACOBSON'S ORGAN OF THE URODELIA, illustrated by a series of transverse sections. F, transverse section through the nose and Jacobson's organ of *Lacerta agilis*; G, the same of a placental Mammal; H, the same of *Ornithorhynchus*, after Symington; I, diagrammatic side view of G.

In A the organ commences medially and basally; in D the lateral position is attained; E, the *Gymnophione*, in which separation from the principal cavity is effected; *na.*, nasal cavity; *jc.*, Jacobson's organ; *cj.*, Jacobson's cartilage; *g.m.*, inter-maxillary gland; *g.n.*, nasal gland; *n.o.*, olfactory nerve; *n.t.*, trigeminal nerve; *d.n.*, nasal duct; *mx.*, upper jaw; *sp.*, septum nasi; *o.d.*, dumb-bell-shaped bone, forming a support for Jacobson's organ.

cavity (*jc.*, Fig. 88, G, H, I). In most Mammals this becomes constricted off and secondarily connected with the buccal cavity. A lateral displacement does not take place, and the organ remains between the floor of the nasal cavity and the roof of the mouth, *i.e.* in its original position. It is always lined with a pronounced sensory epithelium, innervated by the ventral fasciculus of the olfactory nerve (*n.o.*, Fig. I).

Recent investigation has proved, without doubt, that vestiges of a Jacobson's organ are to be found in adult human beings. Before considering these in detail, however, certain structures which attracted the attention of the earlier investigators need to be dealt with.

Huscke's "plough-share cartilage" in Man was formerly regarded as the vestige of the two cartilaginous tubes lying near the base of the nasal septum, which in many lower Mammals envelop the organ of Jacobson. This is incorrect, since, as Spurgat has shown, the same cartilages are found in the human organs of Jacobson as in those of the lower Mammalia, but in a much reduced condition. These organs, together with the Stenson's canals, open into the buccal cavity through the ductus incisivi. The latter are sometimes wide, sometimes constricted, and they communicate with the mouth either independently or by a common orifice. In fresh embryos the passage of the canal is to be found open only in exceptional cases; there are usually two canals present on both the buccal and nasal surfaces of the palate, the former of these are usually the more prolonged. Both pairs are lined with mucous membrane, and, ending blindly, form together an obtuse angle. Traces of the buccal ends of these canals may still be found in some adults in the form of epithelial strands; as a rule, however, they disappear without leaving any trace, while the upper or nasal portions persist.

Between the two canals, or their vestiges, which run up from the buccal cavity just behind the inner incisors, there is on the palate a papilla, the so-called papilla palatina incisiva (*p.p.*, Fig. 95). This has been investigated by Merkel, and found to be a sensory organ, but its physiological significance is not understood.

Returning to the actual organ of Jacobson in Man, the epithelial tubes which form its inner lining agree in every respect morphologically with those of certain lower Mammals (*e.g.* the Rat). The epithelium of the outer wall somewhat resembles that of the regio respiratoria of the nasal cavity, and that of the inner wall, which is almost four times as thick, that of its regio olfactoria. There are no traces, however, of the characteristic filamentous olfactory sense-cells—the cells being much more like the supporting cells of the olfactory epithelium. Between them occur short fusiform elements which do not reach the surface (and may perhaps be incompletely developed olfactory cells). Numerous acinose glands open into the organ.

Although no nerves have been as yet discovered in the organ in the human adult, in the embryo, as in the lower Mammals, a well-defined branch of the olfactory nerve (*n.o.*, Fig. 89, I) runs to it.

All things considered, the organ of Jacobson in Man has certainly all the characteristics of a vestigial structure. This is seen not only in its inconstant occurrence, in its frequent one-sided development, and in its degeneration, which commences even during fœtal life, but in its histological structure (Merkel, Schwink, Chiarugi). In Anthropoids it is still further reduced.

[This organ attains its fullest morphological development in the Monotremes (*Ornithorhynchus*) (Symington).]

THE PROJECTILE NOSE

Whereas the olfactory ridges and Jacobson's organ of Man are to be considered degenerate, the projectile nose and its skeletogenous supports are in a progressive condition; they may indeed be considered as specifically human structures. It cannot as yet be said with certainty what gave the first impulse to their

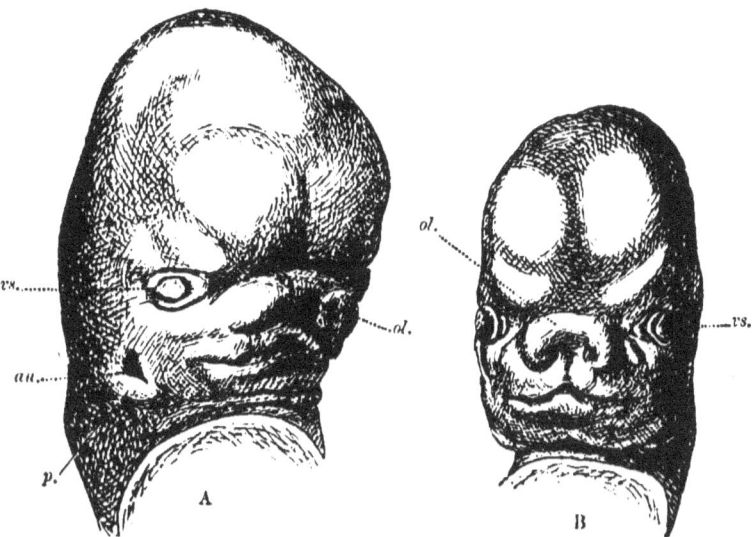

FIG. 90.—HEADS OF TWO HUMAN EMBRYOS.
A, at the end of the second; B, at the beginning of the third month (after W. His). *au.*, external auditory involution, with the pinna (*p.*) seen developing around it. *vs.*, eye; *ol.*, nose.

development. This question awaits an extended morphological inquiry.[1]

THE EYE

The human eye itself shows few vestigial structures; and these, being limited to the embryo, are but transitory. I refer to the arteria hyaloidea which passes through the vitreous body within Cloquet's canal, and which is closely related to the fœtal choroidal fissure. The former plays an important part in the nutrition of the central part of the eye during embryonic life. This is provided for in Fishes and Reptiles by organs known as

[1] This has been undertaken by my pupil F. Spurgat, and a preliminary report on his first series of observations will be found in the *Anat. Anzeiger*, Bd. viii. p. 228.

the processus falciformis and the pecten which are permanently retained, but in Man the corresponding structure undergoes complete degeneration before birth.

We meet with indications of atavism in connection with the accessory parts of the eye. In the fissura orbitalis inferior, for instance, there is an accumulation of smooth muscle, which is the last vestige of the well-developed musculus orbitalis of lower Mammals. In these animals the orbital fossa is usually in open communication with the temporal, *i.e.* the two are not separated by a bony septum (cf. *ante*, p. 58). This sheet-like muscle forms the boundary between the temporal and the orbital fossæ; it is innervated by nerves arising from the sphenopalatine ganglion, and contracting, under their action, causes the eye to protrude.[1]

The occasional presence of laterally and medially diverted offshoots of the levator palpebræ superioris muscle suggests that it may once have been more extensive than at present. It may be regarded as the vestige of the much more strongly developed palpebralis muscle of certain lower Mammals; further investigation of this subject, however, is required.

Great interest attaches to the fold of the conjunctiva which lies at the median angle of the eye, and is known as the plica semilunaris (*pl.*, Fig. 91). This corresponds with the third eyelid, the so-called nictitating membrane, of the lower animals. In Birds, Anurous Amphibians [some Sharks], and in many Reptiles it is highly developed, and, by means of a special muscular apparatus, can be drawn across the eyeball. It serves not only to cover, but to keep clean the surface of the eye, the upper lid [which in Man performs that function] being immovable, and the lower slightly movable or but little developed. In Man, as in the Apes, in association with the absence of a retractor bulbi muscle, this third eyelid has undergone great degeneration, but it may still enclose (more frequently in Negroes than in Caucasians) a cartilaginous support. Among sixteen

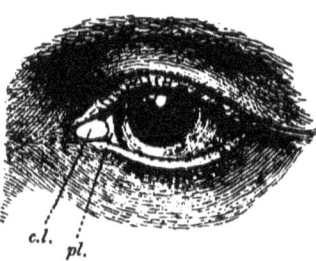

FIG. 91.—HUMAN EYE.
c.l., caruncula lachrymalis; *pl.*, plica semilunaris (vestigial third eyelid).

[1] Nussbaum has recently announced the discovery in a human orbit of a muscle homologous with the retractor bulbi of lower vertebrata. This awaits confirmation.

pure Negroes this cartilage was found by Giacomini in twelve individuals.

The plica semilunaris varies greatly in size at different ages and in different races. In the new-born child, and during the early years of life, it is broader than later, when it does not exceed 1½ to 2 mm. in breadth. One known exception to this rule is, however, found in the Malay tribe of the Orang-Sakai, in which it reaches a breadth of 5 to 5½ mm. It would be worth while to examine other tribes in this respect.

In the caruncula lachrymalis (*c.l.*, Fig. 91), which lies near the plica semilunaris, glands are to be found, which in their structure

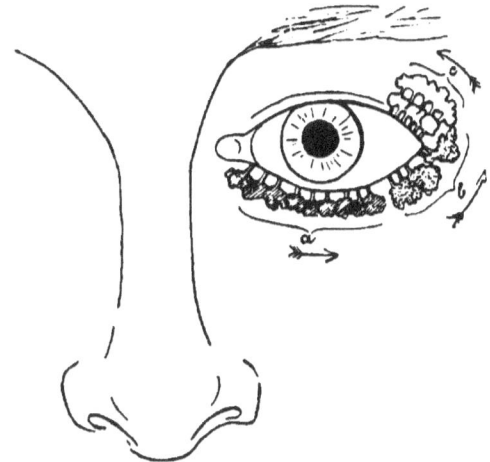

FIG. 92.—DIAGRAM TO ILLUSTRATE THE SHIFTING OF THE LACHRYMAL GLAND, WHICH HAS TAKEN PLACE IN THE COURSE OF PHYLOGENY.
The gland shifts in the direction of the arrows ; *a*, its position in the Amphibian ; *b*, in Reptiles and Birds, and in certain human beings, in which case it may be regarded as atavistic ; *c*, normal position in Man.

greatly resemble the lachrymal glands. These " nictitating glands " constitute a distinct series and are in no way connected with the sweat and Möllerian glands (Peters). Further, sebaceous glands and fine hairs are, in the Primates, found near the caruncula.

Finally, a mention may be made of accessory lachrymal glands which, with their ducts, occasionally lie near the conjunctival sac at the lateral angle of the eye (cf. Fig. 92)—*i.e.* in a position approximate to that of the lachrymal glands of Amphibia and Reptiles, and indicative of a gradual shifting of the lachrymal apparatus in the course of Phylogeny.

Long stiff hairs which occasionally appear in the median

region of the human eyebrow recall from their position the feelers [or supra-orbital vibrissæ] of the lower Mammals. They have been already dealt with (*ante*, p. 4).

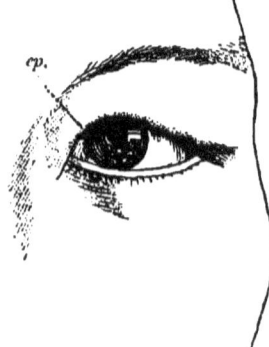

A well-marked variation of the upper eyelid, apparently due to arrested development during fœtal life, is that resulting in the formation of the so-called epicanthus (*ep.*, Fig. 93). This, as its name suggests, is a prolongation of the lid, which extends more especially over the inner angle of the eye. In certain races, such as the Mongolian, this variation is conspicuous, giving rise to the slit-like appearance and oblique position of the aperture of the eye. The obliquity, however, is only apparent, for it vanishes if the skin above the nose be tightly stretched. The epicanthus, as it appears in the Japanese, has been very exactly described by Bälz, who points out that it results from the flatness of the bridge of the nose—the superfluous skin forming the fold in question. It is a matter of interest that a similar condition has been observed among Caucasian children. According to Ranke, about 6 per cent of these exhibit a markedly Mongolian type of eye during the first six months of their lives.

FIG. 93.—EYE OF A MONGOLIAN, WITH THE EPICANTHUS (*ep.*). (After Merkel.)

THE AUDITORY ORGAN

In describing the skeleton of the head, mention has been made (*ante*, p. 49) of the post-oral branchial sacs which characterise a certain embryonic stage, and of the auditory ossicles (p. 64).

The latter arise partly from the original suspensory apparatus of the lower jaw, *i.e.* from the visceral skeleton. As to the former, only the anterior sac persists in Mammals; and from this (the spiraculum [1] of the lower Fishes) the cavity of the middle ear (Eustachian tube and tympanic cavity) develops.

[1] [Considerable interest attaches to the fact that the only living Vertebrates in which this, the "hyo-branchial cleft" of comparative embryologists, is absent, are the Marsipobranchii (Lampreys and Hags) and the Teleostean or Bony Fishes. Its occurrence in the embryos of the former group is now well known (Shipley, *Qu. Jour. Micr. Sci.*, vol. xxvii. p. 349), and Sagemehl has described its apparent vestige in certain adult members of the latter (*Morpholog. Jahrb.*, Bd. ix. p. 213). It is, however, insufficiently recognised that the painstaking researches of Ramsay Wright have

We have thus, in each case, a typical example of change of function.

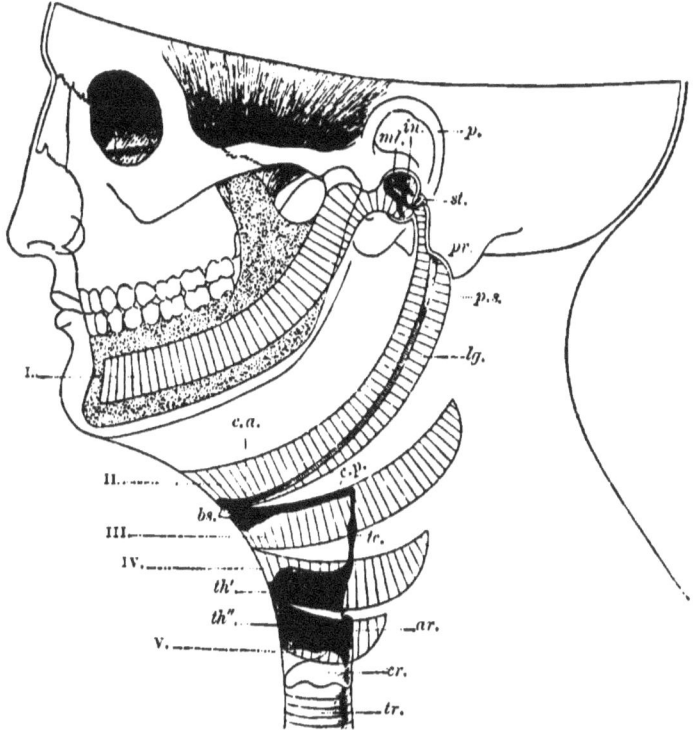

FIG. 94.—DIAGRAM TO ILLUSTRATE THE METAMORPHOSIS DURING DEVELOPMENT OF (I-V) THE FIRST TO THE FIFTH VISCERAL SKELETAL ARCHES.
From the first arch (the so-called Meckel's cartilage) two of the auditory ossicles, the malleus and the incus (*mb.* and *in.*), are represented as arising proximally, but about this there is still considerable doubt (cf. *ante*, p. 64). *p.*, pinna ; *st.*, stapes ; *pr.*, processus mastoideus of skull.
From the second (hyoid) arch arise, proximally, the processus styloideus (*p.s.*), distally the anterior or lesser cornua of the hyoid (*c.a.*), and a portion of the basihyoid or copula (*bs.*). By far the greater portion of this arch becomes the stylohyoid ligament (*lg.*). It is very doubtful whether the arch of the stapes also arises from the proximal portion of the second arch ; the basal plate of the stapes, at any rate, appears to arise independently of it.
The third arch gives rise to the greater part of the body (*bs.*), and the posterior or greater horn, of the hyoid (*c.p.*).
The fourth arch gives rise to the upper segment (*th'.*) of the thyroid cartilage and the fifth to the lower one (*th".*). The aryteuoid cartilage (*a.r.*) is probably a derivative of the fifth arch. *tc.*, the cartilago triticea ; *cr.*, cricoid cartilago ; *tr.*, trachea.

proved its regular occurrence, in a modified form, throughout the living Ganoids ; and further, that in these fishes and certain Selachians it gives off a diverticulum (the canalis tubo-tympanicus), which there is reason to regard as the possible homologue of the middle auditory chamber of the terrestrial Vertebrata (cf. Ramsay Wright, *Jour. Anat. and Phys.*, vol. xix. p. 476).]

The pinna of the ear deserves special attention. In recent years it has been thoroughly investigated by Schwalbe, the results of whose researches are here incorporated. This pinna (p., Fig. 90) is so elaborately modelled a structure that we can hardly imagine it to be degenerate. It undergoes marked variation and adaptation in different races, tribes, and individuals, as well as at different ages. On close examination, variation is found, for the most part, to affect those portions of it which stand out freely from the head in a postero-dorsal direction. Schwalbe calls these parts the "ear-folds," distinguishing the basal region as the zone of the auditory prominence (cf. Fig. 71).

The pinna of Man arises from six prominences which develop near the anterior visceral cleft ($au.$, Fig. 90), and are called the branchial auricular prominences. In the adult pinna they are still evident as the helix, crus antihelicis inferius, crus helicis, tragus, and antitragus (cf. Fig. 71). The human pinna, as compared with that of Apes, would appear to be a degenerate structure; and in reality it is much reduced, being rolled over in such a way as greatly to modify the upper edge of the helix and part of the antihelix.

The variations of the ear-folds are of great interest, and deserve close attention, in connection with the primitive history of Man.

When we examine the highly movable ear of the Ungulata, we find that the ear-fold gives rise to a very efficient sensitive auditory funnel, which lies parallel to the axis[1] of the ear, and ends in a free tip (spina).

In the Primates the pinna is much shortened, and is thrown into folds (helix and antihelix) running at right angles to the axis of the ear. Schwalbe finds two forms of free tip in the Apes. (1) The Macacus or Inuus type (Fig. 71, C); and (2) the Cercopithecus type (Fig. 71, D). In the former (C), which somewhat resembles in shape the ear-fold in human embryos at from the fourth to the sixth month, there is a freely developed edge of the helix which is not rolled over, and a distinct tip, always in the same place.

From the eighth month, the human ear-fold enters upon a degenerative process, which essentially consists in the rolling

[1] By the axis of the pinna (regarded as a standard of measurement) is meant a line which connects the true tip of the ear (Woolner's and Darwin's tip [spina]) with the incisura auris anterior (cf. $s.'$, $s."$, $s."'$, Fig. 71, B). By the breadth of the organ, in both Man and the lower mammals, is understood the measurement of the attached portion (base of the ear).

over of the edge of the ear, and in the greater development of the antihelix. The tip, at the same time, shifts down along the posterior edge of the helix, without, however, becoming rolled in ; and there thus arises the so-called Cercopithecus form (cf. Fig. 71, D) of the human embryo.

If the rolling in of the tip takes place, we have a third type of ear, in which the tip is turned forwards (Darwin's tipped ear). This (Fig. 71, E) is the usual condition of the human adult, but many modifications of it are realised, the tip sometimes entirely disappearing as a free projection.[1]

Besides the degeneration which finds its expression in the reduction of the human ear-fold or pinna,[2] its cartilage is also degenerating. The external auditory passage is among the lower Mammalia (Marsupials) beset by three separate cartilages, movable upon each other. The auditory canal of the child still distinctly reveals this structure, although the alleged complete independence of the basal piece affirmed by Bürkner has not been fully established (Schwalbe). The original clefts between the cartilages are incompletely retained as the incisuræ Santorini.

Secondly, the cartilaginous spina helicis (processus spinosus helicis) is completely fused with the other cartilages of the pinna. It corresponds in position with the free tip of the organ, and is the homologue of a cartilage which, in many Mammals (Ungulata, Carnivora, Rodentia), is independent, and is known as the scutulum (clypeus or rotula). This scutulum fuses with the principal cartilage of the ear in the Lemuroidea and the Apes, as well as in Man.[3]

[1] One curious variation is the occurrence on only one side of Darwin's process. In a batch of military recruits it was found to be of medium size on the right side in 330 men, and on the left only in seventy-nine, and was thus four times as frequent on the former as on the latter. It was found to be remarkably large on the right side in ten individuals, and on the left only in one (Ammon).

[2] The ear-fold may undergo reduction in Mammals which live underground or in water. The rudiment of a pinna has been found in the embryos of some Whales [and a structure which has been similarly interpreted may occasionally appear in the adult Cetacean]. According to this, the ancestors of existing Whales must have possessed an external ear, and since such an organ would occur in land animals, we find in this fact a proof of the descent of the Whales from terrestrial Placentalia (Kükenthal).

[3] In rare cases the scutulum may remain separate, even in Man. The familiar lobulus auriculæ, a non-cartilaginous fatty tegumental fold, first occurs in the Anthropoids. In Man it undergoes many variations of form and size, and is not infrequently entirely absent. It is never found in people of genuine Kyban descent, nor in the Cagots of the Pyrenees (Blanchard).

I have to thank Herr Otto Ammon of Carlsruhe for the following statistics obtained by him in connection with the military recruiting in Baden for 1889 :—

In 4171 ears (of 2086 men) in the military district of Mosbach, the free lobe was

We have every reason for believing that the ancestor of Man could move his pinna to a far greater extent than can his descendant of to-day. The pinna, no doubt, formerly took a great part in the play of the features, and served, as it now undoubtedly does in the lower Mammals, as an excellent instrument for appreciating the direction of sound.

We are justified in this assumption, or rather affirmation, by two facts: (1) the position in which the pinna is still often found with relation to the head; and (2) the presence of an extensive musculature, the primitive history of which has already been given, in describing the platysma myoides (cf. *ante*, p. 105).

With regard to the first point, it is well known that in by far the greater number of individuals the pinna of the ear lies more or less closely applied to the temporal surface of the head. When attention has to be concentrated in a special direction, a person may be seen to correct this physiologically bad arrangement by applying the hollow of the hand to the back of the ear, and so forming an artificial funnel like an ear trumpet.

This proceeding is less necessary in individuals whose ears stand out, wing-like, from the head, *i.e.* are physiologically more correctly disposed. From the modern æsthetic standpoint this is a questionable advantage; but it is a peculiarity which has a great tendency to be handed on by inheritance. In any case, this position is the original one, and the flattened condition must be considered as secondarily acquired.

It is difficult to decide what influences brought about the loss of physiological efficiency of the pinna. It may have been due to a gradual alteration of the resting attitude of Man; and it should be generally known that deformation of the pinna, which often lasts for years, may be produced in children by the same cause.

---

wanting 1511 times, *i.e.* in 36 per cent. It was present in 2461 ears, *i.e.* in 64 per cent; of the median size in 2318, and specially large in 143, *i.e.* in 3 to 4 per cent. Darwin's point was not to be found in 3106 cases, *i.e.* in 74 per cent; it was present in 1066 cases, *i.e.* in 26 per cent; in 1027 it was of median size, and in only thirty-nine (*i.e.* in 9 per cent) unusually large.

THE ALIMENTARY CANAL AND ITS APPENDAGES

PALATAL RIDGES

THE mucous membrane of the roof of the mouth is thrown into a more or less marked median ridge—the raphe, and into a varying number of paired transverse ridges (*r.p.*, Fig. 95), which are especially well developed anteriorly near the incisors, but posteriorly become flattened out. There are five to seven of these transverse palatal ridges on each side, and they are more developed in the embryo and the new-born child than in later life, when their primarily regular arrangement disappears. Those farthest back degenerate, but the anterior ones increase in size and shift nearer to one another as age advances. In very aged persons the whole system of ridges may almost, or even altogether, disappear.

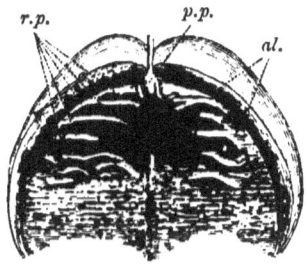

FIG. 95.—PALATE OF A HUMAN EMBRYO AT THE EIGHTH MONTH. *r.p.*, palatal ridges ; *p.p.*, papilla palatina ; *al.*, the later formed alveolar border.

In these ridges which, as has been seen, vary to a great extent, we have the representatives of a larger and more numerous series met with in many lower Mammals (cf. Fig. 96) (in Apes there are as many as ten). They are, as a rule, covered with a tough stratified epithelium, and are functional in helping to triturate and crush the food taken into the mouth (Gegenbaur).

Some years ago I called attention to the fact that in the embryo Cat these ridges develop as rows of papillæ, which later unite, and I put forward the suggestion that we may be here dealing with the remains of palatal teeth handed down even to Man. Closer investigation must show whether these papillæ are actual vestiges of tooth structures or only horny growths, such as are still found among the lower Mammals in the form of horny teeth or ridges (*Ornithorhynchus*, certain Marsupials, and Edentates). The extreme anterior border of the palate bears a median eminence, the papilla palatina (*p.p.*, Figs. 95, 96). On either side of this and of the raphe the naso-palatine canal, already described (*ante*, p. 146), opens.

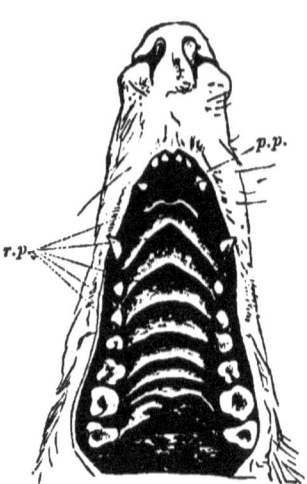

FIG. 96.—PALATAL FOLDS OF THE RACOON (*Procyon lotor*). *r.p.*, palatal folds; *p.p.*, papilla palatina.

TEETH[1]

The teeth are among the most important and the most variable organs of the vertebrate body. Long before the appearance of the osseous skeleton—*i.e.* among the lowest Vertebrates—teeth and tooth-like tegumental scutes are found. We cannot be far wrong in asserting that the acquisition of teeth by the Vertebrata was a most important factor in the struggle for existence. The size and form of the teeth are greatly determined by adaptation to the various conditions of life. It is therefore often difficult to decide whether similar tooth forms in fossil animals are cases of analogy or of homology. It is quite possible for different races of animals, in adaptation to similar modes of life, independently to acquire a similar dentition [as for example in the case of the Crocodilian (*Gavialis*) and the Dolphin (*Platanista*) living side by side in the Ganges]. If, among the lower Vertebrata, we set aside dental ridges resulting from the fusion of several distinct teeth, and the compound teeth of many Fish, the teeth, as far up as the lower Reptiles, are, for the most part, simple pointed cones. In these animals they serve only for seizing the prey, the further disintegration of which takes place in the stomach and intestine. In the Mammalia the food is more or less triturated in the mouth, and that chiefly by the cheek teeth.

The dentition of the Primates is, as compared with that of

[1] In this account of the teeth the researches of Röse have been largely followed.

Mammals generally, but little specialised. The molars in particular are comparatively simple cuspidate teeth, such as are found among the oldest Mammals. Judged from the form of their teeth, the Primates would appear to have branched off very early from the common Mammalian stem. If we can draw conclusions from the fossils as yet found, the Apes were not very widely distributed in earlier periods. They probably lived, as they now do, as climbing animals in tropical climates. In consequence partly of their frugivorous manner of life, and partly of the higher development of their intelligence, their teeth, of no great service for warfare in the struggle for existence, appear to have remained comparatively simple.

The dentition of Man agrees with that of the Old World Apes in number and shape of the teeth. The dental formula is: $i.\dfrac{2.}{2.}c.\dfrac{1.}{1.}p.m.\dfrac{2.}{2.}m.\dfrac{3}{3} = 32$. The New World Apes, on the other hand, have one more premolar in each set, their formula being $\dfrac{2.1.3.3}{2.1.3.3} = 36$. If the teeth of Man are compared with those of the nearly related Anthropoids, it is found that their respective milk teeth agree in form and size more nearly than do their permanent or successional dentitions. In the Anthropoids [with the exception of the Gibbon (*Hylobates*)] the teeth of the second series are larger and stronger than in Man, the contrast being most marked in the size of the canines. The latter serve, in the Ape, as powerful weapons in the struggle for existence,[1] and the premolars of the Apes are also, in consequence of the greater development of their outer cusps, more caniniform than in Man. The molars, on the contrary, are remarkably similar throughout, although they are larger in Anthropoids than in Man; and in *Hylobates*, both in form and size, they can hardly be distinguished from those of the human subject.

[Since, among Mammals generally], the milk teeth, *i.e.* those

[1] We have abundant evidence that teeth were once used by Man or by his ancestors as weapons of defence; traces of such a use have not altogether disappeared in human beings of the present day, and I cannot refrain from quoting in this connection a comment of Darwin which occurs in his book on the *Origin of Man*.

"He who rejects with scorn the belief that the shape of his own canines, and their occasional great development in other men, are due to our early forefathers having been provided with these formidable weapons, will probably reveal by sneering the line of his descent. For though he no longer intends, nor has the power, to use these teeth as weapons, he will unconsciously retract his 'snarling muscles' (thus named by Sir C. Bell) so as to expose them ready for action, like a dog prepared to fight."

of the first series, are as a rule far less modified than the permanent teeth; and since, in view of this, it is found that the former agree in Anthropoids and Man far more than the latter, we are justified in concluding that the teeth of both Man and the Apes point back to a common origin from some more or less intermediate type. The dental formula of the Anthropoid Apes appears to be comparatively fixed; but the

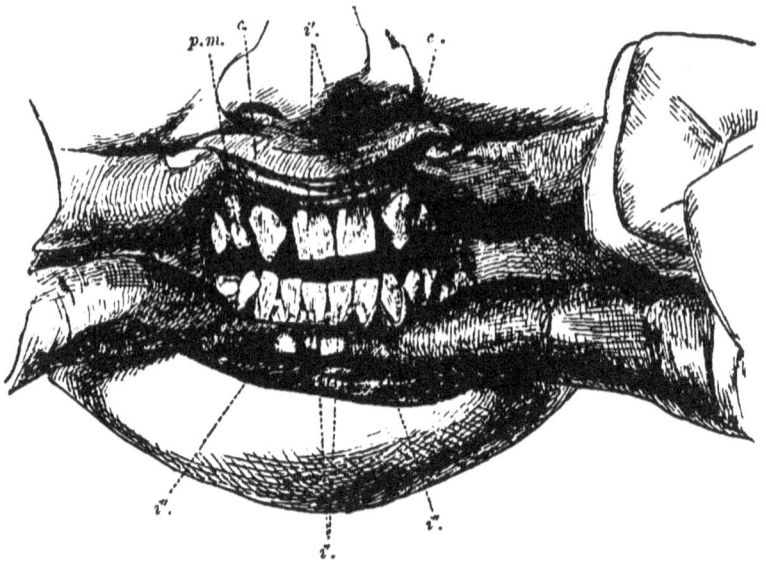

Fig. 97.—HUMAN MOUTH, IN WHICH THE DEVELOPMENT OF THE UPPER OUTER INCISORS HAS BEEN SUPPRESSED.

$i'.$, inner incisors; $i''.$, outer incisors; $p.m.$, first premolar of the upper jaw; $c.$, upper canines which, under the special conditions, come next in order to the upper inner incisors.

teeth of Man show indications of gradual reduction, especially in the variations in the size of the molars and of the upper outer incisors.

The upper outer incisor shows every transition form between a well-developed typical tooth and a short conical stump. In many individuals, however, this tooth is altogether wanting (cf. Fig. 97), and this dental variation may be hereditarily transmitted through several generations.

The recent researches of Röse have revealed reason for believing that the upper molars of Man have been derived from a four-cusped tooth type, and the lower from a five-cusped type, and that the numerical reduction of these cusps has been due to

Man's adoption of a more delicate diet, those degenerating first which were the last to be added to form the compound tooth, In the upper jaw this is the posterior lingual and in the lower the posterior unpaired cusp. In the third molar, the so-called wisdom tooth, the process of reduction may go so far that finally, instead of a tooth with four or five cusps, a vestigial stump alone appears. In a relatively large number of cases, indeed, no wisdom tooth at all appears, it being either not formed, or, if formed, retained within the gum.

Repeated investigations on this subject have all tended to show that these signs of degeneration, so marked in Europeans, are found in non-Europeans also, but not at all to the same extent as among the Aryan race. Quite apart from pathological cases, upper molars with three cusps, lower molars with four, and reduced wisdom teeth, occur more frequently in Europeans than in Negroes, Mongolians, or native Australians. The low race last named, in its dental formula, appears least removed from the hypothetical original type; for in it are still found complete rows of splendid teeth with powerfully developed canines and molars, the latter being either uniform, or even increasing, in size, as we proceed backwards, in such a way that the wisdom tooth is the largest of the series. This is decidedly a pithecoid character, which is always found in Apes. The upper incisors of the Malay, apart from their prognathous disposition, have occasionally a distinctly pithecoid form, their anterior surface being convex, and their lingual surface slightly concave. The ancestors of the Europeans seem to have had the same form of teeth, for the oldest existing fragments of skulls from the Mammoth age (*e.g.* the jaws from la Naulette and Schipka) reveal tooth forms which must be classed with those of the lowest races of to-day.

Apart from those variations in the human dentition, which tend to approximate it to that of Anthropoids, still more startling ones are occasionally found. For example, the appearance of a third premolar is not very rare. In the Freiburg anatomical museum there is an upper jaw with three well-developed premolars on each side, thus showing the dental formula of the New World Apes. An increase in the number of molars is also not very rare in both Man and the Anthropoids. A fourth molar, in a more or less perfect form, is to be met with in every large collection of skulls. Zuckerkandl has shown that the epithelial germ of a fourth molar is not infrequently present in Man, and Röse has since proved that this vestige is on each side coincident with the end of the epithelial dental ridge.

By milk teeth are usually understood the first formed generation of teeth. Röse, however, has recently attempted to show that the milk teeth do not correspond with the first series of teeth of the lower Vertebrates, and that they cannot be homologised with any one special series in Reptiles and allied forms. Milk teeth, according to him, must rather be considered to have arisen by the concrescence of several consecutive generations of teeth of our ancestors, into one single, more solidly constructed, series, the sum of all the remaining rows which were once present having been in Man, as in all diphyodont Mammals, compressed into the second or permanent series. [This is, however, but one of several views put forward during recent years on the subject of the Mammalian tooth genesis. Much more important is the fact that, in Man, while the premolars are comparatively simple teeth, the milk molars which precede them are more complex, and more conformable, in the characters of their fangs and crowns, to the type of the true molars. These facts suggest that the deciduous (milk) molars are of a more primitive (*i.e.* a less reduced) type than the successional.[1]]

Until quite recently, the possibility of Man's developing a third dentition was generally denied, but it is now proved that that may sometimes occur. Baume, Zuckerkandl, and Röse, have discovered a third set of enamelless tooth rudiments on the outer or labial surface of the jaw, [and Schwalbe has lately suggested [2] that they may be the vestiges of a distinct *pre-milk* dentition, of which traces have been found by Kükenthal in the Seal, by Nawroth in the Pig, and, in a more extensive and calcified form, by Leche in the Banded Ant-Eater (*Myrmecobius*). Great interest attaches to further inquiry into these structures.]

In Fishes, Amphibians, and some Reptiles, the first formed

---

[1] [A very interesting allied case is furnished by the common Dog. In the upper jaw of that animal, the characters of the fourth milk (deciduous) molar are almost exactly those of the first true molar, and the characters of the third milk molar those of the fourth premolar. Similarly, the second and first milk molars closely resemble the third and second premolars, allowance being in all cases made for mere difference in size. Indeed, comparison of the premolars with the milk molars and, through these, with the first molar, reveals a marvellous series of progressive stages in simplification and reduction of the type of tooth represented in the adult dentition by the first upper molar. I am hoping shortly to have this most important matter fully worked out in detail.—G. B. H.]

[2] [Cf. Schwalbe, *Morph. Arbeiten*, Bd. iii. p. 531, and Nawroth, "Zur Ontogenese d. Scheweinemolaren," *Inaug. Dissert. Basel*, Berlin, 1893.]

teeth arise in relation to epithelial papillæ, which project above the surface of the mucous membrane of the mouth. A tract of the epithelium of the jaw subsequently sinks down into the mesodermal tissues to form the so-called dental ridge, from which the actual teeth then develop. The dental ridge of the higher Vertebrates commences to form very early, long before the first appearance of the bones. In this early formation of the dental ridge the phylogenetic early appearance of teeth is ontogenetically recapitulated. The occurrence of freely projecting papillæ prior to the formation of the dental ridges seems to have been lost in most Mammals, through abbreviation of the embryonic stages. Röse has, however, lately proved the existence, in Man, of temporary traces of papillæ at a period antecedent to the sinking down of the dental ridge.

The Sublingua

Gegenbaur has devoted special attention to a system of folds on the under surface of the tongue (plica fimbriata), which are very distinctly developed in children at and soon after birth, but in adults are found only in various stages of reduction.

In its general form this organ resembles the sublingua of the Prosimii, in which animals it attains its most independent development in the Slender Loris (*Stenops*) of Ceylon. It is in this creature supported by cartilaginous, fatty, and connective tissue, its investing epithelium being raised into papillæ and showing a tendency to become horny. In the allied *Tarsius* and in *Lemur* degeneration has obviously taken place; since, in the latter, the cartilaginous supporting tissue has altogether disappeared and the organ is no longer independent, so far as its relations with the tongue are concerned. The sublingua would thus appear to have formerly possessed a well-developed supporting skeleton, inherited from the lower classes of animals, and we are, in fact, reminded of the rod-like process of the basihyal which, in Lizards and some Chelonians, passes so conspicuously into the base of the tongue. Thus considered, the sublingua may be regarded as the morphological equivalent of the tongue of the lower Vertebrata, and the actual Mammalian tongue would appear to have been to a certain degree acquired [within the limits of the Mammalian phylum]. The tongue and sublingua thus appear to be organs of very different phylogenetic significance, and there is some reason for thinking that the muscular tongue has probably been developed out of the posterior part of the degenerating sublingua.

The study of Ontogeny has up to the present thrown no light on the sublingua.

Before quitting the tongue the papillæ foliatæ should be mentioned. These, in Mammals, take the form of localised systems of lamellæ, situated on the postero-lateral tongue border, and having their epithelium thrown into a series of flask-shaped depressions. In Man these papillæ vary much in form and size, and since they are occasionally represented by but mere traces they are evidently undergoing reduction.

THYROID AND THYMUS

These two organs are developmentally related to the pharyngeal region.

The thyroid gland, in all Mammals in which it has been examined, arises from two ventral outgrowths, one of which is paired and the other unpaired.

The unpaired constituent is closely connected ontogenetically with the tongue which, during development, bridges over the floor of the buccal cavity, enclosing a space, the wall of which becomes changed into an epithelial vesicle. This is the unpaired or median thyroid gland, and it for a time remains in communication by means of its duct (the ductus thyroglossus) with the posterior surface of the tongue, at its base of attachment. When this duct closes, its orifice may become converted into the so-called foramen cœcum of the adult, and therefore belongs to the class of vestigial structures. The duct itself, as His has shown, may often be retained in the adult for a length of $2\frac{1}{2}$ or more centimetres. Its existence explains the fact that the so-called middle lobe of the thyroid gland is occasionally prolonged upwards into a process, which often becomes constricted so as to form a series of from two to four longitudinally recurrent vesicles (bursæ supra hyoidea and præhyoidea).

The paired portions, or the lateral lobes, of the thyroid gland arise at the region of extreme posterior differentiation of the visceral skeleton, by constriction of the primary floor of the pharynx, near the laryngeal orifice. We have thus, here again, a structure of epithelial origin. At a later stage the lateral and median portions of the thyroid gland become approximated.

The whole organ at first has an undoubtedly glandular character, but after the constriction is completed it undergoes a marked structural change.

The manner in which the thyroid originates justifies us in classing it as a vestigial organ. In the further course of its development, however, it does not degenerate as might be imagined à priori; on the contrary, it develops into a large, highly vascular organ, which, according to recent clinical experience, is of great service in the maintenance of both the bodily and mental health of its possessor.

It would appear to play some important function in relation to the central nervous system, since its removal in animals is attended with the manifestation of an extraordinary number of pathological symptoms,—idiocy, muscular twitchings, tetanic, ataxic, apathic, clonic, and epileptic symptoms being conspicuous, with marked disturbances of the organs of deglutition, circulation, and respiration (cachexia strumipriva). It may further be noted that different classes of animals are differently affected by the destruction of this organ.[1]

This gland may be concerned either in the production of a secretion, or in the removal from the blood of substances which would be injurious to the nervous system; but nothing very definite is known concerning its functions. It is richly supplied with blood, indeed much more so than the brain itself.

In the thyroid gland, then, we have evidence of change of function, and this is also the case, at least to a certain extent, with the thymus. In Mammals, and especially in Man, this gland is chiefly formed from a hollow epithelial outgrowth of the third branchial pouch, although the fourth, and to a certain extent the second also, take part in its formation.

The thymus thus far resembles in its origin a gland; but it loses this character, and a thorough histological change takes place in consequence of the wandering into it of lymphoid cells. This change renders its physiological significance still more difficult to explain. Towards the end of the second year the thymus (the greater part of which now lies behind the sternum, i.e. ventrad of the heart and of the roots of the larger blood-vessels) reaches its highest development, and after that period it, as a rule, undergoes retrogressive metamorphosis; in very old

---

[1] It is difficult to decide whether and to what extent the frequent pathological affections of the thyroid gland (the formation of a "crop" with secondary disorganisation of the tissues) may or may not be referred to change of function within it.

people, however, epithelial, lymphoidal, and fatty vestiges of it always occur.

We cannot at present determine what was the original significance of the thyroid and thymus glands, and the like is true of an allied body, the so-called carotid-gland (glandula intercarotica), which is found at the bifurcation of the common carotid artery.

[Concerning the thymus, however, Beard, working chiefly at the lower Fishes, in which it attains its greatest development, has recently been led to the brilliant suggestion [1] that it may be in them primarily protective of the branchial organs of respiration, by a process of phagocytosis, in a manner akin to that in which the tonsils and associated cytogenous tissues are protective of the main respiratory passages of the pulmonary organs of the terrestrial Vertebrata.]

BURSA PHARYNGEA

The primitive history of this organ cannot at present be certainly determined. In Man it appears at about the third month of fœtal life, on the posterior pharyngeal wall, as an epithelial evagination, directed upwards and backwards towards the occipital bone. During embryonic life this structure becomes shifted in the course of its growth; its canal lengthens, and finally approaches the tonsils; after this it participates in all the changes which affect these organs. Chief among these is degeneration, which normally takes place before the time of puberty. The degenerative processes bring about shrinkings, fusions, the formation of crypts and cysts, and other modifications so diverse that hardly any two cases are alike, and the most different accounts are consequently given of them in the literature of the subject.

The following lower Mammals are known to possess a bursa pharyngea; the Alpine Marmot (*Arctomys marmota*), the Pig (*Sus scrofa*), the Roebuck (*Capreolus*), and the Bear (*Ursus*). In no other Mammals examined has anything of the kind been found, and since no traces of the organ are to be observed in the lower Vertebrata, its primitive history and physiological significance remains problematical (Killian).

ŒSOPHAGUS AND STOMACH

In their fully developed condition the œsophagus and stomach show no anatomical peculiarities which need be specially

[1] [*Anat. Anzeiger*, Bd. ix. p. 482.]

mentioned here. Attention may, however, be drawn to the saccus cæcus, which is, as it were, indicative of the commencement of a process of chambering in the stomach, the antrum pyloricum, and a constriction (c'., Fig. 98) which but very rarely occurs [1] near the middle of the pyloric region.

The œsophageal mucous membrane, which after birth is covered with a dense stratified epithelium, is in the embryo beset by a columnar ciliated epithelium, and thus recalls very primitive conditions. In Amphioxus and the young Lamprey (Ammocoetes), for example, nearly the whole intestine is still lined with a similar ciliated epithelium. In the adult Lamprey it is somewhat more limited, and it is still to be found at various parts at least of the intestine, in a large number of the Anamnia. Ciliated epithelium is also frequent in the œsophagus of Reptiles, and it has even been proved to exist in the intestinal canal of some Mammals, at least over small areas.

[A similar replacement of ciliated by stratified non-ciliated epithelium may take place over localised areas of the mammalian trachea. In the Dog and Cat, for example, this change is effected over areas of attrition, resulting from a folding over of the tracheal wall; and this and other allied considerations have led to the application of the term "frictional" to stratified squamous epithelium (cf. Haycraft and Carlier, *Qu. Jour. Misc. Sci.*, vol. xxx. p. 519).]

Muscle bundles often occur between the posterior wall of the windpipe and the œsophagus, at the point where the left bronchial tube crosses the latter, and at other parts of the intestinal canal, *e.g.* the duodenum. Their significance is undetermined; but their inconstancy, variability, and feeble development suggest that they may be among those organs which are being gradually lost by Man.

The comparative anatomy of the stomach, and of the course and ultimate distribution of the vagus nerve, prove that the former, like some other organs of the viscera (*e.g.* the heart, the thyroid, and the thymus glands), originally lay farther forward, *i.e.* nearer the head, and that it has secondarily shifted back (cf. *ante*, p. 38 and Fig. 31).

It not infrequently happens that a blind diverticulum (diverticulum ilei or diverticulum of Meckel) arises from the

---

[1] I noticed this constriction twice during the ordinary dissecting course in this University in the winter of 1892 and 1893; and careful dissection showed that there was at the constricted part a ring-like specialisation of the circular musculature.

lower part of the small intestine.[1] This diverticulum is connected during the embryonic period, and sometimes still longer, with the navel, by a cord, containing the last vestiges of the ductus omphalo-mesentericus, which connected the yolk-sac with the intestine. We have in this a mere vestige of a fœtal organ.

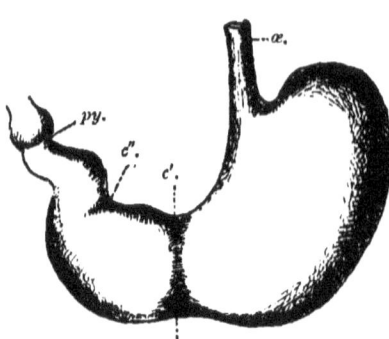

FIG. 98.—HUMAN STOMACH.
œ., œsophagus ; *py.*, pylorus ; *c'.c".*, constrictions of the pyloric chamber.

[On examination of 769 bodies, at the instigation of the Collective Investigation Committee of the Anatomical Society of Great Britain and Ireland,[2] the diverticulum ilei has been encountered in but sixteen cases, or in little more than 2 per cent. Special interest attaches to Rolleston's report upon the examination of 337 individuals (nearly 44 per cent of the whole number) which were equally representative of the two sexes, as nine of the ten possessed of the diverticulum were males.]

[A remarkable case has more recently been put on record by Buchanan,[3] of an adult male subject in whom this appendage had a total length of 9 cm. and a basal circumference of 11 cm., and contained a spacious central cavity having a wide aperture of communication with the ileum. The remaining alimentary viscera were strikingly aberrant, the colic head and the cœcum being directed towards the left hypogastric region (instead of the right), the cœcum terminating in an appendix vermiformis which measured 13½ cm. in length.]

---

[1] According to Sappey, the length of the intestine in white men of middle height is 9600 mm.,—8000 of which are to be reckoned to the small intestine, and 1600 to the large one. According to the researches of Chudzinski, who examined nine Negroes, the total average length was 8667 mm., *i.e.* almost 1000 less. There were, however, great variations in length in different individuals. If the length of the intestine is affected by the height of the individual, it can hardly be so to any great extent.

The fact that the total length of the intestine is less in Negroes is due to the comparative shortness of the small intestine, for the large intestine is longer in the black than in the white races.

[2] [*Jour. Anat. and Phys.*, vol. xxvi. p. 91.]

[3] [*Ibid.* vol. xxvii. p. 559.]

THE VERMIFORM PROCESS

The processus vermiformis (*ap.*, Fig. 99) is a feebly developed organ which lies at the end of the short cœcum (*cœ.*), and possesses a considerable morphological interest. In Man its average length is 8½ cm., but it may be but 2 cm., or on the other hand, some 20 to 23 cm. long.

Considerable variation also occurs in its width and disposition

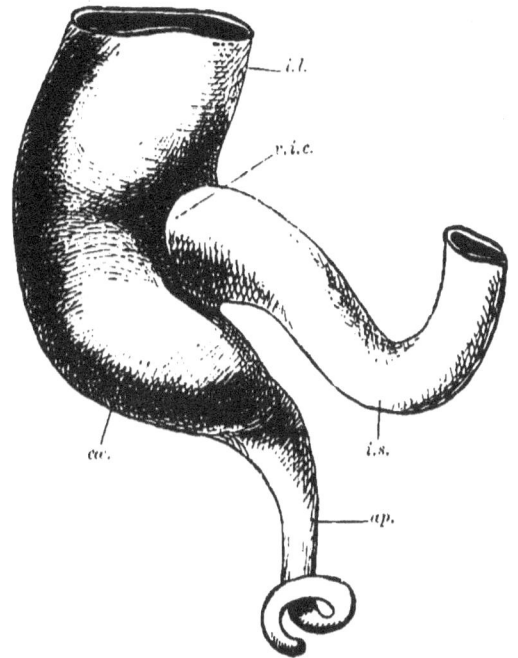

FIG. 99.—THE CŒCUM AND PROCESSUS VERMIFORMIS OF A HUMAN EMBRYO.
i.l., large intestine ; *i.s.*, small intestine ; *cœ.*, cœcum ; *ap.*, vermiform process.

(cf. p. 166), and in the folds of mucous membrane which bound its ostium. Indeed, everything points to the retrogressive character of this appendage, and justifies us in concluding that the total length of the alimentary tract was formerly greater than it now is. The great variations in the form and size of the cœcum (*cœ.*) also support this view.

According to Ribbert the processus vermiformis at different ages measures as follows :—

168 THE STRUCTURE OF MAN

At birth . . . . . . 3⅖ cm.
Up to the 5th year . . . . 7⅔ „
From 5—10 . . . . . 9 „
From 10—20 . . . . . 9¾ „
From 20—30 . . . . . 9½ „
From 30—40 . . . . . 8¾ „
From 40—60 . . . . . 8¾ „
In old people over 60 . . . 8¼ „

In embryos and new-born children on the one hand, and in adults on the other, the vermiform process varies in length in

FIG. 100.—THE CŒCUM AND VERMIFORM PROCESS OF A HUMAN EMBRYO.
References as in Fig. 99.

proportion to that of the rest of the intestinal canal; and since it is a degenerating organ, it is not surprising to find that it is most strongly developed in fœtal times, and does not grow at a rate proportionate to advancing age. In the embryo its length, in proportion to that of the large intestine, is approximately one to ten, and in the adult one to twenty. Further light is thrown on these facts by Ribbert's interesting discovery of the frequent occlusion of the vermiform process. He found it either partially or totally closed in 25 per cent of the cases examined,

THE ALIMENTARY CANAL AND ITS APPENDAGES   169

with accompanying very decidedly retrogressive changes (pathological cases excluded) in the related tissues.[1]

Taking only adults into consideration (i.e. omitting individuals under twenty years of age in whom variations are comparatively rare), out of 100 vermiform processes 32 were found partially or wholly closed. Complete occlusion throughout the whole organ was found in a very small number, about $3\frac{1}{2}$ per cent. Partial occlusion is much more frequent, all degrees being found, from the first narrowing to the complete closing of the lumen.

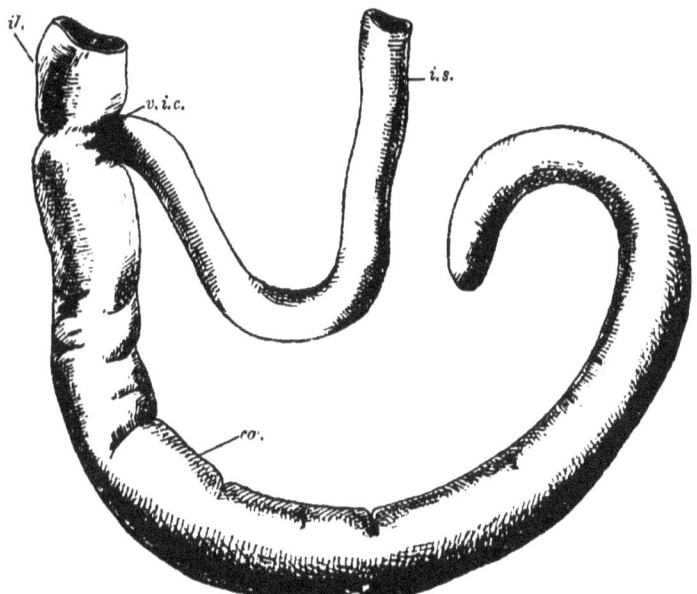

FIG. 101.—THE CŒCUM AND VERMIFORM PROCESS IN A KANGAROO.
i.l., large intestine ; *i.s.*, small intestine, *v.i.c.*, position of the ileo-colic valve ; *cœ.*, cœcum.

In rather more than half of the cases the occlusion affected a quarter of the length ; in nearly half of the remainder its extent varied between one quarter and three quarters, and in only a very small number did it affect more than three quarters, or close up the tube.

This process of occlusion is equally marked in both sexes, and the statistics concerning its occurrence at different ages are very striking. They make it clear that there is marked increase

[1] Actual pathological obliteration, nevertheless, occasionally occurs at the end of the vermiform process.
The occlusions which result, and which are probably always due to inflammation, are less frequent than the typical obliteration (Ribbert).
I cannot again in this connection refrain from referring to the coincidence of the existence of vestigial organs and the tendency to disease caused by them.

in the frequency of its occurrence in advanced age, as will be seen from the following table :—

From the 1st—10th year occlusion observed in 4 per cent.
,, 10th—20th ,, ,, 11 ,,
,, 20th—30th ,, ,, 17 ,,
,, 30th—40th ,, ,, 25 ,,
,, 40th—50th ,, ,, 27 ,,
,, 50th—60th ,, ,, 36 ,,
,, 60th—70th ,, ,, 53 ,,
,, 70th—80th ,, ,, 58 ,,

It follows from the foregoing table that in more than 50 per cent of people over sixty years of age there is degeneration of the vermiform process. In new-born children, on the other hand, this phenomenon has never been observed, and the youngest child in whom it has been found commencing was five years old. Total occlusion is also similarly connected with age, though not in nearly so marked a manner as partial closure. It has never been observed before the thirtieth year; and while it was not found once in individuals between fifty and sixty, it was most frequent in those whose ages ranged from sixty to seventy. Among these, nine out of the twenty-one cases recorded showed complete occlusion; and since besides them there were seven just on the point of closure, we may conclude that more than 50 per cent were thus affected.

A relation has further been proved to exist between the length of the appendix and its degeneration. The longest appendices (21 to 15 cm. long) kept their lumen throughout; in those 14 and 13 cm. long, commencing obliteration of the lumen was observed in four cases, and in those 12 and 11 cm. long it was not found. From this point, however, occlusion again increased as the length decreased. If we leave out of account individuals under five years of age, in whom occlusion has not been observed, we find that it occurs as under, viz.—

Where the length of the appendix is 20 cm. in 34 per cent.
,, ,, ,, 9 ,, 18 ,,
,, ,, ,, 8 ,, 32 ,,
,, ,, ,, 7 ,, 40 ,,
,, ,, ,, 6 ,, 30 ,,
,, ,, ,, 5 ,, 70 ,,
,, ,, ,, 4 ,, 66 ,,
,, ,, ,, 3 ,, 100 ,,

Although this connection between length and frequency of occlusion is, as the table shows, somewhat irregular, we may at least conclude that, as a rule, the shorter appendices show occlusion more frequently than the longer (Ribbert).

The Liver and the Pancreas

These two organs, which are genetically closely related, occasionally show variations in the manner of their lobation which may amount to constriction, and in the relations of their ducts.

[Recent investigation at the hands of a number of independent workers has revealed the fact that the pancreas, in all classes of Vertebrates, is a compound organ, derivative of from one to four diverticula of the gut, and in most cases from three, as is said by Felix[1] to be the case in Man himself. One (or more) of these primitive outgrowths gives rise to the chief duct (or ducts) of the adult organ, the rest usually becoming obliterated with advancing development. Pending the working out of further details, considerable interest attaches to the recent discovery by Rolleston,[2] that the duodenum of the human adult may sometimes bear a diverticulum (proved to be distinct from the "ampulla Vateri") which enters the substance of the pancreas, and which there is reason to suspect may be a persistent vestige of one of the pancreatic outgrowths of the embryo.]

The average weight of the liver is said to be 1451 grs. in the white races, 1266 grs. in the black.

The Respiratory System

The visceral skeletal arches, which lie ventrad of the cranium proper and are intimately related to the cephalic portion of the gut, have been already mentioned in dealing with the head skeleton, and their great phylogenetic importance has been pointed out (cf. *ante*, pp. 49 and 64, and accompanying Figs.). A few additional remarks, however, are here necessary.

Whereas certain Fishes (primitive Selachians) have from six to seven pairs of branchial pouches,[3] Vertebrata somewhat higher in the scale (Turtles, Lizards, and Snakes) develop but five pairs,

[1] [Cf. Stöhr, *Anat. Anzieger*, Bd. viii. p. 205.]
[2] [*Jour. Anat. and Phys.*, vol. xxviii. p. xii.]
[3] [It is insufficiently recognised that the "Hag Fishes" may bear many more than this, and that in one species of these (*Bdellostoma polytrema*) from thirteen to fourteen pairs are present (cf. Günther, *Brit. Mus. Cat. of Fishes*, vol. viii. p. 512, and Schneider, *Archiv f. Naturgesch.*, Bd. xlvi. p. 115.)

which are destitute of branchial organs, and of these (*e.g.* in the Lizard) only the three anterior, as a rule, break through the outer integument. The fourth, in exceptional cases, may also break through, but this never occurs with the fifth. The same is the case in Birds, except that in them the third pair of sacs open externally only in exceptional cases, and that the fourth and fifth pairs, which are inconstant in their appearance, never break through. In Mammals and Man only four pairs of branchial sacs arise, and here also those which lie most posteriorly are decidedly vestigial in character. For this reduction a parallel is forthcoming in the branchial apparatus of the Anamnia; and there is thus evidence both in Phylogeny and in Ontogeny of a progressive suppression of the branchial pouches and arches in postero-anterior succession.

The branchial pouches and the skeletal arches which support them thus belong, in the higher Vertebrata and Man,[1] in which they never bear functional respiratory organs, to the category of typical vestigial structures [inherited and for the most part lost —unintelligible, as Gegenbaur long ago insisted, except in the knowledge, furnished by comparative morphology, that in certain lower animals their full development is indispensable to existence].

There occasionally occur in the anterior cervical region in Man " fistulæ," which may penetrate a greater or lesser distance in from the integument, or may bound canals which even open into the pharynx. These are abnormal structures, due to arrested development, under which branchial clefts have not become completely obliterated. In dealing with the auditory organ details have already been given (*ante*, p. 150) of the relationship of the cavity of the middle ear (Eustachian tube) to the modified remnant of the first visceral cleft, which in the higher Vertebrata has undergone a new development, in adaptation to a change of function.

THE LARYNX

The study both of the innervation of the musculature of the larynx, and of the genesis and Comparative Anatomy of its cartilaginous framework, strongly suggest its origin, for the

---

[1] The branchial sacs, and the external branchial furrows in the outer integument which correspond with them, are most distinctly visible in human embryos of 3-4 mm. in length.

greater part, from branchial or visceral structures.[1] It may be considered as certainly proved that the upper part of the thyroid cartilage arises out of the fourth and the lower out of the fifth primitive (*i.e.* the second and third branchial) visceral arch, and it is probable that the fifth branchial arch gives rise to the arytenoids.

With regard to the Mammalian epiglottis, it seems now tolerably certain that it does not owe its origin merely to the mucous membrane of the floor of the mouth, but that it represents an originally paired skeletal element which, in the course of phylogeny, has passed from the condition of hyaline- to that of fibro-cartilage. [This view receives support from the investigations of Göppert, who has recently given reasons[2] for believing that the cartilages of Wrisberg and the epiglottis, which are frequently in organic continuity among the lower Mammals, are specialised portions of one original structure.] Any attempt, however, to derive the epiglottis from the branchial skeleton seems, in the present state of our knowledge, beset with difficulties.[3]

[It is now demonstrated that the upward prolongation of the Mammalian epiglottis involves that organ in a relationship with the velum palatinum (furnishing a *raison d'être* for the existence of the latter), for the purpose of restricting the respiratory passage (narial pharynx). Special inquiry has also shown that in both the young and adults of representatives of all orders of Mammals, the epiglottis, when at rest, lies above the velum in an intra-narial position. Man is, however, an exception to this rule, at least in the adult state, and there is reason for believing that the velum and epiglottis have, in him, suffered a loss of connection by the specialisation of the latter more particularly for vocalisation. It is yet uncertain whether the epiglottis of the human embryo does or does not occupy the intra-narial position[4]]. It

---

[1] The hyoid and the thyroid skeletal apparatus are still closely connected in *Ornithorhynchus*, and bear distinct traces of their branchial origin, as not only lateral arches, but portions of their median elements or copula can clearly be recognised. In the higher Mammalia the hyoid separates from the thyroid, although the two continue to be related (cf. the cartilago triticea, *ante*, Fig. 94). In Mammals above the Monotremata the thyroid cartilage appears to consist of a single plate; but it gives some indications of its primary origin from two consecutive branchial arches which still remain distinct in the Monotremata (Gegenbaur).

[2] [*Morph. Jahrb.*, Bd. xxi. p. 68.]

[3] [Gegenbaur has recently come to the conclusion that the epiglottis is a derivative of the fourth pair of branchial arches, *Die Epiglottis*, Leipzig, 1892.]

[4] [Cf. Howes, *Jour. Anat. and Phys.*, vol. xxiii. p. 594.]

would, therefore, be very interesting to follow closely, in Man's development, the changes of position and inter-relationship between the larynx and the upper part of the pharynx (choanæ). I am indebted to my colleague, Professor Killian, for knowledge of the fact that the larynx of the human embryo may occupy a high position, the upper edge of the epiglottis reaching even to the uvula.

The musculature of the human larynx appears to a great extent to have been derived from the simple sphincter and dilator apparatus of lower Vertebrata, of Lizard-like type. Under the more subtle differentiation of the laryngeal skeleton in Man, the musculature has also undergone corresponding changes—for example, there is no longer one single muscle for constricting the glottis, but a whole system of such muscles. In other words, the reptile-like sphincter laryngis has gained new points of origin and insertion in the cartilage; and Fürbinger has proved that while this is especially the case with the deeper layers of the sphincter, the superficial do not undergo any such marked differentiation, but retain to a greater extent the original condition. It is in these superficial tracts that the greater number of variations are to be found.

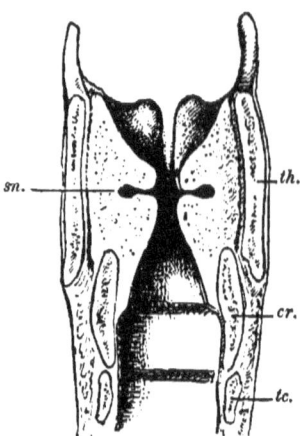

FIG. 102.—HUMAN LARYNX IN FRONTAL SECTION.
th., thyroid cartilage ; *cr.*, cricoid cartilage ; *tc.*, first tracheal cartilage ; *sn.*, sinus of Morgagni.

The close connection between the laryngeal and the pharyngeal musculature is evidenced not only by their common relationships to the vagus nerve, but by the frequent occurrence of fibres connecting the crico-thyroideus muscle with the constrictor pharyngis inferior.

Between the true and false vocal cords there arises on each side of the larynx a diverticulum known as the ventriculus or sinus of Morgagni (*sn.*, Fig. 102). This evagination is directed outwards and somewhat forwards; it also projects upwards more or less, and may even in rare instances reach the upper edge of the thyroid cartilage.

These Morgagni's pouches are susceptible of marked variation, and we have little difficulty in recognising in them the homologues of the "vocal sacs" of the Monkeys. The latter can be filled with air from the larynx, and in certain Anthropoids they may extend far down in the neck, or even to the shoulder or thorax. These sacs, which, when distended, are really immense, may be partly enclosed in an osseus capsule produced by the transformation of the hyoid (*Mycetes*). It seems to me that they may not only act as resonators when the animal howls, but that, when inflated, they may serve to intimidate enemies.

Gruber [and Rudinger] have described cases, in Man, in which the sacs broke through the thyroid membrane and came to lie, like those of the Apes, outside the larynx. [In one case of Rudinger's the sac of the right side was alone present. The same variation has been observed by Bischoff in the Gorilla; and it is interesting to note that inequality in growth of the two sacs has been recorded in the Chimpanzee, the Orang, and in Man.[1]]

On examination of the larynxes of a number of Negroes, Giacomini asserts that the ventriculus in no way differs from that of Europeans. [This is, however, in strange contradiction to the conclusions of Gibb,[2] that the larynx of the Negro differs from that of the white races in the invariable presence of the cartilages of Wrisberg, the obliquity of the true vocal cords, and the pendent condition of the ventricles, which latter, according to him, are situated below the plane of the true vocal cords, instead of above it as in the whites.]

Myologically, Giacomini's inquiry is very interesting. The Italian investigator also examined the Anthropoids, and found that while the Chimpanzee's larynx most nearly resembles that of Man, the Orang's is the least akin to it, and that of *Macacus* and *Cercopithecus* occupies an intermediate position.

LUNGS

Aeby, from a careful study of the structure of the lungs and of the arrangement of the pulmonary vessels, has concluded that in Man the upper lobe of the left lung is homologous with the middle lobe of the right, and that the upper lobe of the right has no counterpart on the left side. The question therefore arises whether this asymmetry is a primitive condition, or whether the left lung may not once have possessed a counterpart to the extra lobe now borne by the right, *i.e.* whether the original plan of the tractus respiratorius, as judged by the subdivision of the trachea, may not have been strictly symmetrical? This would

[1] [Cf. Ehlers, *Abhandlg. K. Gesellsch. d. Wiss. Göttingen*, Bd. xxviii. p. 48.]
[2] [*Mem. Anthropolg. Soc.*, Lond., vol. ii. p. 1.]

appear at first sight the more likely, from the fact that whereas in man an eparterial bronchus is present only on the right side, in some Mammals it occurs (either bronchial or tracheal in origin) on both right and left.[1]

But all these animals, as Gegenbaur has remarked, in the rest of their organisation do not by any means show primitive conditions which can be considered to bear on the genealogy of Man; and great care is therefore necessary in dealing with the question in hand. Cases, in Man, like those described by Dalla Rosa and Bohls, in which an eparterial bronchus is present on both sides [2] must not therefore be hastily classed as atavistic.

It is, further, a very remarkable fact that the Marsupials, Rodents, Insectivora, Lemuroidea, and Apes, show no sign of original bilateral symmetry of the lungs. Further, the ontogeny of Man throws no light on the subject. We therefore at present can neither decide along what line of descent the Mammals above referred to may have inherited their symmetrical eparterial bronchi, nor in what manner the existence of these is to be explained. It is, however, certain that if the human lungs originally bore homologous superior lobes, this symmetry must have been early lost. In face of these facts it is idle to speculate as to probable causes which may perchance have effected a gradual loss of symmetry of the bronchi.

[1] *E.g. Bradypus, Equus, Elephas, Phoca, Phocæna communis, Delphinus delphis,* and *Auchenia.*

[2] The presence on both sides of an eparterial bronchus has only twice been observed in Man—once where the viscera were in the normal position, and once in a case of *situs inversus.* In both instances there were also marked anomalies of the trunks of the larger arteries in the thorax. On each side three well-defined pulmonary lobes were found, and bilateral symmetry was complete (Dalla Rosa).

Complete absence of the eparterial bronchus, and the existence of a tracheal near a bronchial eparterial bronchus, have been observed in Man. In the latter case, according to Chiari, it would appear that one of the collateral (dorsal) branches of the normal bronchial eparterial bronchus had become independent, and wandered up to the trachea. This view receives support from the well-known tendency of the lateral bronchus to give up branches to the principal, and from the study of cases in which two eparterial bronchi, one above the other, are found. The upper of these is evidently a branch of the ordinary eparterial bronchus shifted on to the main bronchus, and in this phenomenon we have an intermediate stage between the normal condition and that of the tracheal bronchus. The latter may therefore be regarded as a branch of the ordinary eparterial bronchus which has wandered farther up. I put forward these views with all reserve.

[His has shown that in Man the first hyparterial bronchus of the left lung divides immediately after its origin, giving off an ascending branch (unrepresented on the right side) which runs forwards to the apex of the lung. Robinson has shown (*Jour. Anat. and Phys.,* vol. xxiii. p. 240) that the same is true of the Rat, and he suggests that this ascending branch may, as it were, compensate for the absence of a distinct eparterial bronchus.]

In dealing with the lung of the Primates, considerable importance attaches to the growing together of the pericardium and the diaphragm, for this brings about a constancy, or, if I may be allowed the expression, a certain rigidity in the form of the pleural cavities. As a consequence of this, a stricter limit is placed upon the extension of the lobes of the lungs than in the lower Mammals, in which the lung is able, either constantly or during inspiration, to penetrate between the heart and the diaphragm, into the sinus subpericardiacus. This applies especially to the right lung, at the base of which a special lobe may be more or less distinctly developed. This, the lobus subpericardiacus (or azygos impar), is occasionally present in Man, most frequently, it appears, in the lower races and in microcephalous individuals. The probability that its presence may be indicative of atavism is not lessened by the fact that indications of it often occur, in the form of a blunt process lying in front of the ligamentum pulmonale, which sinks into a depression in the mediastinum, just as in the Orang.

Hasse has not only confirmed Aeby's observations in all essential points, but, by the aid of very ample material, has extended and revised them. According to him, the principal bronchi of the human lung run downwards, backwards, and slightly outwards, the direct current of inspired air following the same course. He raises the question whether this has always been the disposition of these bronchi, and inquires into its cause. The first question he answers in the negative, and seeks to prove that a very gradual change took place in the position of the bronchi; indeed, that the position which has been acquired in the course of Phylogeny is exactly the reverse of the primitive one. The facts discovered by His in the study of the human embryo lend support to this view. In other words, comparison of the embryonic with the adult condition shows most clearly that a depression of the right and an elevation of the left chief bronchus takes place. The condition of the adult, so far as the branching of the bronchi is concerned, is effected as early as the end of the second month of intra-uterine life, the change being in the main due to the twisting of the heart upwards, backwards, and to the left.

Hasse is, however, unable to prove any more satisfactorily than his predecessors why the right lung-sac is from the first more spacious than the left, and what caused the right eparterial bronchus to appear. He has, however, made an attempt at explanation which, since it appears to me to possess a certain degree of probability, may be here recapitulated. He writes: "Since the heart and its immediate connections push the right primary pulmonary sac, which from the first is larger than the left, backwards and upwards, the branches of the fifth aortic arch —the arteriæ pulmonales—(which, as fig. 15 in His's work shows, descend quite symmetrically) come to lie somewhat differently on the two sides. The right artery must cut across and overlie the primary lung-sac earlier than the left, and become therefore the sooner connected with it. Herein, perhaps, also lies the explanation of the greater growth of the right sac, and of the fact that this gives rise to a special outgrowth, the foundation of the eparterial bronchial system. I am the more inclined to this belief, and to that in the above-named determining causes, by the fact that in cases of *situs inversus* and reversal of the heart and great blood-vessels, the relationships of the right and the left main bronchi, and indeed of the two lungs as wholes, are also reversed (Weber, Leboucq, Aeby)."

This is not the place to consider further either the relationships of the bronchial system, the differences in its distribution in relation to the planes of the body, or the changes which it undergoes after birth. For these details I must refer the reader to the original monograph. In the same work is to be found a discussion of the arrangement of the bronchial system in adult human beings, the explanation of which may be summarised as depending upon the direction of movement of the single points of the thoracic walls lying round the lung. Hasse concludes his interesting account as follows:—"If it be admitted that the tendency towards modification conditioned by the mechanism of the walls of the thorax is inherited, then we must allow that the facts point back to the form of lung of the earliest ancestors of Man among the Amniota, and to the changes which the respiring organs have gradually undergone in the course of time in the ancestral series. The principal direction of the bronchi is at first downwards and backwards. From this it follows, it seems to me, that in the ancestors of Man the diaphragm first played the principal part in respiration. Then the system of branches running outwards and downwards is developed in an ascending degree. From this I conclude that thoracic respiration next supervened in increasing degree, this being most marked in the lower, or better, the posterior part of the thorax, and least marked near its upper and anterior region. By degrees the upper and anterior part of the thorax took an increasing part in respiration, and this led to the mechanism of respiration which is illustrated in Man. This course of the development of respiration and of the respiratory movements, it appears to me, is in exact correspondence with the development of the respiratory organs as I have explained them, and with the facts brought to light by Aeby's investigation of the bronchial tree of the lower animals."[1]

---

[1] I put forward these views of Hasse with all reserve, and I would draw attention once more to a point already touched upon in dealing with the thoracic skeleton

(*ante*, p. 43), *i.e.* the structural variation of the first rib, and the feeble respiratory activity and consequent slight movement of the tips of the lungs. I consider that these phenomena should be regarded as degenerative, on the assumption that the remote ancestors of Man were still provided with cervical ribs, and that their lungs extended farther towards the head than they now do. There must thus, as I think, have been effected in the Phylogeny of Man first a shifting of the respiratory organs in a caudal direction, and next in order the formation of the diaphragm, and, in connection with the latter, a modification of the respiratory mechanism originally restricted to the lungs and the walls of the thorax. The contrast between this theory and that of Hasse is obvious, and although I am as little able as he is to furnish proofs, I believe that my explanation receives support from the facts of development and Comparative Anatomy.

THE CIRCULATORY SYSTEM

IN no other system of organs does the fundamental law of biogenesis find such wide application as in the circulatory, and to go into details concerning it would be merely to repeat what has been often said before. Attention may therefore be confined to the following facts.

THE HEART

The heart arises (*cd.*, Fig. 31, A), at an early embryonic stage, far forwards in the cervical and indeed in the cephalic region. This recalls its position in adult Fishes and Amphibians. The comparison with these animals is the more fully justified, in that the heart of the early human embryo, like that of the lowest Anamnia, has throughout a single lumen, and its further differentiation is gradually undergone in correspondence with the phylogenetic development of the organ.

The structure of the heart, originally very simple, soon becomes complicated, but even then certain peculiarities of the right auricle point back to the condition found in the Amphibia. These are, for example, the inconstant vestiges of valves at the opening of the left vena cava superior (Thebesian valve), and the almost constant remains of the valves of the sinus at that of the vena cava inferior (Eustachian valve). The same applies to the traces of the incorporation of the sinus venosus and of the pulmonary veins into the opposite divisions of the atrium (auricles). In short, Comparative Anatomy furnishes not only interesting parallels with, but an explanation of the various stages in the Ontogeny of the heart of the higher Vertebrata. There are, however, some conditions which occur in the Mammalian heart, especially during the early periods of its development, which cannot be explained by inheritance, but which have arisen secondarily through adaptation; among the chief of these are the secondary perforation of the septum atriorum and the formation of the annulus ovalis or isthmus of Vieussens.

THE ARTERIAL SYSTEM

The arterial system of Man bears traces of primitive conditions. It is indeed an astonishing fact, for example, that the aortic arch system of the embryos of the higher Vertebrata, up to Man himself, appears in the same manner as in the Anamnia. Six pairs of aortic arches in all are formed in the young Mammalian embryo, but the representatives of the first and second of these and the vestige of the fifth degenerate early,[1] and consequently only three pairs remain to undergo final transformation.

[Conspicuous among the variations occurring in Man is the occasional presence in the adult of paired aortic arches, the arch of the right side, which usually disappears during development, being retained. Twelve cases of double aortic arch have been recorded in Man,[2] and this variation may be accompanied by the obliteration and reduction to a fibrous band of the ordinarily functional (left) arch,[3] the resulting condition of the parts being essentially that characteristic of Birds.] In a similar manner, many of the variations to which the vessels derivative of the primitive arterial system of the human embyro are liable, can only be explained by the fact that embryonic trunks, which under normal conditions become occluded and vestigial, may remain functional throughout life. In this respect the Anthropoids altogether agree with Man.

On the inner surface of the abdominal wall in Man three cord-like structures pass from near the bladder to the navel. These are known as the ligamentum vesicale medium and the ligamenta vesicalia lateralia. The first urachus corresponds with the stalk of the allantois of the embryo; the latter, however, are the last vestiges of the umbilical or hypogastric arteries, which during intra-uterine life, *i.e.* from about the time when the posterior limbs are just beginning to appear as buds, convey the

[1] [The recent researches of Boas and others have proved that in all classes of terrestrial Vertebrates the pulmonary artery is a derivative of the sixth aortic arch (the fourth branchial), and that the arch in front of it is suppressed; and Zimmermann has shown that Man himself is no exception to this rule (*Verhandlg. Internat. Medic. Congresses X.*, Berlin, 1891, Bd. ii., Abth. i. p. 145).]
[2] [Cf. Leboucq, *Ann. Sci. Med. Gand.*, 1894, p. 7.]
[3] [Cf. Morrison Watson, *Jour. Anat. and Phys.*, vol. xi. p. 229.]

blood from the aorta to the placenta. The basal portions of these vessels often remain patent throughout life, and function as superior vesical arteries; the remainder of each, however, i.e. by far its greater portion, loses its lumen altogether and becomes a solid strand of connective tissue.

[Considerable interest attaches to those veins of the very variable "vesico-prostatic plexus" which, in the adult, in proximity to the above-named arteries, carry back the blood from the urinary bladder to the internal iliac veins. The detailed relationships of certain varieties of these would seem to suggest, by analogy to the lower vertebrata, that they may be associated with the "anterior abdominal" venous system regularly present in Birds, Reptiles, and Amphibians, and represented by at least its main trunk, in the Monotreme *Echidna*[1] among Mammals.]

The continuation proper of the axis of the human aorta is represented by a weak vestigial vessel, of very variable relationships[2]—the arteria sacralis media. In long-tailed animals, in which the posterior end of the body has not undergone reduction, this vessel is represented by the caudal artery, which is a direct, gradually diminishing, continuation of the aorta, originally giving off, like it, segmentally recurrent branches.

When we consider the polymeric origin of the limbs (cf. *ante*, p. 67) dating back to an originally segmented condition of the trunk, it is evident that their principal arteries must have arisen in relation to segmental arteries of the body wall, and that originally they in no way differed from these. This assumption finds actual proof in the mode of origin of the arteria subclavia; but while it is comparatively easy to prove this for the fore-limb, in the hind-limb a difficulty presents itself, since its corresponding vessel at a very early period undergoes a great increase in size and marked specialisation in relation to the development of the umbilical artery.[3] In any case it is certain that the

---

[1] [Cf. Fenwick, *Jour. Anat. and Phys.*, vol. xix. p. 320 ; and Beddard, *Proc. Zool. Soc.*, Lond., 1884, p. 553.]

[2] [These have been recently tabulated for 400 autopsies worked out by collective investigation in medical schools, under the auspices of the Anatomical Society of Great Britain and Ireland. In one instance the vessel appears to have been entirely absent, cf. *Jour. Anat. and Phys.*, vol. xxvii. pp. 184-187.]

[3] I cannot here enter further either into the question of primary origin, direct from the aorta, of the arteria umbilicalis, or into that of the secondary connection between this vessel and the arteries of the limbs. It must suffice to refer the reader

artery known as the common iliac is the first formed of the posterior limb, and that it arises as a segmental vessel of the aorta.

The artery which, in the embryo Mammal, including Man, runs into the developing posterior limb bud, does not directly become the arteria femoralis of the adult. It accompanies the ischiadic [or crural] nerve in its distribution; on the posterior side of the limb it runs down to the bend of the knee, and from this point is continued into the upper part of the thigh. This artery should be called the ischiadic [or crural] as it corresponds with the vessel of the same name in most Birds, and with the principal vessel of the hind-limb in Reptiles and Amphibians.

"The femoral artery develops later as a branch of the iliac. At first it spreads only over the inner or ventral portion of the thigh; it, however, soon grows rapidly in a distal direction, along the inner surface of the cartilaginous femur, to the bend of the knee, where it unites with the ischiadic artery. The femoral artery thus formed rapidly increases in size, while that section of the ischiadic related to the upper leg degenerates. It is thus that the definitive condition is attained; and but a short vestige of the arteria ischiadica persists in the adult, as the "ischiadic" or "inferior gluteal" (Hochstetter). Mechanical causes may have perhaps brought about this change in the principal artery of the hind-limb in the ancestors of Mammals, but we have no clear knowledge on the subject.

In no other part of the body are the variations in the arteries so frequent as in the fore-limb, especially in the hand. The arteries of the foot present numerous variations, and, in correlation with the variations of the skeleton and musculature, some of these may be classed as progressive and others as retrogressive.

Where a supracondyloid process of the humerus exists (cf. *ante*, p. 78) the brachial artery lies behind it. The latter is thus covered by the head of the pronator teres muscle which extends upwards, and the condition resembles that of those Mammals in which the brachial artery and median nerve pass through an invariably developed foramen supracondyloideum.[1]

A comparison of the arteries of the hand with those of the foot shows that there are in the hand two palmar arches, a

to the recent series of very careful studies by Hochstetter, published in the *Morphologisches Jahrbuch*.

[1] For further details on this point, cf. Ruge, *Morpholg. Jahrb.*, Bd. ix. p. 329.

deeper and a superficial, but in the foot only a deep plantar one. It is evident on reflection that a superficial arch cannot exist in the foot on account of its functions as an organ of support, and that the larger pedal arteries, to be free from interference with the circulation, may have had to withdraw into the recesses of the foot. Indications, however, are not infrequently encountered that the foot formerly possessed a superficial arterial arch, and that the arteries for the toes arose from it, in a manner identical with that in which the arteries for the fingers arise from the superficial palmar arch of the hand.

Finally, as to the intestinal arteries, although our knowledge of the development of these is still very limited, all things point to the fact that originally they were numerous and segmental, and that their final reduction in Man and Mammals to three trunks, the cœliac, omphalo-mesaraic (which later becomes the superior mesenteric), and the inferior mesenteric, is to be considered as secondary.

THE VENOUS SYSTEM

The developing venous system of Man, like the arterial, shows unmistakable traces of a very primitive condition inherited from the lower Vertebrates. In this connection the anterior and posterior cardinal veins, the ductus Cuvieri, and the sinus venosus cordis, are especially conspicuous.

The system of the vena cava inferior is a late acquisition, dating [in its fully differentiated form] from the higher Fishes (Dipnoi) and Amphibians. Its phylogenetically recent origin is, even in Man, denoted by the variation and arrested development which it occasionally exhibits. Several cases of [that which Hochstetter's researches prove to be] the persistence of an early stage in its development have been recorded. I refer to those in which the caval vein, from about the level of the superior mesenteric, is continued downwards towards the pelvis, owing to the retention of the posterior cardinals.

In these cases we may speak of persistence of the posterior cardinals in the form of a double vena cava inferior.

In other cases of what we may now regard as arrested development, the distal portion of the inferior vena cava is formed out of the left instead of the right cardinal vein, there is then a vena cava inferior passing to the left [of the aorta].

In very rare cases, where development is arrested at a very

early stage (eighteen to twenty-one days after fertilisation), the post-caval vein never develops, and the posterior cardinals take its place.

In one such case, described by Kollmann, the two posterior cardinal veins persisted to the level of the third lumbar vertebra. At the crura of the diaphragm, within the aortic foramen, the right cardinal vein was connected with the left by three branches. The trunk thus related lay to the left of the aorta, and ran on as a persistent portion of the left cardinal. At the level of the tenth thoracic vertebra the vessel turned to the right, and after this it was the right cardinal vein which was continued to its point of entrance into the vena cava superior. The ductus venosus Arantii was absent; and the circulation in the liver remained entirely embryonic, the hepatic veins still entering the heart separately. This remarkable case was that of a man of twenty-eight, who had committed suicide.

In Man, and certain Mammals (Apes, Lemurs, Carnivora, Whales, and Edentates), the left vena cava superior early degenerates and disappears, with the exception of its basal portion, which remains as "the coronary sinus," so-called on account of its receiving the intrinsic cardiac veins. [The great veins of the head, neck, and fore-limb on the left side become connected with those of the right by a transverse trunk, derived from the left innominate vein—the two innominate or brachio-cephalic veins uniting to form the single "superior cava."] In this we have to deal with the modification of a condition which in other Mammals (Rodents, Insectivora, Bats, and Ungulates) is retained throughout life; [and it is an interesting circumstance that among these a transverse connection between the great veins of the neck strongly suggestive of that above described may not infrequently be established (ex. *Lepus*), without any accompanying reduction of the left pre-caval.]

The venous system, so rich in variations, is well known to possess valves which prevent regurgitation, [and thus ensure the maintenance of the single circle of the circulation.] In keeping with this we should expect to find such valves chiefly in the limbs, *i.e.* where the venous stream—I refer especially to the lower limbs—already has great difficulties to overcome. This expectation is fulfilled; but when we reflect that the ancestor of Man himself had a quadrupedal ancestry, it follows that there must have been a time in which his thoracic, and abdominal, and dorsal surfaces, now disposed antero-posteriorly, were turned downwards and upwards and were disposed ventro-dorsally. Circulation within the intercostal and lumbar veins must then have been placed under much less favourable conditions than at present: it had to be maintained, as the venous circulation in the lower limbs now has, against the action of gravity. This justifiable assumption has led me to investigate the intercostal veins in Man closely, by way of ascertaining if they possess valves, and my observations in all essentials confirm those of Henle recorded in his *Handbuch der Anatomie*. That is, I found great variation both in the number and the development of the valves, so that the impression of a retrogressive condition became irresistible.

It is well known that in other parts of the body, valves of the veins appear in a reduced and evidently degenerating or vestigial form, and also that in the embryo there arise many more valves than attain complete development. [The valves of the portal system are among the number thus suppressed, but they may be occasionally retained.[1]]

THE SPLEEN

Throughout the Mammalian series three lobes of the spleen may be detected, viz. an anterior, a posterior, and a middle, all of which vary greatly in size and form, in the various types. In Marsupials the posterior lobe stretches far down towards the rectum. In the Placental mammals the lobes are increasingly reduced, and finally, in the Primates, the posterior lobe has almost disappeared; but the anterior and the median are represented even in Man, while the posterior lobe is in him reduced to a projection of its margo obtusus (Klaatsch).

The average weight of the spleen in the white races is said to be 195, and in the black but 171 grs.

[1] [These valves are typically bicuspid. They are most numerous at birth, in the vessels of the large intestine. After birth they disappear rapidly, and when present in the adult they appear to be most abundant on the small intestine. Cf. Hochstetter, *Archiv f. Anat. und Phys.*, 1887 ; *Anat. Abth.*, p. 137 ; and Bryant, *Boston Medical and Surgical Journal*, vol. cxix. p. 400. Hyrtl long ago drew attention (*Sitzungsb. Wien. Akad.*, Bd. lxi. p. 27) to the existence in the Rodentia of a spiral valve-like fold within the portal vein.]

THE URINOGENITAL SYSTEM

THE PRONEPHROS AND THE PRIMITIVE KIDNEY

IN all classes of Vertebrates the Urinogenital System first appears [in the form of a duct (Wolffian or Segmental duct) which is primarily related to a urinary apparatus confined to the head region. In the Amniota and Selachii the latter is wholly degenerate in character; among the remaining Anamnia, however, it may for a longer or shorter period persist as a distinct firstformed functional excretory organ. It is accordingly regarded as a possible larval kidney, and termed the pronephros, as it appears to be of very ancient origin]. While the secreting glandular portion of this system never lasts for more than a short period, its duct persists and appears in some cases (cf. *infra*, p. 190) to give rise to the leading duct of a much more extensive urinary system that develops later and is known as the middle kidney or mesonephros.

This second nephridial system, which becomes the definitive urinary system of Fishes and Amphibia, consists like the pronephros of metamerically recurrent tubes. The two systems are so constituted as to suggest for the Vertebrata of to-day an origin from a lowly segmented ancestor.[1]

The higher Vertebrates pass through an embryonic stage, in which they possess first a pronephros and then a mesonephros, which is an irrefragable proof that in their ancestors, and con-

[1] [This view receives support from the general tendency towards corresponding metamerism of the muscular, skeletal, nervous, and vascular systems of the vertebrate body. There are, however, reasons for thinking that the recurrent symmetry of at least the skeletal and muscular apparatus may be of secondary significance; and there are not wanting competent investigators who deny *in toto* the origin of Vertebrates from multi-segmented animals (cf. especially W. K. Brooks "The Genus Salpa," *Mem. Biol. Lab., Johns Hopkins Univ.*, II. pp. 182-203). The whole question must remain in abeyance, pending further inquiry into the origin of metamerism in general, with a view to the formation of a sounder conception concerning that.]

sequently in the ancestors of Man, each of these organs once constituted in turn a permanent urinary system.[1]

[The definitive kidney and ureter of Mammals arises at a comparatively later period (eleventh to twelfth day of intra-uterine life) in relation to an outgrowth of the base of the mesonephric duct.[2] This kidney, by extension, reaches to the mesonephridial region. On account of its distinct origin from the rest of the excretory system it is generally termed the metanephros, and its duct the metanephric duct.]

The definitive adult kidney of Man is, as a rule, a compact organ, with smooth walls; but its surface is not infrequently more or less distinctly furrowed, and thus apparently lobed. Lobation of the kidney is characteristic of certain lower Mammals [*e.g.* Cetacea and Ungulata]. The regular appearance of furrows in the kidney of the human embryo, giving rise to the so-called "renculi," and the not infrequent occurrence of an increased number of renal arteries, justify the conclusion that the lobate structure may have been typical of the ancestors of Man.

It is not yet evident what first led to the degeneration of the pronephros and to the loss of a renal function by the mesonephros in the amniota. So far as the mesonephros was concerned, the degeneration did not originally affect the whole organ, but only a part of it. The remainder, undergoing a change of function, became secondarily related to the male reproductive[3] apparatus. It gave rise with its duct to the epididymis and vas deferens, and became otherwise transformed into a series of vestigial appendages to the urinogenital organs of both sexes.

[1] This view, so far as it involves the conclusion that the mesonephros of the Amniota is the representative of the excretory organ of their ancestors, receives its chief support from the condition of the excretory apparatus in Reptiles. These animals pass through a period in which the greater part of the mesonephros continues functional, side by side with the later definitive kidney. In the Lizards, for example, it shrivels up after the first hibernation, *i.e.* in the second year.

[2] [The metanephric tubules of Mammals are stated to arise as outgrowths of this diverticulum itself, but in other animals there is good reason for regarding them as, at any rate in part, distinct in origin—*i.e.* as arising independently of the duct with which they subsequently become connected, in the manner typical of the mesonephric series. The recent researches of Semon (*Jenaische Zeitschrift*, Bd. xxvi. p. 89) and Field (*Bullet. Mus. Comp. Zool. Harvard*, vol. xxi. p. 201) have revealed striking details of similarity in development between the pro- and meso-nephridia, rendering it more difficult than hitherto sharply to discriminate between them. Indeed, recent discovery tends to suggest that the pro-, meso-, and meta-nephridia are portions of one continuous system, and that their apparent independence is due to the assumption of secondary relationships with independently formed ducts.]

[3] The initial stages in this process have been permanently retained as the adult condition by the Elasmobranchs and Amphibia.

In the wholly vestigial condition the mesonephros is not infrequently the seat of origin of pathological affections (formation of cysts).

The vestigial portions of the mesonephros in men are the paradidymis, Giraldé's organ, and the stalked hydatids of Morgagni; in women it gives rise to the greater part of the parovarium and the whole of the paroophoron. Further, in women, the last vestiges of its duct are found, either confined to the region of the parovarium, or, where suppression is least marked, in the form of "Gärtner's canal" which reaches the vagina.

MÜLLERIAN DUCT

Van Wijhe, believing that the ancestors of the vertebrate were hermaphrodite, has argued that the first appearance of the Müllerian duct probably dates back to a period in the evolution of the phylum when, as a means of preventing self-fertilisation, there were distinct ducts for the transmission of the sperm and the ova. Be this as it may, the secondary nature of the Müllerian duct is shown by its comparatively late development in the individual. It originates in the Amniota by evagination of the cœlomic epithelium, to form a structure which, becoming constricted off into a tube, gradually elongates in a caudal direction to reach the cloaca.

In the male, the duct of the mesonephros, and in the female, as is well known, the whole of the Müllerian duct, forms the adult genital duct (cf. Fig. 103). In the male the greater part of the Müllerian duct degenerates or entirely disappears, thus losing nearly all physiological significance. Its proximal vestige becomes in Man the unstalked hydatid of Morgagni, a small appendage of the testis; its distal end, however, is believed to unite with that of its fellow of the opposite side to form a vesicle, the "uterus masculinus," which becomes embedded in the prostate, and later opens, conjointly with the vasa deferentia, into the urinogenital sinus (urethra).[1]

[1] [The term "uterus masculinus" is applied, by analogy, to a somewhat similarly placed median vesicle, opening into the prostatic portion of the urethra in other Mammals. One well-known case is that of the common Rabbit. The so-called "uterus masculinus" of that animal certainly does superficially resemble that of Man, but the two differ fundamentally in their relationships to the vasa differentia, *i.e.* in Man the bases of these pass behind the vesicle and open at its sides, while in the Rabbit they pass in front of it and open within its anterior lip. Kölliker from the study of its development, has claimed for the so-called "uterus masculinus" of the Rabbit) (*Entwicklungsgesch. d. Menschen u. d. höhern Thiere*,

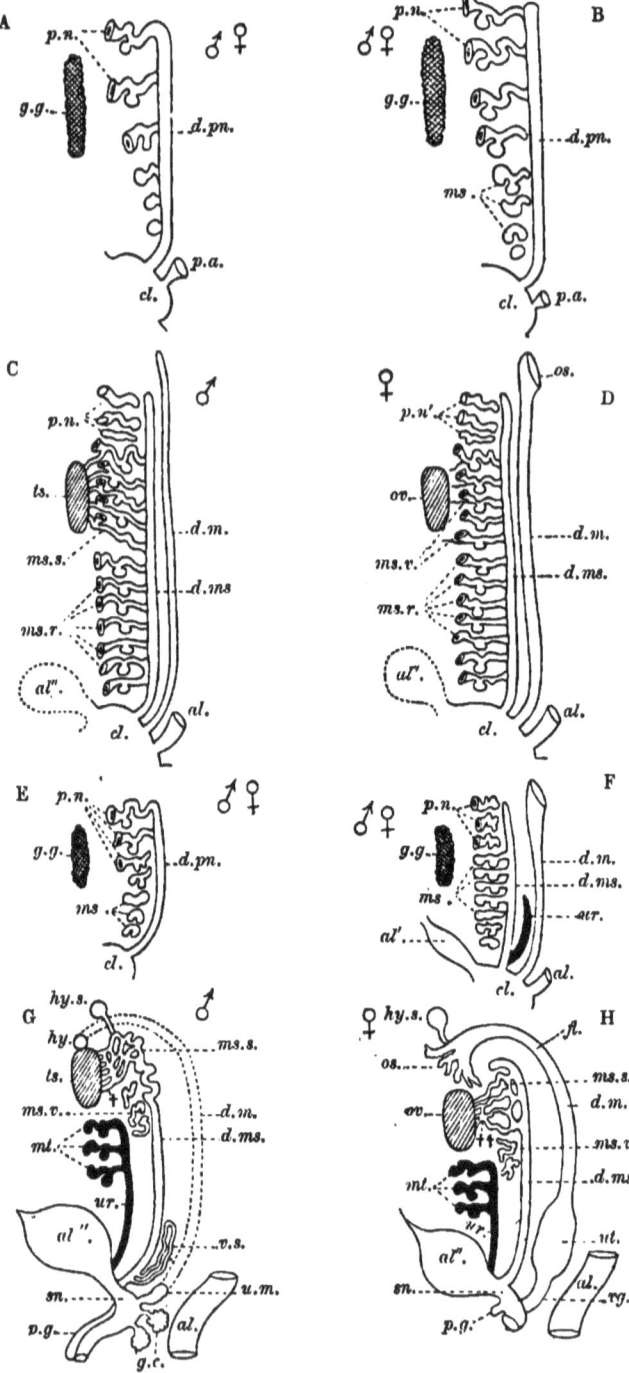

THE URINOGENITAL SYSTEM

FIG. 103.—A SERIES OF WHOLLY DIAGRAMMATIC FIGURES TO ILLUSTRATE THE COMPARATIVE MORPHOLOGY OF THE URINOGENITAL ORGANS OF THE VERTEBRATA.

A, The pronephros stage of the Anamnia ; B, a later stage of the same ; C, the urinogenital apparatus of the male Amphibian ; D, the same of the female ; E, pronephros stage of the Amniota, the mesonephros as yet rudimentary ; F, urinogenital apparatus of the Amniota, at a stage at which the sexes are not differentiated ; G, urinogenital apparatus of the male Amniota ; H, the same of the female ; $p.n.$, pronephros ; $d.pn.$, duct of the pronephros ; $ms.$, the developing mesonephros ; $ms.s.$, part of the mesonephros, becoming converted into the epididymis and parovarium ; $ms.r.$, vestiges of the mesonephros, the paradidymis and the paroophoron ; †, rete and vasa efferentia testis ; ††, a network homologous with these structures at the hilus ovarii ; $hy.s.$, stalked hydatid ; $ms.r.$, portion of the mesonephros which in Amphibians and Selachians becomes the so-called pelvic kidney ; $d.ms.$, duct of the mesonephros, which in male Amphibians and Selachians becomes (Fig. C) the urinogenital, and in females (Fig. D) the urinary duct. In the male Amniota it gives rise to the seminal duct (Fig. G), and in the female to the Gärtner's duct (Fig. H). $v.s.$, the seminal vesicle, an outgrowth of the duct of the mesonephros ; $d.m.$, Müllerian duct, which in Mammals becomes differentiated (Fig. H) into the Fallopian tube ($fl.$), the uterus ($ut.$), and the vagina ($vg.$) ; $os.$, its ostium abdominale tubæ ; $hy.$ and $u.m.$ (Fig. G), unstalked hydatids and uterus masculinus (vestiges, in the male, of the Müllerian duct, $d.m.$) ; $mt.$, the definitive kidney or metanephros of the Amniota, asserted to arise from the ureter ($ur.$), itself an outgrowth of the mesonephric duct ; $al''.$, allantois (urinary bladder) ; $sn.$, sinus urogenitalis ; $p.g.$, genital prominence ; $g.g.$, genital glands, undifferentiated stage ; $ov.$, ovary ; $ts.$, testis ; $cl.$, cloaca ; $al.$, hind-gut ; $p.a.$, porus abdominalis ; $g.c.$, Cowper's glands.

Tabulated Résumé of the Facts pictorially illustrated on the opposite Page.

		Anamnia.	Amniota.
Pronephros.	Male and Female.	Develops in all Anamnia, but in all probability never persists as a permanent excretory organ.	Still develops in the Amniota, but as an excretory organ undergoes entire degeneration in the embryo.
Duct of Pronephros.	Male and Female.	In Elasmobranchii, appears to give origin by subdivision to both Mesonephric (Wolffian) and Müllerian ducts. In Amphibia, becomes converted into the Mesophric duct. Its fate in other Anamnia is not yet fully investigated.	Probably persists as the Mesonephric (Wolffian) duct, and contributes in some to the formation of the Müllerian duct. Great differences of interpretation still exist concerning it.
Mesonephros.	Male and Female.	Functions in all Anamnia as a urinary gland. In Elasmobranchs, Amphibians, and one or two higher Fishes, its anterior portion becomes related to the male genital apparatus, the posterior portion persisting as a permanent kidney.	Loses its renal function in all Amniota (as a rule in the embryo), and becomes vestigial, except so far as it becomes an accessory portion of the reproductive apparatus in the male, [and enters into the formation of the suprarenal body.]

		Anamnia.	Amniota.
Mesonephros.	Male.	The proximal portion becomes in most related to the testis, and functional in the transmission of the semen, the distal functioning as a kidney.[1]	The proximal end becomes the rete and vasa efferentia testis, and the caput epididymis, and perhaps also the stalked hydatid of Morgagni: the distal end becomes the paradidymis (Giraldé's organ).[2]
	Female.	Persists as the kidney.	The greater part of the proximal portion becomes the parovarium, the distal the paroophoron.[2]
Duct of Mesonephros.	Male.	Functions in most higher Fishes merely as the urinary duct. In Selachians, Amphibians, and some Ganoids, serves as the urinogenital duct.	The proximal portion becomes the corpus and cauda epididymis, and the distal the seminal duct (vas deferens).
	Female.	Functions exclusively as the duct of the mesonephros, i.e. the urinary duct.	The greater part, as a rule, degenerates; the proximal portion may be retained in a vestigial form in the region of the parovarium. In certain cases it may persist as a whole, as Gärtner's canal. The distal end becomes the organ of Weber.
Müllerian Ducts.	Male.	In Elasmobranchs, for certain, it degenerates in post-embryonic life, vestiges of its proximal portion being retained. (Its fate in most other Fishes is doubtful.) In Amphibia it is retained for its whole length, in a functionless and often but little degenerate condition.	The proximal portion becomes the unstalked hydatid of Morgagni, the distal, in some Mammals, the so-called "uterus masculinus." In exceptional cases the whole is retained as Rathke's duct. In Sauropsida the distal part usually disappears.
	Female.	Becomes the whole genital duct.	Becomes the whole genital duct.
Metanephros & Ureter.	Male and Female.	Probably unrepresented.	Development not yet fully worked out. It appears to arise in part (ureter) from the distal end of the mesonephric duct, and in part (secreting elements) as a caudad extension of the mesonephros.

[1] [The males of the Bony Fishes and of the Marsipobranchii are exceptions to this rule, the mesonephros being in them functional only as a kidney].

[2] [Allowance being made for its entering into the constitution of the suprarenal body (cf. previous page).]

THE URINOGENITAL SYSTEM 193

In Amphibia, Reptiles, and Birds, the Müllerian ducts in the female remain separate throughout life, and this is also the case in the lowest living Mammals (Monotremata), which are partly on this account called the Ornithodelphia. In all Mammals above the Monotremes, however, they early become to a lesser or greater

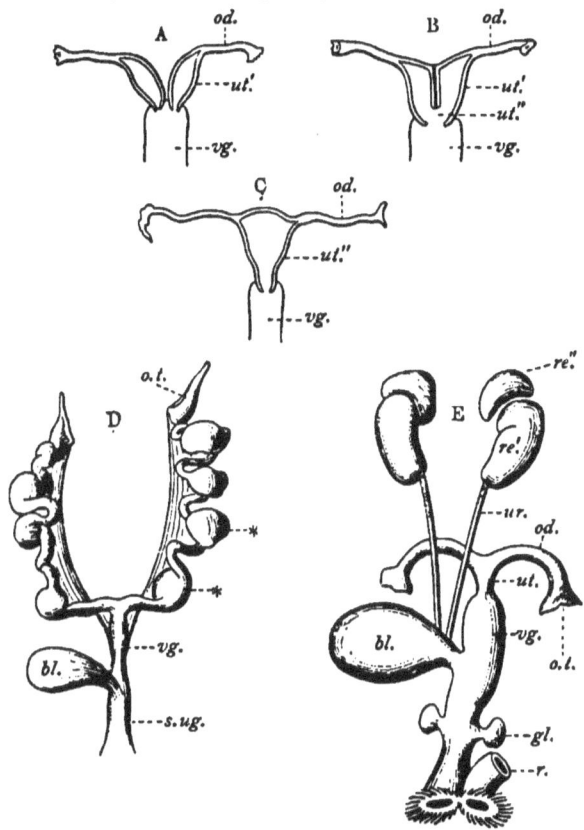

FIG. 104.—A to C, DIAGRAMMATIC REPRESENTATIONS OF THE CHIEF TYPES OF UTERUS OCCURRING IN THE PLACENTAL MAMMALS. A, UTERUS DUPLEX; B, UTERUS BIPARTITUS; C, UTERUS SIMPLEX; D, URINOGENITAL APPARATUS OF A FEMALE MUSTELINE; E, THE SAME OF THE HEDGEHOG, THE FORMER WITH EMBRYOS (* *) IN THE UTERUS.

od., oviduct (Fallopian tube); *ut.*, uterus; *ut'.*, cornua uteri; *ut".*, corpus uteri; *vg.*, vagina; *ot.*, ostium tubæ; *gl.*, accessory gland; *r.*, rectum; *s.ug.*, sinus urinogenitalis; *re'.*, kidney; *re".*, suprarenal body; *ur.*, ureter; *bl.*, bladder.

Aufl. II. p. 981) a paired origin from the bases of the mesonephric ducts, and in respect to this it exactly harmonises with, and would appear to represent in a confluent form, the human vesiculæ seminales. The fact that among other Rodents it is represented (*e.g.* Guinea-Pig) by a pair of elongated cœca, or (*e.g.* Muridæ) by two folded and more glandular diverticula, having the detailed relationships of the seminal vesicles of the other mammalia, fully bears out this view.—G. B. II.]

O

extent united, the union being first effected at a middle point, before the ducts themselves open into the urinogenital sinus. [Those portions of the oviducts situated above this point of union become converted into the uteri and Fallopian tubes, and those below into the vaginæ.]

Among the Marsupials there arises at this point a median vaginal sac, and neither the upper (uterine) nor the lower (vaginal) portions unite further. For this reason these animals are frequently classified as the Didelphia. In all the higher and truly placental Mammals the union extends backwards to form a single median vagina [as is expressed in the application to them of the term Monodelphia]. It also extends forwards, giving rise to a single median uterus as we ascend in the series (cf. Fig. 104). Man and the Primates are among those monodelphous Mammals in which the two uteri as a rule completely unite; but abnormal forms of uterus, known as uterus duplex, bilocularis, subseptus, bipartitus, incudiformis, arcuatus, and bicornis, not infrequently occur, at any rate in Man. These are but the expression of arrested development,—arrested, that is, at stages corresponding with those of the gradual fusion of the originally separate Müllerian ducts effected during the course of long geological periods. The uterus simplex is the normal condition in the Primates of the present time.

In the uterus simplex, traces of the primitive paired condition of the Müllerian duct are still found in the paired Fallopian tubes (*od.*, Fig. 104, C), and in the longitudinal ridges of the cervix uteri and of the vagina (columnæ rugarum).

HYMEN

The primitive significance of the fold of mucous membrane termed the hymen, which lies within the entrance of the vagina in the female and more or less completely closes it, is by no means clear. The only thing that can be stated with certainty is that it is coincident in disposition with the elevation of the urethral mucous membrane of the male known as the colliculus seminalis.

[It is an interesting fact that a similar and complete fold is present within the base of the oviduct in the virgin state of the lower Fishes (Sharks and Rays).]

THE CLOACA

At a certain stage in the development of Man the urinogenital ducts and intestine open posteriorly into a common chamber, the cloaca. This points back to a condition which must have existed in the remote ancestors of Man, for a cloaca persists throughout life in Amphibians, Reptiles, and Birds, as well as in the lowest Mammals, which last are on this account called the Monotremata.

In the further course of development the cavity of the cloaca becomes divided into two, the posterior chamber serving as a prolongation of the rectum, the anterior forming a sinus urinogenitalis, from the anterior wall of which the genital eminence is developed (cf. Fig. 103, G and H).

EXTERNAL GENITAL ORGANS OF THE FEMALE

Concerning the external genital apparatus of the female, the labia majora are probably to be regarded as partially developed homologues of the scrotum of the male. Indications of them are found even in the Lemuroidea and the Apes; but in most Apes it appears that only the lesser system of folds found in women, the labia minora, form the boundary of the genital aperture. The labia minora, which form a strong præputium and frenulum clitoridis, belong ontogenetically to the genital eminence, and are developed upon its lower surface. They thus fall under a different morphological category from the labia majora.

The clitoris in Apes is both relatively and absolutely larger than in human beings, and its under surface is furrowed as far as the urinary aperture. This primitive condition is recalled by the occasional condition, due to arrested development of the genital eminence, known as hypospadias.

In certain branches of the Ethiopian race the females are distinguished by a very slight development of the labia majora and of the mons veneris, and of hair about these parts. On the other hand, among the female Hottentots, a marked hypertrophy of the labia minora and of the præputium clitoridis is well known, giving rise to what is known among Bushwomen as the "Hottentot apron." [This, however, is most probably due to manipulation, and to the wearing of a split stick with a weight attached.] The vagina appears (as in Apes) smoother, it being less strongly folded than in unmarried Europeans. In Japanese women the labia majora and the mons veneris are feebly developed and but little hairy, and the labia minora seem also to be but slightly developed (Bischoff).

MALE GENITAL GLANDS (DESCENSUS TESTICULORUM)

Among Mammals the genital glands of the male (testes) agree in their place of origin with those of the female (ovaries). Both are developed out of the germinal epithelium, differentiated near the dorsal wall of the cœlom to the right and left of the vertebral column. But while, during further development, the ovaries, as a rule, shift down towards the pelvis, the testes may wander still farther (*descensus testiculorum*). This descensus is closely connected not only with the history of the testis, as the result of interaction between the organ and the parts immediately surrounding it, but also with the relations of the testis to other organs more or less remote from it.

Many variations occur among Mammals in the manner of descent of the testis, and in the changes in the ventral body wall which accompany it. It seems possible, however, as Klaatsch has shown, to reduce these variations to a simple ground plan. The descent of the testes, which is a new development peculiar to Mammals, is effected in its most primitive manner in Insectivores and Rodents; and everything points to the fact that it was originally a periodic phenomenon occurring in the adult. For instance, in the Hedgehog the testes retain their original intra-abdominal position up to the rutting period; but as that period approaches they come to lie in evaginable portions of the inguinal body wall. After the rutting season they always return into the abdominal cavity, but the mechanism by which this is accomplished is not yet clearly understood.

In connection with the shifting of the testis, a structure termed by Klaatsch the "conus inguinalis" is of the greatest significance. This organ is best developed in the Muridæ, and consists of a conical invagination of the muscular abdominal wall, at first connected not with the three lateral abdominal muscles, but only with the obliquus internus and transversus. Its internally projecting point, or at least its surrounding tissue, fuses with a cord-like structure called by Klaatsch the ligamentum inguinale (cf. Fig. 105). This ligamentum inguinale (which must not be confused with the gubernaculum or round ligament of earlier writers) is a subperitoneal strand containing smooth muscle, which arises, in both sexes, on each side of the genital ducts, and runs to the inguinal region of the abdominal wall, *i.e.* to that point which corresponds with the aperture of the canalis inguinalis interna. This "ligament," for which a parallel exists in other differentiations of the cœlomic musculature (*e.g.* the musculus suspensorius duodeni, musculature of the genital ducts), leaves the genital duct at the point where the ligamentum testis or ovarii reaches it. This coincidence of position by no means always obtains; but the fact that it may do so has led to the erroneous idea that the ligaments of the genital ducts hitherto known as the ligamentum rotundum and the gubernaculum always and alone connect the ovary and testis with the inguinal region. The study of Ontogeny proves that in origin they are distinct from the ligamentum inguinale. The latter, in the female, becomes the ligamentum rotundum uteri. Besides this,

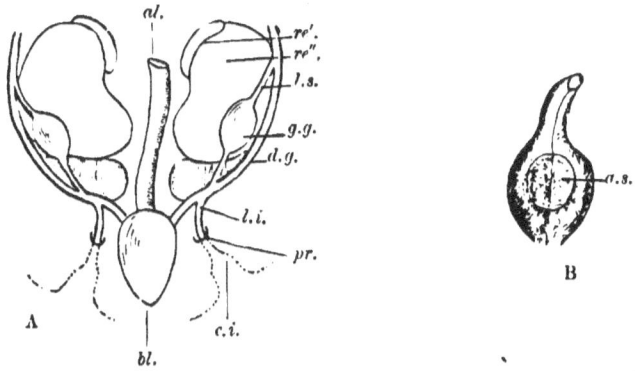

FIG. 105.—A, A PARTLY DIAGRAMMATIC REPRESENTATION OF THE EMBRYONIC URINOGENITAL APPARATUS OF A MALE MAMMAL, SHOWING ITS RELATIONS TO THE VENTRAL ABDOMINAL WALL.
B, THE PENIS AND SCROTUM OF A HUMAN EMBRYO 15 CM. LONG, WITH THE AREÆ SCROTI (*a.s.*) MEETING IN THE MIDDLE LINE.
(BOTH FIGURES FOUNDED ON THE WORK OF KLAATSCH.)
al., intestine ; *re'.*, suprarenal body ; *re".*, kidney ; *l.s.*, suspensory ligament of testis ; *g.g.*, testis ; *d.g.*, genital duct ; *l.i.*, ligamentum inguinale ; *pr.*, processus vaginalis ; *c.i.*, conus inguinalis ; *bl.*, urinary bladder.

the ligamentum inguinale, as well as the conus inguinalis of Klaatsch, were called gubernaculum testis by former authors; in fact, the term gubernaculum was originally applied to the most heterogeneous structures.

In the Insectivora and Rodents, the descent of the testis is accompanied by an evagination of the conus due to muscular contraction, so that the ligament may in this case rightly be termed a "gubernaculum." This evagination gives rise to a more or less marked bulging of the integument, to form the "bursa inguinalis" of Klaatsch. This pouch, which represents the point of least resistance in the abdominal wall, is composed of (1) the evaginated abdominal integument (scrotum, sac of the testis), (2) evaginated derivatives of the internal oblique and transversus muscles (cremaster), and its cavity is connected with the cœlom by a special canal (canalis vaginalis in the male, canalis Nuckii in the female).

The differentiation of these parts, which was in all probability originally effected only in the adult, in some cases takes place at an earlier (Mouse) or even embryonic period (Squirrel).

It is conceivable that next in order to the type represented by Rodents and Insectivores, there may have existed forms in which the descensus occurred periodically in youth, but in which, in more advanced age, in consequence of the loss of the reditus testium at the rutting season, it became fixed. Such forms are not actually known; but the hypothetical stage is very nearly realised in Man, as in him, by the partial reinvagination of the bursa, and by the consequent formation of a conus inguinalis, we are still reminded, ontogenetically, of the periodical descensus and reditus testium, although it is but a very feeble process. There is thus reason for thinking that, among the Prosimii and Primates, forms corresponding with this hypothetical stage might be found.

The definitive descensus is due to a further evagination of the conus. The bursa inguinalis, however, which was once (as in the Rodents and Insectivora) the direct product of this very shifting of the testis, in Man first arises independently at some distance from it, forming what is known as the genital ridge or the outer genital fold.

Among the lower Mammals the development of a permanent scrotum has become established in the Marsupialia, Ungulata, and Carnivora. Among the Edentata only the Orycteropodidæ possess a testis sac into which the testes periodically enter. In *Dasypus, Bradypus*, and *Myrmecophaga* the testes are abdominal; in *Manis* they are subintegumental, and lie in the inguinal region. In the Monotremes a descensus testiculi is not known to occur.

In considering the phylogenetic origin of the descensus testiculorum, Klaatsch has formulated the following ingenious argument :—The mammary organ, which in the form of a somewhat circular patch of the integument, characterised by glands and smooth musculature, first became differentiated in the inguinal region, exercised a great influence on the abdominal wall. He has suggested that among the ancestors of the Mammals there occurred, as he believes is shown by the Monotremata, a transference of the mammary organ from the female to the male;[1] and that this may have

---

[1] In other words, Klaatsch interprets as the homologue of this Mammary area a circumscribed wrinkled portion of the integument, only scantily covered with hair,

exercised a great influence on the lower portion of the abdominal wall. This would appear to have involved the invagination of a more or less circumscribed portion of the lateral abdominal muscles by the glandular apparatus (which in the Monotremata has already attained large proportions), leading up to the differentiation of a compressor of the mammary organ out of the transversus muscle. He further surmises that this, which represented a primitive conus inguinalis, was retained in the Marsupials to assist in the extra-uterine nourishment of the young, and that it disappeared in the Placentalia owing to the substitution of other methods of providing for the offspring. The invagination of the conus into the cœlom must, like the maturation of the glandular complex, have occurred periodically. The male conus became related to the male genital gland, and the periodic displacement of the latter (towards the point of the least resistance) must thus be associated with its great increase in size at the times of sexual activity. For the ovaries this last factor has not to be taken into account, as they do not undergo such great variations of size; and further, their power of descent is greatly diminished in consequence of their position in relation to the Müllerian ducts.

The essential, that is the first, cause of the descensus remains unexplained, and the origin of the ligamentum inguinale is still a complete enigma. On the other hand, its connection with the uterus, its periodical increase in size during pregnancy, and especially its near relation to the conus inguinalis, and thus to the mammary organ, make it very probable that it originally arose in the female, and was transferred to the male with the other parts belonging to the mammary organ.

SUPRARENAL BODIES

These organs are probably to be traced to a double origin, partly from the mesonephros and partly from the sympathetic nervous system. Their physiological significance is as little known as their primitive history, and it is not certain whether, so far as Man is concerned, they are phylogenetically in a progressive or in a retrogressive condition.

The latter assumption is the more probable when we consider their great development during embryonic life. On the other hand, their rich blood-supply indicates some important physiological function performed throughout life.

which is to be found on the level of the scrotum in the young stage of all Mammals, including Man, and which at a later stage meets the corresponding area of the other side in the middle line. The numerous smooth muscles which constitute the tunica dartos appear to correspond with the smooth muscle layer of the glandular area in the Monotremata. In all Mammals the area scroti is distinguished by the fact that the hair grows on wart-like elevations which are closely crowded together — a peculiarity which gives the area a characteristic appearance. The hairs are provided with very small sebaceous glands; the coiled tubular glands are much larger, and open near hairs disposed singly. In Man the tubular glands are less conspicuous.

CONSPECTUS OF THE ORGANS MENTIONED IN THE TEXT, ARRANGED ON THE BASIS OF THEIR PHYSIOLOGICAL CONDITION

I. ORGANS SHOWING RETROGRESSIVE CHARACTERS

A. Retrogressively modified, the Organs still performing clearly recognisable Functions

Certain muscles of the lower leg and foot.
Adductor transversus of the foot.
Opponens of the ball of the little toe.
Serratus posticus superior and inferior.
The flexors proper of the fingers.
M. pyramidalis (when comparatively well developed as accessory to the rectus abdominis).
M. levator palpebræ superioris.
Intestinal cœcum.
Eighth sternal rib.
The eleventh and twelfth ribs.
Sternum.
The fifth toes.
The fibula.
Olfactory lobe of the brain and (in part) the olfactory organ.
The canines and upper lateral incisors; the molars, in so far as there is a decrease in the number of their cusps.
The pre-maxillary bone.

B. Retrogressively modified, the Organs having become wholly or in part functionless, some appearing in the Embryo alone, others present during Life constantly or inconstantly. For the greater part Organs which may be rightly termed Vestigial.

Os coccygis. Cauda humana.
Superfluous embryonic notochord and associated somites.

Embryonic cervical, lumbar, and sacral ribs.
The thirteenth rib of the adult.
The seventh cervical rib in the adult.
The interarticular cartilage of the sterno-clavicular joint (probable vestige of the episternal apparatus).
Ossa supra-sternalia.
Certain centres of ossification in the manubrium sterni.
The branchial clefts (for the most part) and branchial ridges.
Processus styloideus ossis temporis, and the ligamentum stylo-hyoideum.
Anterior cornua of the hyoid, for the greater part.
Foramen cœcum of the tongue.
Processus gracilis of the malleus.
Post-frontal bone (?)
Ossa interparietalia (and ? præ-interparietalia).
Processus paramastoideus of exoccipital.
Torus occipitalis.
Processus frontalis of the temporal.
Processus coracoideus [meta- and epi-coracoid bones].
Os centrale carpi.
Processus supracondyloideus humeri.
Trochanter tertius femoris.
The phalanges of the fifth toe, and less conspicuously of the third and fourth toes.
Muscles of the pinna and the Musculus occipitalis.
M. transversus nuchæ.
Facial muscles transformed into tendinous expansions.
Mm. plantaris and palmaris longus, when completely tendinous.
M. ischio femoralis.
The caudal muscles.
M. epitrochleo-anconæus.
M. latissimo-condyloideus.
M. transversus thoracis (triangularis sterni).
M. palmaris brevis.
The transition bundles between the trapezius and the sterno-cleido-mastoideus.
M. levator claviculæ.
M. rectus thoracis.
M. cremaster.
The primitive hairy covering or lanugo.
Vestiges of vibrissæ.

THE STRUCTURE OF MAN

The vertex coccygeus, the foveola and glabella coccygea.
Certain vortices of hair on the breast.
Nipples in men.
Supernumerary mammary glands in women.
Alleged vestiges of mammary pouches [?]
Supernumerary olfactory ridges.
Jacobson's organ, and ductus naso-palatinus.
Papilla palatina and foliata.
Plica semilunaris of the eye.
Vasa hyaloidæ (Cloquet's canal) of the embryo—the choroidal fissure.
Lachrymal glands, in part.
The epicanthus.
M. orbitalis.
Certain varieties of the pinna of the ear.
The filum terminale of the spinal cord.
Glandula pinealis and parietal organ.
The parieto-occipital fissure of the brain [doubtful].
The obex, ponticulus, ligula, tæniæ medullares, and velum medullare anterius and posterius, of the brain.
The hypophysis cerebri (pituitary body).
The dorsal roots and ganglia of the hypoglossus nerve.
The rami recurrentes of certain cranial nerves.
Certain elements of the brachial and lumbo-sacral plexuses.
The coccygeal nerve.
The glandula coccygea.
Palatal ridges.
The sublingua.
The formation of rudimentary dental papillæ before the sinking of the dental ridge.
The wisdom teeth.
The occurrence of a third præmolar (reversionary).
The occurrence of a fourth molar (reversionary).
The vestiges of a third dentition.
The ciliated epithelium of the embryonic œsophagus.
Bursa sub- and præhyoidea (ductus thyroglossus).
Musculi broncho-œsophagei.
The appendix vermiformis.
Ventricle of the larynx (Morgagni's pouch).
Lobus subpericardiacus of the lung (reversionary).
Certain valves of the veins.
Certain structures of a vestigial nature in the heart.

CONSPECTUS OF ORGANS MENTIONED IN THE TEXT 203

Arteria sacralis media.
Arteria ischiadica.
Superficial plantar arterial arch of the foot.
The vena cava superior sinistra.
Venæ cardinales posteriores, and ductus Cuvieri.
Vestiges (in the female) of the mesonephric system, and (in the male) of the Müllerian ducts.
Conus inguinalis, and ligamentum inguinale.
The area scroti.

C. Modified under Change of Function, though this cannot in all cases be proved

Suprarenal bodies.
Glandula thyroidea.
Glandula thymus.
Bursa pharyngea.
Anterior lobe of the hypophysis cerebri (pituitary body).
Carotid and coccygeal glands.

D. Characters Indicative of Change of Position or Shifting

Proximal shifting of the pelvic girdle, and, correlatively, the shortening of the lumbar region of the vertebral column (assimilation of the fifth lumbar vertebra by the sacrum).
Distal shifting of the shoulder girdle.
Abbreviation of the cœlom.
Proximal and distal abbreviation of the osseous thorax.
Power of abduction in the embryo and at birth of the first metatarsal and great toe.
Shifting of the eye from the lateral surface of the head to the anterior.
Wandering of the lachrymal glands.
[Variations in arrangement] of the platysma myoides muscle.
[Variations in arrangement] of the sphincter colli.
Shifting of the navel.
Shifting of the heart, the stomach, and the thyroid and thymus glands.
Descent of the genital glands (testes and ovaries).
Shifting of certain muscles of the lower leg on to the dorsum and plantar surface of the foot.
Torsion of the humerus, radius, and ulna.

Disposition of the foot at a sharp angle to the leg.
Secondary separation of the orbit from the fossa temporalis.
Shifting of the lachrymal bone on to the surface of the face.
The disposition of the palatine bones in relation to the palatal processus of the maxilla.
The fusion of the nasal bones.
The position of the pinna on the adult head.
The ultimate positions of the ribs upon the vertebral column.
(Widening of the thorax, as an accompaniment of an alteration in the positions of the organs within the thoracic cavity.)

II. ORGANS SHOWING PROGRESSIVE CHARACTERS, *i.e.* TENDING TOWARDS MORE PERFECT ADAPTATION

Higher differentiation and more subtle development of the muscles of the thumb—both of those which pass from the forearm along the volar and dorsal surfaces to the thumb, and of those of the ball of the thumb.

Increase in physiological efficiency of the hand in general, especially of the flexors of the hand and of the fingers, the palmaris longus excepted.

Increased development and strengthening of the arch of the foot, of the tarsus, heel, and great toe.

Secondary lateral extension of the malleolus fibularis.

The perfecting of the whole lower limbs for support and ambulation (in adaptation to the upright gait).

Development of the iliac expansions in the female, with widening of the sacrum and of the aperture of the pelvis.

Curvature of the lumbar vertebral column.

Gluteal muscles and muscles of the calf (gastrocnemius and soleus).

More subtle differentiation of the facial muscles proper (as opposed to the muscles of the pinna and of the scalp).

The projectile nose.

Certain nerve tracts in the brain and spinal cord.

The occipital lobes of the brain (posterior cornua of lateral ventricle and calcar avis ?)

Higher degree of development of the brain cortex (histological differentiation concomitant with increasing intelligence).

The more subtle differentiation of the muscles of the larynx. Articulate speech.

On glancing through this summary, it will be seen that the arrangement of the subject matter is not altogether a natural one; indeed, in introducing it, I have only sought to give a classified survey of the contents of this book.

Physiological considerations must determine the ultimate method of grouping the facts, especially because, as was pointed out in the introduction, the term vestigial is, as a rule, only applied to such organs as have lost their original physiological significance. Retrogressive organs, on the contrary, are such as may still remain functional, though, as a rule, only to a limited extent. It has further been seen that both these conditions in the process of degeneration may be, in different individuals, realised in one and the same organ. The palmaris longus and plantaris muscles furnish a case in point; for while these, and especially the former, are not infrequently so well developed that there can be no doubt of their being functional, cases occur in which one or the other of them has become quite transformed into tendinous tissue and really vestigial. And in yet other cases these muscles may altogether have disappeared. On this subject Osborn makes the following appropriate remark :—
"Both in the muscular and skeletal systems we find organs so far on the down grade that they are mere pensioners of the body, drawing pay (*i.e.* nutrition) for past honourable services without performing any corresponding work—the plantaris and palmaris muscles for example."[1]

Many similar examples might be given. Confining our attention to muscles alone, it may suffice to recall the pyramidalis and certain muscles of the head.

[1] Cf. this author's Cartwright Lectures, Lect. I. "The Contemporary Evolution of Man," *Medical Record*, Feb. 20, 1892.

LIST OF THE ORGANS AND TOPICS CONSIDERED IN THE TEXT, CLASSED ACCORDING TO THE SYSTEMS TO WHICH THEY RELATE

I. INTEGUMENT AND INTEGUMENTAL ORGANS

(a) *Horny Structures.*
Vibrissæ (tactile hairs).
Primitive hairy covering (lanugo).
Converging hair vortices, ex. vertex coccygeus.
Glabella and foveola coccygea.
Pseudohypertrichosis.
Hypertrichosis vera.
Nails (the fifth claw-like).

(b) *Glands.*
Montgomery's glands.
Mammary pouches.
Mammary line.
Supernumerary mammary glands and nipples (polymasty, polythely).
Pectoral hair vortices (probably indicating the former position of supernumerary nipples).

II. SKELETAL SYSTEM

(a) *Vertebral Column.*
Cauda humana.
Os coccygis.
Curvature of the lumbar portion of the spinal column.
Forward shifting of the sacral portion of the spinal column (assimilation of the last lumbar vertebra).
Numerical increase of the lumbar vertebræ.
Outgrowth of the transverse process of the sixth cervical vertebra.

(b) *Thorax.*
Quadrupedal form of the thorax in the child, with greater dorso-sternal diameter.
Disappearance of the lumbar ribs.
Disappearance of the cervical ribs.

Reappearance of cervical, lumbar, and sacral ribs formerly present.
Variations in development of the upper and lower ribs.
Former greater extension of the pleuroperitoneal cavity, both anteriorly and posteriorly.
The eighth sternal rib.
Reduction of the sternal ribs to six.
Reduction of the sternum.
Vestiges of the episternal apparatus.

(c) *Skull.*
Post-frontal bone.
Os interparietale.
Os præinterparietale.
Processus parnmastoideus.
Torus occipitalis.
Suppression of the parietal process of the alisphenoid.

LIST OF ORGANS ACCORDING TO SYSTEMS 207

Fusion of nasal bones.
Participation of the os lachrymale in the superficial facial skeleton.
Variation of the os lachrymale.
Downward prolongation of the nasal process of the frontal bone.
Lower bridge to the nose.
Ductus naso-palatinus.
The pre-maxillary and maxillary bones.
Ossa palatina, in relation to the palatine processes of the maxillæ.
Distinctness of the ossa palatina, and the spina nasalis posterior.
Vestiges of the branchial skeleton (thyro-hyoid apparatus, ossicula auditus).

(d) *Skeleton of the Limbs.*

Processus coracoideus [epi- and meta-coracoid bones].
Extension of the basis scapulæ.
Great development (divergence) of the iliac expansions.
Length of the forearm in the embryo and in the lower races of Mankind.
Perforation of the olecranon fossa.

Processus supracondyloideus (entepicondyloideus).
Os centrale carpi.
Trochanter tertius femoris.
Variations in the length of the lower leg.
Platyknemia.
Exclusion of the fibula from articulation with the femur.
Marked convexity of the condylus externus tibiæ.
Great development of the malleolus tibialis in the embryo, the lower races of Mankind, and Anthropoids.
Predominance of the great toe.
Great development of the tarsal elements.
Parallel disposition of the great toe with the others, in the adult.
The great toe in the embryo and the lower races.
Reduction of the fifth (or fourth and fifth) toes (fusion of their terminal and penultimate phalanges).
Comparison of the position of the limbs in the human embryo and the lower Vertebrates.

III. MUSCULAR SYSTEM

M. serratus posticus superior et inferior.
Mm. caudæ humanæ.
Traces of metamerism in the abdominal muscles.
M. rectus abdominis.
M. pyramidalis.
Mm. scaleni.
M. triangularis sterni.
M. cleido-occipitalis.
M. subcutaneus colli (platysma myoides).
Mimetic muscles.
M. sphincter colli.
M. transversus nuchæ.
M. epicranius.
Muscles of the pinna.
M. palmaris longus.

M. plantaris.
M. flexor sublimis digitorum.
M. flexor profundus digitorum.
M. flexor brevis digitorum pedis.
M. extensor brevis digitorum pedis.
Mm. interossei pedis.
M. adductor hallucis.
M. opponens minimi digiti.
M. latissimo-condyloideus.
M. sternalis.
M. epitrochleo-anconæus.
M. levator claviculæ.
M. ischio-femoralis.
Muscles of the thumb (especially the flexor longus pollicis).
Mm. glutei (esp. gluteus maximus).
M. gemellus superior.
Mm. soleus and gastrocnemius.

IV. Nervous System

(a) Central Nervous System

Filum terminale.
Glandula coccygea.
Pyramidal tracts.
Parieto-occipital fissure ("Affenspalte").
Pineal gland (epiphysis cerebri).
Pituitary body (hypophysis cerebri).
Lobus olfactorius.
Roof of the fourth ventricle.
Obex, ligula, vela medullaria, tæniæ medullares.
Occipital lobe of cerebrum.
Posterior cornu of lateral ventricle.
Calcar avis.

(b) Peripheral Nervous System

Roots and ganglia of hypoglossus.
Rami recurrentes of certain cerebral nerves.
Traces of tegumental sense organs in fœtal life.
Variations in the brachial and lumbosacral plexuses.

V. Sense Organs

Disappearance of an olfactory ridge in the embryo.
Papilla palatina and foliata.
Jacobson's organ.
Vasa hyaloidea (Cloquet's canal).
The projectile nose.
Orbitalis muscle.
Levator palpebræ superioris muscle.
Plica semilunaris.
Supernumerary lachrymal glands.
Epicanthus.
Auditory ossicles (relations to the visceral skeletal arches).
The middle ear (hyoid visceral cleft).

VI. Alimentary System

Palatal ridges.
Milk dentition.
Indications of a third dentition.
Wisdom teeth.
Possible indications of free dental papillæ before the down-growth of the dental ridge.
Canine teeth.
Outer upper incisors.
Cheek teeth (reduction of cusps and fangs).
Appearance of a third premolar and a fourth molar.
Sublingua.
Glandula thyroidea.
Glandula thymus.
Foramen cœcum and base of the tongue.
Ductus thyroglossus.
Bursæ supra- and præhyoideæ.
Carotid gland.
Bursa pharyngea.
Constriction of the stomach.
Ciliated epithelium in the œsophagus.
Diverticulum ilei.
Cœcum.
Vermiform appendix.

VII. Respiratory System

Metamorphosis of the aortic arch system.
Branchial pouches and cervical fistulæ.
Sinus Morgagni (laryngeal resonant chamber).
Sinus and Lobus subpericardiacus.

LIST OF ORGANS ACCORDING TO SYSTEMS

VIII. CIRCULATORY SYSTEM

Vestiges of valves in the embryonic heart.
Vestiges of the sinus venosus, in the heart.
Intestinal arteries.
Arteria sacralis media.
Arteria ischiadica (genesis of femoral artery).
Superficial vascular arch of the foot.
Cardinal veins.

Ductus Cuvieri.
Sinus venosus cordis.
Persistence of the post. cardinal veins in the form of a double vena cava, inferior.
Metamorphosis of superior caval veins.
Valves of the intercostal and intestinal veins.

IX. URINOGENITAL SYSTEM

Pronephros and mesonephros.
Vestiges of the mesonephros.
Uterus duplex, bipartitus, bicornis, and simplex.
Hypospadias.

Descensus or reditus testiculi.
Conus inguinalis.
Ligamentum inguinale.
Area scroti.
Suprarenal bodies.

SOME ORGANS AND VESTIGES OF ORGANS, WHICH SHOW [STRUCTURAL COMMUNITY WITH] VERY PRIMITIVE VERTEBRATE TYPES

CONDITIONS DEFINITIVE IN FISHES (ELASMOBRANCHS) ARE INDICATED BY

(1) The free dental papillæ projecting above the surface of the mucous membrane before the sinking of the dental ridge.

(The appearance ontogenetically of the dental ridges, long before the first osseous rudiments, points back to the extremely early phylogenetic appearance of teeth, in Vertebrates, before any of the other hard structures of the body.)

(2) The pineal gland and pineal organ (a parietal foramen in the roof of the skull is found in Fishes as early as the Devonian period, and the organ occurs in the Marsipobranchii).

(3) The pituitary body (hypophysis cerebri).
(4) The branchial pouches.
(5) The vessels of the visceral arch system.
∪ (6) The vasa hyaloidea of the vitreous body (Cloquet's canal).
(7) The cardinal veins.
(8) Certain structures, appearing in the development of the heart, vestiges of which are found in the fully developed organ.
(9) The arteria caudalis (A. sacralis media).
(10) The pro- and meso-nephric excretory apparatus.
(11) The possible vestiges of a third set of teeth (pointing back to a probable successive renewal of teeth, such as characterises Fishes, Amphibians, and Reptiles).

INDICATIONS OF DEFINITIVE CONDITIONS

CONDITIONS DEFINITIVE IN AMPHIBIA AND REPTILES ARE INDICATED BY

(1) The arteria ischiadica [cruralis].
(2) The double rectus abdominis muscle.
(3) The foramen supracondyloideum (entepicondyloideum) humeri (found in Amphibians and Reptiles as early as the Permian period).
(4) The presence of (supernumerary) lachrymal glands below the eye.

CONCLUDING REMARKS

In the course of Phylogeny the body of Man has undergone a series of modifications which still in part find expression in his Ontogeny. There are indications that changes in his organisation are still continuing, and that the Man of the future will be different from the Man of to-day. It is the more necessary to emphasise this, because it has only recently been asserted by one in authority in the anthropological world, that "since the Neolithic Age Man has been a fixed type."

I willingly admit that nothing is gained by the mere demonstration of "animal likenesses," and that the final and only satisfactory solution of the great riddle of Man must lie in the demonstration of his genealogy and the line of his inheritance.

Although small and insignificant in their first appearance, structural changes become more and more distinctly marked from generation to generation, and more and more definitely fixed according to the laws of heredity and selection. There exist different degrees of the degenerative process: first an organ begins to degenerate in the adult body, then this degeneration finds expression in the embryo, then the organ in question only occurs in a certain percentage of the individuals as a reversion, and finally even such occasional occurrence ceases, and all trace of the organ is lost. Osborn calls this process of gradual extinction the "long struggle of the destructive power of degeneration."

Although these changes are so manifold and follow such different directions (take, for example, those of the musculature), one principle lies at the bottom of them all, viz. the endeavour to shake off, as far as possible, all that is unnecessary and superfluous, in order to make room for further development. Weismann very justly remarks: "If Nature were not able to effect the disappearance of superfluous organs the transformation of species would have been well-nigh impossible, for the existing parts which had become superfluous would have been in the way of other active parts, and would have hindered their development. Indeed, had all parts which the ancestors possessed been necessarily retained, an abnormal animal would at last have been produced—a monster no longer capable of living. The degeneration of parts which have become superfluous is thus a condition of progress."

But what is it that actually initiates these various changes? What is their first cause? This question cannot be answered offhand on account of the great number of circumstances which have to be taken into account. First, we have to consider external influences of the most varied kinds which affect the different organs, or systems of organs, in a progressive or retrogressive manner, leading to new acquisitions or to gradual losses. These changes, however, have, as it were, to be introduced by the occurrence of slight variations, and then (if I may use a military term) when once a breach has been made in any part, a point of least resistance is formed for pathological affections, as I have tried to prove in the foregoing pages, and a substitute for the gradually degenerating organs has to be found. In other words, as soon as a transformation takes place in any part of the body, correlative alterations in some other part commence, so that, as it were, a wave of modification passes from one system of organs to another. For example, when the dentition of our ancestors degenerated, and the canines became reduced, the important weapons of attack and defence thus lost had to be replaced, if the struggle for existence was to be advantageously maintained. Concurrently with the reduction of powerful jaws the brain was developing, and the intelligence attained a sufficiently high degree of perfection to invent weapons, at first no doubt of a very simple character. Or again, as the foot gradually changed from a seizing organ into one for support of the body, and its musculature consequently changed, then, in adaptation to the new function, great alterations had to be effected not only in the skeleton of the limb, but also in its muscular and nervous system, *e.g.* the muscles of the calf and buttocks attained a massive development. Such examples might be multiplied, but the above will suffice to show that these modifications are not mere freaks of chance, mere *lusus naturæ*, but are the expression of law-abiding processes, even if we cannot always succeed in determining their first cause. At all events, these processes need immense periods of time for their accomplishment, so that, as a rule, they are removed from direct perception by means of the senses, and can only be inferred from the evidence of Phylogeny, Comparative Anatomy, and Ontogeny.

This applies not only to Man, but to the whole animal kingdom, which yields us a long series of examples of degeneration. Here also we find evidence of the great importance of the external conditions of life to which the organism responds. One of the most striking proofs of this is afforded by the degenerate condition, or even entire absence, of eyes in animals living in the depth of the ocean or in caves. Such animals also illustrate how the loss of one organ is compensated for by the increased development of other organs. From the same point of view are to be considered the limbless Amphibia, and the Slow-worms, and another group of Reptiles of essentially similar adaptive organisation, the Amphisbænidæ, and finally the more familiar Earthworm itself.

Whereas, among the above-mentioned cases, it is the organ of sight which atrophies; in other animals, the olfactory organ disappears, and I may especially refer to those Fishes known, from the characters of their jaws and teeth, as the Plectognathi Gymnodontes. Here,[1] in adaptation to a diet of Crustacea and Molluscs which are very difficult to crush, the musculature of the jaws develops to an extraordinary degree, displacing the olfactory apparatus to such an extent that the olfactory nerve is reduced to a minute thread, which branches either within a mere tegumental olfactory process or simply under the surface integument of the olfactory region.

Until quite recently, the question wherein lay the cause of the degeneration of an organ was thought to be satisfactorily answered as follows: the organ is not used, and the degenerating effect of disuse, passed on from one generation to another, gains in intensity, until it leads to the total removal of the organ in question. This answer presupposes what is often stated, but has never been proved, viz. *the inheritance of acquired characteristics.*[2]

---

[1] Cf. Wiedersheim, "*Das Geruchsorgan der Tetrodonten.*" Kölliker *Gratulationsschrift*, 1897.

[2] [This statement requires qualification. It is true that we have no very satisfactory concrete instance of a chance structural modification of an individual having been transmitted by inheritance to its own immediate offspring. But, on the other hand, as Herbert Spencer has argued with great force, there seems no way of explaining the phenomena of highly organised life, except on the supposition of some transmission of characters acquired in adaptation to the environment.]

Weismann has recently conclusively proved that this answer is not sufficient, and that it must first of all be shown how it can come to pass that a portion of the body which up to a certain time is indispensable to existence, should disappear as soon as it is not needed. The real cause, according to Weismann, lies in a converse process, that is, the cessation of Natural Selection— in Panmixia (general cross-breeding). In other words, as soon as, by change in its external surroundings, an organ is excluded, its condition becomes retrogressive. Then the general interbreeding between individuals in which the organ in question is well developed and others in which it is but feebly developed, which latter have survived in spite of this, leads to its slow but steady degeneration.[1]

The numerous above-mentioned cases of degeneration in the organs of the human body should also, without doubt, be regarded from this point of view. The fact that the degree of development of this or that organ (*e.g.* the sense organs, which are incomparably more highly developed in savages than in civilised men) is no longer of supreme importance to the individual, *i.e.* no longer necessary for his prosperity, leads to a degeneration, which, in the struggle for existence, could only be compensated for by a high degree of civilisation. Weismann gives the following striking example of this: "We can at the present day earn our bread quite independently of the acuteness of our hearing and the delicacy of our scent, indeed, even the sharpness of our sight is no longer a decisive factor in our success in the struggle for existence. Since the invention of spectacles, short-sighted men suffer hardly any disadvantage as compared with the long-sighted in their capacity for earning a living, at any rate in the higher circles of society. This is why so many short-sighted people are to be found among us. In ancient times a short-sighted soldier, or still more a short-sighted general, would have been simply an impossibility, as would also a short-sighted huntsman; indeed, in nearly all branches of human society short sight would have been a considerable obstacle, and would have rendered it difficult or impossible for a man to thrive and prosper. This is now no longer the case; the short-sighted man can make his way like

---

[1] [This argument is unsatisfactory. Panmixia alone could not lead to the disappearance of any organ. Natural selection may effect an increase in an organ, by eliminating those below a certain average; or the diminution of a structure, by eliminating all above a certain average. But it is not easy to see how Panmixia, or the cessation of Natural Selection, could alter the average in any way.]

every other, and his short sight, so far as it involves hereditary tendency, will be handed on by him and will help to make hereditary shortness of sight a widely-spread characteristic in certain classes of society."

The above sufficiently illustrates the fact that progressive variations are closely connected with retrogressive variations, indeed that to a great extent the former are rendered possible by the latter. If it be true that the adaptation of a creature to its surroundings depends on the process of Natural Selection, we must also consider that Natural Selection is the determining factor in both retrogressive and progressive processes. We have, then, to fall back on the general law of Selection propounded by Charles Darwin, which may be summed up as follows: survival only of the fittest, transmissibility by inheritance, and the gradual improvement of what is advantageous from generation to generation, till the highest possible degree of perfection is reached.

But wherein lies Man's special "perfection"? Does such perfection exist, and if so, is it, in comparison with other living beings, as universal as is generally assumed? Let us look at this matter a little closer.

There would appear to have been a time when our ancestors were protected against the inclemencies of the weather by a natural covering of hair, and against insects and other injurious influences by an extensive tegumental musculature, when the pinna of the ear, more advantageously disposed than at present, and moved by numerous and powerful muscles, collected the sounds of approaching danger incomparably better than at the present day, and when the sense of smell, probably intensified by Jacobson's organ, was more highly developed than now. Indeed, at a very low stage of phylogenetic development, when the visual organs were placed laterally on the head, and were furnished with a third eyelid, and regulated by more numerous muscles, there may even have been a "third eye" which could perceive what took place above the head (cf. the pineal organ, p. 133). The intestinal tube may have been longer, and thus better suited than at the present day for vegetable diet, the ancestor of Man enjoying at any rate more favourable conditions of existence as a vegetarian than his successor now does (compare also the former greater number of cheek teeth). He may also have had the further advantage of not possessing a vermiform process of the cœcum which predisposes to disease, and causes the destruction of a considerable percentage of his fellows.

The herbivorous stage was followed by an omnivorous one, characterised by the development of powerful canines. In this way, as skill in hunting and slaying animals developed, and carnivorous diet became of continually greater importance, the intestinal tube would appear to have begun to shorten and the processus vermiformis to become constricted.

Laryngeal sinuses may have been developed, which, acting as resonators, lent the voice greater strength and carried it farther, and thus made it a means of frightening or enticing. The lower jaw, the neck and its musculature, were far more powerfully developed than now.

In the male the genital glands may have remained, as they now normally do in the female, within the abdominal cavity, and been thus better protected from injury than at present. At a later stage even, when they had changed their position, and had reached the pouch-like appendages of the abdominal integument, they could still be withdrawn into the cavum abdominis, at least temporarily, by means of a well-developed muscle (cremaster). This is still indicated by ontogenetic processes.

There can be no doubt that the ancestors of Man were provided with a more extensive mammary system and more numerous mammæ than he to-day possesses, and the significance of this fact is equally clear. It can only be explained by the assumption that a greater number of young were originally produced at a birth. This, of course, was of advantage in the preservation of the species.

It follows from the above that in the course of a long geological period, Man has gradually lost a great number of advantages once possessed by his ancestors, and the question arises whether he has acquired any others in exchange for those lost. This certainly is the case, and this indeed must have been so, otherwise the species *Homo* would have failed in the struggle for existence. We thus have a series of exchanges, based (if we take only the most important organ into consideration) upon the unlimited capacity of development of the human brain. This one acquisition, supported by an increased functional efficiency of the hand and by the development of articulate speech, has entirely compensated for the loss of the great series of advantageous arrangements mentioned above. They had to be sacrificed in order that the brain might successfully develop, and that the *Homo sapiens* of to-day, with his surprising adaptability to the most varied conditions of life, might be produced.

This momentous exchange took place slowly and only after

great opposition. It was not accomplished without a struggle, in which every inch of the already occupied territory had to be painfully fought for; and the extraordinary tenacity with which certain favourable positions once attained are clung to, is seen in the fact that some of them are still taken up by the organism as dim reminiscences of the past, perhaps only during fœtal life. These ancient ancestral pictures,—for such indeed they are—are eloquent witnesses of a time long since past. They keep our vision clear, when we have, as in this present case, to be impartial judges of ourselves.

As Testut appropriately says: Let us not unjustly reproach anatomists with lowering Man, with drawing him down from his high position: it is true that Anatomy does rank Man in the class of the Mammalia, but it places him in the highest order of that class, that of the Primates; and although it cannot entirely separate him from these, it gives him the highest possible position among them. Anatomy not only makes Man the most perfect of Primates, but also proclaims him first of the foremost of all living beings.[1] As Broca has said: "That may well suffice for his ambition and his glory." I cannot do better than conclude with the following words of the last-named author, which are no less worthy of consideration:—" Pride, which is one of the most characteristic traits of our nature, has in many minds prevailed over the calm testimony of reason. Like those Roman Emperors who, intoxicated with their universal power, ended by denying their manhood, and by believing themselves to be demigods, so the king of our planet pleases himself with the thought that the nature of the vile animal which is subject to his caprices cannot have anything in common with his own. The proximity of the monkey is to him inconvenient; he is no longer satisfied to be the king of animals, he desires that an immense unfathomable abyss should separate him from his subjects; and, sometimes, turning his back on the earth, he takes refuge, with his endangered majesty, in the nebulous sphere of the Reign of Man. But Anatomy, like that slave who followed the triumphal car, repeating the words 'Memento te hominem esse,' comes to agitate him in this self-admiration, and reminds him that reality, visible and tangible, links him with the animals."

[1] [Cf., however, Minot, "Is Man the Highest Animal"?—*Proc. Americ. Assoc. for the Advancement of Science*, 1881, p. 240.]

GLOSSARY OF TECHNICAL ZOOLOGICAL TERMS OCCURRING IN THE TEXT.

AMBLYSTOMA.—A Tailed Amphibian of the United States and Mexico.
AMMOCŒTES.—The sexually immature larva of the Lamprey.
AMNIOTA.—The three higher classes of Vertebrates, *i.e.* Reptiles, Birds, and Mammals, the embryos of which are enveloped in an amnion.
AMPHIOXUS. THE LANCELET.—[The lowest animal possessing, in the adult state, a vertebral skeleton (notochord).]
AMPHISBÆNIDÆ.—Lizards with Snake-like bodies, which live underground.
ANAMNIA.—The two lowest classes of Vertebrates, *i.e.* Fishes and Amphibians, the embryos of which are not enveloped in an amnion (cf. Amniota).
[ANATOMY.—The study of gross structure.]
ANTHROPOIDS, also ANTHROPOMORPHA.—The highest "man-like" Apes (Gibbons, Orangs, Gorillas, and Chimpanzees).
ANURA.—Tailless Amphibians (Frogs and Toads).
APLACENTALIA (*Mammalia aplacentalia*).—The lowest Mammals, *i.e.* the Ornithodelphia (Monotremata) and the Marsupialia. The Monotremata are oviparous. The Marsupials produce immature young, which are in most of them carried about after birth in a pouch (marsupium) formed by the abdominal integument. [In neither Monotremata nor Marsupials is an allantoic placenta developed like that of all the higher Mammals (Placentalia).]
ARCTOMYS MARMOTTA.—Marmots; [terrestrial Rodents inhabiting Europe, North Asia, and North America.]
[ATAVISM.—The reversion to the condition of a lower type.]
ATELES.—The Spider Monkey of South America.
AUCHENIA.—The Llama.

[BIOLOGY.—In English, the study of all phenomena manifested by living organisms.[1]]
BOVINA.—Oxen.
BRADYPUS.—A South American Sloth.
BRANCHIOSAURUS.—A Tailed Amphibian of the Permian period.

CAPROMYS.—Arboreal Rat-like animals found in Cuba and Jamaica.
CARNIVORA.—Beasts of prey (flesh-eaters). Especially Felidœ and Canidœ.
CAVIA.—The Guinea-Pig.
CEBUS.—The "Capuchin," a leading genus of American Monkeys.

---

[1] [The term "Biologie" of continental observers is usually applied to the study of life itself, *i.e.* it is more nearly equivalent to our English term Physiology.]

CERCOPITHECUS.—A family of African Apes—[the "Green Monkeys" of menageries].
CERVUS CAPREOLUS.—The Roebuck.
CETACEA.—An order of Aquatic Mammals (Whales, Dolphins, and Porpoises).
CHELONIA.—Turtles and Tortoises.
[CHIMPANZEES.—Anthropoid Apes, readily remarkable for the relative shortness of the fore-limb. Confined to West and Central Equatorial Africa.]
CHIROPTERA.—Bats.
CHOLŒPUS.—The two-toed Sloth of Northern South America.
CŒLOGENYS.—The "Paca," a large Rodent somewhat resembling the Guinea-Pig, inhabiting Central and South America.

DASYPROCTA.—The "Agouti," a near relative of the Cœlogenys.
DASYPUS.—One of the Armadillos.
DELPHINUS.—The common Dolphin.
DICOTYLES.—The Peccary, or New World Pig.
DIDELPHIA.—Marsupials, Mammalia having two vaginæ.
DIPNOI.—Fishes having not a few points of resemblance to the Amphibia. [Remarkable among fishes for the conversion of the air-bladder into a functional lung] (confined to certain rivers of Queensland, Tropical Africa, and South America).
DUCKBILL.—The "Platypus" of Australia, one of the Monotremata. (Cf. Aplacentalia and Ornithodelphia.)

ECHIDNA.—The "Spiny Ant-Eater" of Australia, one of the Monotremata. (Cf. Aplacentalia and Ornithodelphia.)
EDENTATA.—An order of Mammals, comprising the Ant-Eaters, Armadillos, and Sloths.
[ELASMOBRANCHII.—The lowest living order of true Fishes, includes the Sharks, Rays, and Herring Kings, with their allies.]
[EMBRYOLOGY.—The study of the earlier growth stages of living organisms, in the higher animals up to the completion of organ formation. A department of the wider study of Development.]
ERINACEUS.—The Hedgehog.

GANOIDEI.—A group of living Fishes, [including the Sturgeons, the Bony Pikes of North America, and the Polypterus or "Bichir" of the Nile, and their allies.]
GORILLAS.—[The largest of the Anthropoid Apes. Confined to West Equatorial Africa.]
GYMNOPHIONA.—Limbless Amphibians (Cœcilians) with Snake-like bodies, some of which are known to live a subterranean life.

HATTERIA.—The "Tuatara" of New Zealand. A "Lizard" of very primitive structure.
[HISTOLOGY.—The study of the minute structure of tissues and organs.]
HOMŒOSAURUS.—A Fossil Lizard [of the Jurassic of the European Continent].
HYLOBATES.—The Gibbons ["Long-armed Apes." Anthropoid Apes, confined to South-east Asia. The only Apes which habitually walk upright].
HYPEROÖDON.—A toothed Whale of the North Atlantic, sometimes called the "Bottlenose."
HYSTRIX.—The Porcupine.

GLOSSARY OF TECHNICAL ZOOLOGICAL TERMS

INUUS.—[A genus of Old World Apes, allied to the only European Ape—the Barbary Ape (*Macacus*) of Gibraltar.]
INSECTIVORA.—[A heterogeneous order of Mammals, which includes the Hedgehogs, Shrews, and Moles.]

LEMUROIDEA.—Arboreal animals of the Old World, chiefly of Madagascar, with dentition approximate to that of certain Insectivora, and as a rule with Monkey- and Ape-like prehensile (cf. Tarsius) limbs. (The "Tarsier" and "Aye Aye" are of this sub-order.)

MACACUS.—(Cf. Inuus.)
MANATEE.—The "Sea Cow," an aquatic Mammal, famous for having given rise to the fable of the Mermaid.
MANIS.—One of Scaly Ant-Eaters of the Old World.
MARSIPOBRANCHII.—The Lampreys and Hags.
MARSUPIALIA.—A sub-class of Mammalia, the females of most of which are provided with a marsupium, or pouch, enclosing the teat-bearing area of the body-wall. (Cf. also Didelphia and Aplacentalia.)
MONODELPHIA.—Mammals possessed of a single vagina, *i.e.* all those above the Marsupials.
MONOTREMATA.—The lowest sub-class of Mammals. (Cf. Aplacentalia and Ornithodelphia.)
[MORPHOLOGY.—The study of form and arrangement of the parts of the body.]
[MURIDÆ.—A family of Rodents, embracing the Rats and Mice.]
MUSTELIDÆ.—A group of Carnivores, including the Weasels, Pole-Cats, and Martens.
MYCETES.—The Howling Monkeys of South America.
MYOGALE.—[The "Desman," an aquatic Insectivore, related to the Moles and Shrews, occurring in the Pyrenees and South-East Russia.]
MYRMECOPHAGA.—[One of the Hairy Ant-Eaters of South America.] (Cf. Edentata.)

[ONTOGENY.—The developmental history of the individual.]
ORANGS.—[Anthropoid Apes confined to the Oriental region. The "Red Haired Apes" of Sumatra and Borneo.]
[ORNITHODELPHIA.—The lowest living Mammals (Australian). Oviparous Mammals, having non-united oviducts and a cloaca. (Cf. Monotremata, Duckbill, and Echidna.)]
ORYCTEROPODIDÆ.—The "Aaardvark," or hairy Ant-Eaters of the Old World. (The Cape Ant-Eater.)

PALÆOHATTERIA.—A fossil "Lizard" [of the Permian beds in Saxony] related to Hatteria.
PETROMYZON.—The Lamprey (cf. Ammocœtes and Marsipobranchii).
PHALANGISTA VULPINA.— The Australian "Opossum," or "Vulpine Phalanger." A climbing Marsupial.
PHOCA.—The Seal.
PHOCÆNA.—The Porpoise.
PHYLLOMYS.—An extinct Rodent, from the Brazilian caves.
[PHYLOGENY.—The developmental history of the race.]

THE STRUCTURE OF MAN

[PHYLUM.—A term applied to any great race or assemblage of genetically related forms of life, which conform to the same fundamental type.]

[PHYSIOLOGY.—The study of the functions of living matter, i.e. of the living in action.]

PINNIPEDIA.—Marine Carnivora, having feet transformed into paddles. The Seals, Sea-lions, and Walruses.

[PLACENTALIA.—The highest sub-class of Mammals. Those Mammals which develop an allantoic placenta.]

PRIMATES.—The highest order of Placental Mammals, including the Lemuroidea, Monkeys, Apes, and Man.

PROSIMII.—(Cf. Lemuroidea.)

REVERSION.—(Cf. Atavism.)

RODENTIA.—An order of gnawing Mammals (Rabbits, Rats, Porcupines, Squirrels, and their allies).

SAURIANS.—Lizards.

SELACHIANS.—Sharks and Dog-fishes. (Cf. Elasmobranchii.)

SIRENIA.—An order of Aquatic Mammals. (Cf. Manatee.)

SLOW WORMS.—A group of Limbless Lizards.

STEGOCEPHALA.—Fossil Amphibians, most abundantly represented in the Carboniferous, Permian, and Triassic strata.

STENOPS.—The "Slender Lori" of Ceylon, one of the Lemuroidea.

SUS SCROFA.—The Domestic Pig.

TARSIUS.—[The "Tarsier" of Borneo, Sumatra, and the Celebes.] One of the Lemuroidea.

TELEOSTEI.—The Bony Fishes.

TETRODONTA.—Aberrant Bony Fishes, belonging to the family Gymnodontes.

TOOTHED WHALES.—A group of the Cetacea, including the Cachelots or Sperm Whales, Dolphins, and Porpoises. (Cf. Cetacea.)

UNGULATA.—The Hoofed Mammals.

URODELA.—The Tailed Amphibians. Newts, Salamanders, and their allies.

URSUS.—The Bear.

ZIPHIUS.—[A long-snouted Toothed Whale met with in most of the great seas.]

INDEX

Acetabulum, 74
Affenspalte, 127
Ainos, 10
Alimentary canal, 155
Amasty, 22
Ankle-joint, 84
Aorta, 181
Areæ scroti, 197, 199
Arterial system, 181
Arteries, intestinal, 184
  of fore-limb, 182
  of hind-limb, 183
Artery, hyaloid, 147
  hypogastric, 181
  median sacral, 182
Astragalus, 84
Atrium, 180
Auditory organ, 150

Bone, alisphenoid, 58
  coracoid, 71, 72
  cotyloid, 74
  epicoracoid, 72
  epipteric, 59
  frontal, 55, 61
  hyoid, 65
  interparietal, 55
  lachrymal, 60
  malar, 58
  metacoracoid, 72
  nasal, 60
  palatine, 63
  post-frontal, 55
  premaxillary, 61
  sphenoid, 58
Bones, metatarsal, 88
  turbinal, 60, 141
  Wormian, 60

Brain, 127
  fissures of, 127
  growth of, 53
  olfactory lobe of, 137
  transitory fissures of, 138
  weight of, 51, 128
Branchial arches, 66, 151
  pouches, 171
  skeleton, 172
Breasts, supernumerary, 18
Bronchus, eparterial, 176
Bursa inguinalis, 197, 198
  pharyngea, 164
Bursæ præ- and supra-hyoid, 162

Cæcum, 167
Calcaneum, 84
Canalis inguinalis, 196
Canals, naso-palatine, 145, 156
  Nuckii, 198
  tubo-tympanicus, 151
  vaginalis, 198
Carpus, 79
Caruncula lachrymalis, 149
Cauda humana (*see* Tail)
Cerebellum, 131
Cerebrum, lobes of, 131
Cervical groove, 66
Choanæ, 61
Chorda dorsalis, 49
Circulatory system, 180
Clavicle, 71, 73
Clitoris, 195
Cloaca, 194
Coccyx, 28, 32
Colliculus seminalis, 194
Conus inguinalis, 196
Cranium, capacity of, 51

224   THE STRUCTURE OF MAN

DENTAL RIDGE, 161
Descensus testiculorum, 196
Diaphragm, 38, 177
Diverticulum ilei, 165
Duct, Müllerian, 189, 193
  Wolffian, 187
Ductus Cuvieri, 184
  thyroglossus, 162

ENSIFORM PROCESS, 44
Epicanthus, 150
Epididymis, 188
Epiglottis, 173
Epiphysis cerebri, 131
Episternum (*see* Interclavicle)
Eustachian tube, 150
Eye, 147
Eyebrows, 4, 150
Eyelids, 148, 150

FALLOPIAN TUBE, 194
Femur, 81
Fibula, 83, 93
Filum terminale, 124
Finger nails, 11
Fissura orbitalis, 148
Fistulæ, cervical, 172
Foot, skeleton of, 85, 87
Foramina, condylar, 78
Fore-limb, skeleton of, 77
Fossa, olecranon, 77
  orbital, 58, 148
  temporal, 58, 148
Foveola coccygea, 5, 23, 28
Frog, 11
Frontal organ (*see* Paraphysis)

GÄRTNER, canals of, 189
Genital duct, 189
Gill clefts, 49 (*see also* Branchial pouches)
Giraldé, organ of, 189
Glabella coccygea, 5, 23, 28
Gland, coccygeal, 126
  pineal (*see* Epiphysis cerebri)
  pituitary (*see* Hypophysis cerebri)
  thymus, 163
  thyroid, 162
Glands, genital, 196
  lachrymal, 149
  mammary, 12
  Montgomery's, 12

Glands, nictitating, 149
Glaser, fissure of, 65
Great toe, 85
Gubernaculum, 196, 197
Gynækomasty, 17

HAIR, 3
  tracts, 5
  vortices, 5, 23
Hairs, tactile (*see* Vibrissæ)
Hairy men, 9
Hallux (*see* Great toe)
Hand, skeleton of, 79, 86
Heart, 39, 180
Hind-limb, skeleton of, 80
Hip-girdle (*see* Pelvic girdle)
Hottentot apron, 195
Humerus, 77
  torsion of, 91
Hymen, 194
Hyoid arch, 65, 151
Hypertrichosis, 7, 10
Hypophysis cerebri, 135

ILIUM, 74, 76
Incus, 64, 151
Integument, 3
  sense organs of, 140
Interclavicle, 46
Intestine, 166
Ischium, 71, 74

JACOBSON, organ of, 143

KIDNEY, definitive, 188

LABIA majora, 195
  minora, 195
Lamina papyracea (*see* Os planum)
Lanugo, 9
Larynx, 172
  musculature of, 174
  skeleton of, 66, 151
Ligament, interclavicular, 48
Ligamentum inguinale, 196, 199
Ligula, 137
Limbs, comparison of fore- and hind-, 91
  displacement of, during development, 92
  disposition of, in adult, 91
  disposition of, in fœtus, 85
Limb girdles, 68

INDEX

Limb skeleton, 67
  genesis of, 68
Little toe, 89
Liver, 38, 171
Lobus olfactorius, 141
Lumbar curvature, 32
Lungs, 175

MALLEOLUS, fibular, 83
  tibial, 83
Malleus, 64, 151
Mammary glands, development of, 13
  supernumerary, 16
Mammary line, 14
  pouch, 14
Meckel, cartilage of, 64, 151
Mesonephros, 187
Metanephros, 188
Monotremata, mammary organ of, 12, 14, 17, 198
Mouth, development of, 136
Muscle, adductor hallucis, 112
  agitator caudæ, 99
  biventer maxillæ, 102
  cleido-occipitalis, 102, 112
  coccygeus, 98
  cremaster, 198
  curvator caudæ, 27
  curvator coccygis, 99
  depressor caudæ, 99
  epicranius, 107
  epitrochleo-anconæus, 113
  extensor brevis digitorum, 111
  extensor carpi radialis, 119
  flexor brevis minimi digiti, 112
  flexor digit. communis, 110, 117
  flexor digit. profundus, 110, 117, 119
  flexor digit. superficialis, 110, 119
  flexor longus hallucis, 117
  flexor longus pollicis, 117
  frontalis, 107
  gastrocnemius, 120
  gemellus superior, 119
  gluteus maximus, 82, 99, 119
  ischio-femoralis, 114
  latissimo condyloideus, 112
  latissimo dorsi, 38
  levator claviculæ, 114
  levator palpebræ, 148
  mylohyoid, 102
  opponens hallucis (and o. pollicis), 88

Muscle, opponens minimi digiti, 112
  orbitalis, 148
  palmaris, 109, 110
  panniculosis carnosus, 103, 113
  pectoralis, 45, 113
  plantaris, 109, 110
  platysma, 103, 105
  pyramidalis, 101
  pyriformis, 119
  rectus abdominis, 99
  semimembranosus, 120
  semitendinosus, 120
  serratus magnus, 45
  serratus posticus, 38
  soleus, 120
  sphincter colli, 106
  sternalis, 113
  subcutaneus colli (see M. platysma)
  transversus abdominis, 198
  transversus nuchæ, 105
  triangularis sterni, 102
Muscles, caudal, 27, 98
  cervical, 103, 113
  cutaneous, 103
  gluteal, 119
  intercostal, 43, 99
  interossei pedis, 111
  laryngeal, 174
  mimetic, 103, 109, 114
  of head, 103, 107, 115
  of limbs, 109, 116, 120
  of pinna, 107, 154
  progressive, 114, 121
  retrogressive, 98, 121
  scaleni, 102
  serrati, 98
Muscular system, 97
Myelon (see Spinal cord)

NAILS, 11
Nerve, hypoglossus, 138
  trigeminal, 139
  vagus, 138
Nerves, caudal, 32
  sympathetic, 139
Nervous system, 123
Nictitating membrane, 148
Nose, bridge of, 61
  the projectile, 147

ODEX, 137
Œsophagus, 164

Olfactory organ, 141
Os acetabuli (*see* Bone, cotyloid)
  antiepilepticum, 57
  centrale carpi, 80
  fronto-parietale, 57
  planum, 60
  præinterparietale, 57, 60
Ossa suprasternalia, 48
  suturaria (*see* Bones, Wormian)
Ossicula auditus, 64, 151
Ovary, 196

PALATE, hard, 63
Palate, ridges of soft, 155
Pancreas, 171
Papilla foliata, 162
  palatina, 146, 156
Paradidymis, 189
Paraphysis, 134
Parietal organ (*see* Pineal organ)
Pectoral girdle, 68
Pelvic girdle, 68
  development of, 74
  shifting of, 31, 95
Pericardium, 38, 177
Pineal gland (*see* Epiphysis cerebri)
Pineal organ, 133
Pinna, 108
  development of, 152
  muscles of, 107, 154
Pituitary body (*see* Hypophysis cerebri)
Platyknemia, 82
Pleural cavities, 39
Plexus, brachial, 95
  ischiadic, 95
  lumbo-sacral, 95
  pudendal, 95
  vesico-prostatic, 182
Plica fimbriata, 161
  semilunaris, 148
Polymasty, 17, 19
Polythely, 17
Ponticulus, 137
Post-anal gut, 32
Præputium, 195
Process, coracoid, 72
  paramastoid, 57
  styloid, 63
Processus supra-condyloideus, 78
  vermiformis, 167
Promontory, of sacrum, 32, 34
Pronephros, 187

Pseudohypertrichosis, 9
Pubis, 71, 74
Pyramidal nerve tracts, 125

REDITUS TESTICUM, 198
Respiratory system, 171
Ribs, cervical, 41, 102
  lumbar, 39
  sacral, 40
  sternal, 45, 46
  supernumerary, 39, 44
  thoracic, 39
Round ligament, 196

SACRAL DIMPLE (*see* Glabella coccygea)
Sacrum, 33, 40
Scapula, 71, 72
Scrotum, 198
Sense organs, 140
  integumental, 140
Shoulder girdle (*see* Pectoral girdle)
Sinus, Morgagni's, 174
  venosus, 180
Skeleton, 26
Skull, 48
Spinal cord, 123
Spleen, 186
Stenson, canals of (*see* Canals, naso-palatine)
Sternum, 44, 46
Stomach, 164
Sublingua, 161
Suprarenal bodies, 199
Sutures, cranial, 55
  maxillo-palatine, 63
  premaxillo-maxillary, 62
Sympathetic system, 139

TAIL, human, 5, 26, 31
Tarsus, 79
Teats, development of, 13
  supernumerary, 18, 20
Teeth, genesis of, 156
  milk, 160
  pre-milk, 160
  wisdom, 159
Tegumental organs, 3
Testis, 196
  descent of, 196, 198
Third eyelid (*see* Nictitating membrane)
Thorax, types of, 36

Thyroid cartilage, 66, 151
  gland, 162
Tibia, 82, 93
Tongue, 161
Torus occipitalis, 57
Trochanter, third, 82
Tympanic cavity, 150

URACHUS, 181
Urinogenital system, 187
Uterus, 194
Uterus masculinus, 189

VAGINA, 194, 195
Vas deferens, 188
Veins, intercostal, 186
  posterior cardinal, 184
  valves of, 185
Velum medullare, 137
Vena cava inferior, 184

Vena cava superior, 185
Venous system, 184
  anterior abdominal, 182
Vertebræ, caudal, 31
  coccygeal, 27
  thoracic, 43
  sacral, 33
Vertebral column, 26
Vertex coccygeus, 5, 26
Vibrissæ, 4
  supra-orbital, 150
Visceral skeletal arches, 49, 64, 66, 151
Visual organ (*see* Eye)

WHISKERS (*see* Vibrissæ)

XIPHISTERNUM, 45

YOLK SAC, 166

THE END

www.ingramcontent.com/pod-product-compliance
Lightning Source LLC
Chambersburg PA
CBHW031736230426
43669CB00007B/358